# COMMANDING THE WATERWAYS

## THE STORY OF

# SEA RAY

# COMMANDING THE WATERWAYS

## THE STORY OF

# SEA RAY

JEFFREY L. RODENGEN

Edited by Stanimira Stefanova
Design and layout by Ryan Milewicz

*Dedicated to John Keim, friend, confidant, marine-industry mentor, and links master.*

Write Stuff Enterprises, Inc.
1001 South Andrews Avenue
Fort Lauderdale, FL 33316
**1-800-900-Book** (1-800-900-2665)
(954) 462-6657
www.writestuffbooks.com

The publisher has made every effort to identify and locate the source of the photographs included in this edition of *Commanding the Waterways: The Story of Sea Ray*. Grateful acknowledgment is made to those who have kindly granted permission for the use of their materials in this edition. If there are instances where proper credit was not given, the publisher will gladly make any necessary corrections in subsequent printings.

**Publisher's Cataloging in Publication**
*(Prepared by The Donohue Group, Inc.)*

Rodengen, Jeffrey L.
   Commanding the waterways : the story of Sea Ray / Jeffrey L. Rodengen ; edited by Stanimira Stefanova ; design and layout by Ryan Milewicz ; [foreword by C.N. Ray].

   p. : ill. ; cm.

   Including bibliographical references and index.
   ISBN-13: 978-1-932022-33-9
   ISBN-10: 1-932022-33-3

1. Sea Ray (Firm)--History.  2. Boating industry--United States--History.  I. Stefanova, Stanimira. II. Milewicz, Ryan.  III. Ray, C. N. (Cornelius Nathaniel), 1925-  IV. Title. V. Title: Sea Ray

HD9993.B633 R63 2008
338.7/62382023/0973          2008931621

Completely produced in the
United States of America
10 9 8 7 6 5 4 3 2 1

## Also by Jeffrey L. Rodengen

*The Legend of Chris-Craft*

*IRON FIST:*
*The Lives of Carl Kiekhaefer*

*Evinrude-Johnson and*
*The Legend of OMC*

*Serving the Silent Service:*
*The Legend of Electric Boat*

*The Legend of Dr Pepper/Seven-Up*

*The Legend of Honeywell*

*The Legend of Briggs & Stratton*

*The Legend of Ingersoll-Rand*

*The Legend of Stanley:*
*150 Years of The Stanley Works*

*The MicroAge Way*

*The Legend of Halliburton*

*The Legend of York International*

*The Legend of Nucor Corporation*

*The Legend of Goodyear:*
*The First 100 Years*

*The Legend of AMP*

*The Legend of Cessna*

*The Legend of VF Corporation*

*The Spirit of AMD*

*The Legend of Rowan*

*New Horizons:*
*The Story of Ashland Inc.*

*The History of American Standard*

*The Legend of Mercury Marine*

*The Legend of Federal-Mogul*

*Against the Odds:*
*Inter-Tel—The First 30 Years*

*The Legend of Pfizer*

*State of the Heart: The Practical Guide*
*to Your Heart and Heart Surgery*
*with Larry W. Stephenson, M.D.*

*The Legend of Worthington Industries*

*The Legend of IBP*

*The Legend of Trinity Industries, Inc.*

*The Legend of*
*Cornelius Vanderbilt Whitney*

*The Legend of Amdahl*

*The Legend of Litton Industries*

*The Legend of Gulfstream*

*The Legend of Bertram*
*with David A. Patten*

*The Legend of Ritchie Bros. Auctioneers*

*The Legend of ALLTEL*
*with David A. Patten*

*The Yes, you can of Invacare Corporation*
*with Anthony L. Wall*

*The Ship in the Balloon:*
*The Story of Boston Scientific and the*
*Development of Less-Invasive Medicine*

*The Legend of Day & Zimmermann*

*The Legend of Noble Drilling*

*Fifty Years of Innovation: Kulicke & Soffa*

*Biomet—From Warsaw to the World*
*with Richard F. Hubbard*

*NRA: An American Legend*

*The Heritage and Values of RPM, Inc.*

*The Marmon Group: The First Fifty Years*

*The Legend of Grainger*

*The Legend of The Titan Corporation*
*with Richard F. Hubbard*

*The Legend of Discount Tire Co.*
*with Richard F. Hubbard*

*The Legend of Polaris*
*with Richard F. Hubbard*

*The Legend of La-Z-Boy*
*with Richard F. Hubbard*

*The Legend of McCarthy*
*with Richard F. Hubbard*

*Intervoice: Twenty Years of Innovation*
*with Richard F. Hubbard*

*Jefferson-Pilot Financial:*
*A Century of Excellence*
*with Richard F. Hubbard*

*The Legend of HCA*

*The Legend of Werner Enterprises*
*with Richard F. Hubbard*

*The History of J. F. Shea Co.*
*with Richard F. Hubbard*

*True to Our Vision*
*with Richard F. Hubbard*

*The Legend of Albert Trostel & Sons*
*with Richard F. Hubbard*

*The Legend of Sovereign Bancorp*
*with Richard F. Hubbard*

*Innovation is the Best Medicine:*
*The extraordinary story of Datascope*
*with Richard F. Hubbard*

*The Legend of Guardian Industries*

*The Legend of*
*Universal Forest Products*

*Changing the World: Polytechnic*
*University—The First 150 Years*

*Nothing is Impossible: The Legend*
*of Joe Hardy and 84 Lumber*

*In it for the Long Haul:*
*The Story of CRST*

*The Story of Parsons Corporation*

*Cerner: From Vision to Value*

*New Horizons:*
*The Story of Federated Investors*

*Office Depot: Taking Care of Business—*
*The First 20 Years*

*The Legend of General Parts:*
*Proudly Serving a World in Motion*

*Bard: Power of the Past,*
*Force of the Future*

*Innovation & Integrity:*
*The Story of Hub Group*

*Amica: A Century of Service*
*1907–2007*

*A Passion for Service:*
*The Story of ARAMARK*

*The Legend of Con-way:*
*A History of Service, Reliability,*
*Innovation, and Growth*

# TABLE OF CONTENTS

# FOREWORD

by

## C. N. RAY
SEA RAY FOUNDER

I CLEARLY REMEMBER THE first time Sea Ray boats were displayed at the 1960 Chicago National Boat Show. The Sea Ray logo at the time was a stylized stingray, so our booth at the Cow Palace had a large aquarium tank with a live stingray swimming around, attracting attention from the aisles. As it turned out, our new boat models, designed by the studio of Harley Earl, attracted much more attention. We were already setting ourselves apart from our competition with strict attention to the basics: superior products, superior dealers, and a sincere appreciation of our customers.

We were an immediate hit—in fact, I was having a difficult time sorting out the many dealerships that wanted to represent Sea Ray. I didn't want to sign a dealer in Omaha, Nebraska, that I had never seen. So you know what I did? I had promised many people that I would look at their dealerships, so I flew my airplane to check out all these different people and find out whether they would represent our products well. We were shooting for a Mercedes- or Cadillac-quality dealer in the boat business and looking for organizations that had really nice showrooms. I realized that the dealer was the key to our success, assuming we could build a good boat. A bad dealer could take a good boat and get nowhere with it. Size wasn't too important because we were so small, but I was willing to grow up with them. I was fussy about giving them a lot of territory, however, so they weren't competing against each other. Most important was the character of the individual, how they approached matters, and what they had done in the past.

The dealer, of course, has a great responsibility to the customer. I realized that if we could establish a strong enough bond with the dealer, the dealer would develop equally strong bonds with their customers. Sea Ray customers knew that no matter what their service issue or unusual quality issue, both the dealer and Sea Ray would stand behind them. I had an unwritten rule: If a complaint was serious enough, we authorized the dealer to offer to buy back the boat on the spot. That built another bridge of confidence and loyalty between the customer and the dealer, as well as the dealer and Sea Ray. I sent a letter out to each customer when they sent in their warranty card. I thanked them, of course, for their purchase and sent them a nameplate to stick on the dashboard of their boat that read, "This Sea Ray

Boat Was Built Especially for Joe Smith." My signature was on the letter, and I would tell them that if there was ever a problem, they could call me directly, and we would make it right. They knew they could rely on the top man in the company to look out for them.

Of course, it's much easier to offer assistance when the quality of your product is unusually high. From the very beginning, I would impress both the dealer and consumer by doubling up my fist and whopping the side of the boat as hard as I could. That made a huge impression because the boat was solid as a rock. We actually put more laminate in our boats than our competitors did, even though it's an expensive part of the boat. If you leave a couple of layers out, the boat becomes lighter. You can put a smaller horsepower engine in it and give it the same speed. The problem is, as it bounces through the water over the years, the dashboard starts shaking, the instruments get messed up, the steering wheel becomes loose, and so on. With Sea Ray, you know you have a substantial piece of equipment under your fanny when you're bouncing along on the waves. Beyond superior design and construction, we used top-of-the-line accessories, knowing it's often the little things that will ruin a good ride and a good consumer experience.

Enduring in this business for 50 years, however, and maintaining a strong reputation and the loyalty of both dealers and consumers is not an easy matter. It takes constant vigilance with every aspect of running the business. You have to concentrate on the most minute details—not one can be overlooked. I was constantly preaching to those who worked for me, as well as our dealers, that if they were going to beat the dealership down the street, they had to do a better job of service. There are some other really fine boat companies. You just have to be better at everything.

We didn't try to be all things to all people though. We didn't get into the bass-boat business. We never designed a boat that was set up for a crew, with separate quarters from the rest of the boat and so forth. We thought about building a boat larger than 68 feet, even up to 80 feet. Ultimately, we decided not to extend ourselves into unfamiliar waters, keeping our focus on maintaining the high standards of the core Sea Ray products.

Being a part of the boat business is a lot of fun. People really enjoy our products, and the friends you make in this business are the best you can find in your lifetime. Sure, there are times when it can be frustrating, but those times are overshadowed by the warmth that surrounds the whole Sea Ray universe, from fellow Sea Ray employees to great dealer relationships to proud and loyal owners. It's amazing how fast 50 years can glide by.

# ACKNOWLEDGMENTS

MANY PEOPLE ASSISTED IN THE RE-search, preparation, and publication of *Commanding the Waterways: The Story of Sea Ray.* The development of historical timelines and a large portion of the principal archival research was accomplished by Research Assistant T. Wayne Waters. His thorough and careful work made it possible to publish a great deal of interesting information on the origins and evolution of this unique company.

The research, however, much less the book itself, would have been impossible without the dedicated assistance of Sea Ray executives and associates. Principal among these are Mike Hungerford, Rob Parmentier, and Sharon Blazer, whose affable guidance made it possible for our research team to locate and identify records and individuals crucial to the Sea Ray legacy. Others who were of great assistance in completing the book include Dusty McCoy, Amanda Balman, Jim Carpinelli, Terri Domain, Kelly Henry, Greg Garland, Gretchen Wolpert, and Don Rush. A special thank you goes to C. N. Ray, Sea Ray founder, for contributing the book's foreword.

The interest and courtesy of the many interview subjects for the book was most gratifying. All the people interviewed—whether current employees, associates, or retirees—were generous with their time and insights. Those who shared their memories and thoughts include Bill Barrington, Pete Beauregard, Sr., Pete Beauregard, Jr., Barry Bensz, Rodney Bensz, Ed Boncek, Mike Burke, Dwight Cobble, Roger Giles, Ken Harrell, Carrie Hedberg, Stephen Helwig, Mike Hungerford, John Keim, Nancy Luster, Rod Malone, Howard "Mac" Mc Donald, Bill McGill, Arch Mehaffey, Mike Meyer, Jerry Michalak, Gary Montavon, Mike Morrison, Rob Noyes, Rob Parmentier, C. N. Ray, Larry Russo, Sr., Larry Russo, Jr., Bob Scott, Murray Shektman, Shane Stanfill, Jim Steffens, Rick Stone, Göran Sundberg, Lars Sundberg, Bruce Thompson, Bob VanNorman, Joe Wakeen, Mary Wakeen, Forrest Weyant, Ian Williamson, and Jozef Wiszniewski.

Finally, special thanks are extended to the dedicated staff at Write Stuff Enterprises, Inc., who worked on the book. Thanks are due to Stanimira "Sam" Stefanova, executive editor; Elizabeth Fernandez, Anne Forsyth, and Heather Lewin, senior editors; Sandy Cruz, vice president/creative director; Elijah Meyer and Ryan Milewicz, graphic designers; Roy Adelman, on-press supervisor; Abby Hollister, proofreader; Mary Aaron, transcriptionist; Elliot Linzer, indexer; Amy Major, executive assistant to Jeffrey L. Rodengen; Marianne Roberts, executive vice president, publisher, and chief financial officer; Steven Stahl, director of marketing; and Tania Overby, bookkeeper.

A great tradition of building high-quality boats started in 1959 when a young C. N. Ray founded Sea Ray, which has grown to become one of the largest recreational boat- and yacht-building companies in the world.

## CHAPTER ONE

# BOATING BRAINSTORM

## 1959–1963

*There's no romance in sand and gravel.*

—C. N. Ray, Sea Ray founder[1]

THE PLEASURE-BOATING industry of the 1950s was still in its infancy and experiencing the type of instability associated with the birth of a newly emerging market sector. A few marine manufacturers seemed firmly established, but many more had quickly appeared only to disappear soon thereafter. In the last year of the decade, however, a new competitor arose—one whose commitment to quality and innovation made an immediate impact on the industry.

Sea Ray was launched in October 1959 when boat lover and entrepreneur Cornelius "Connie" Nathaniel Ray III, or "C. N." as most would come to know him, purchased the assets of Carr-Craft, a small fiberglass boat company based in Detroit. Initially operating out of a garage, Ray, without any previous boatbuilding experience, began manufacturing fiberglass boats with just three employees, including old college friend and subsequent business partner Arch Mehaffey as well as Carr-Craft's fiberglass specialist and designer, Jerry Michalak. Within a few months, he moved the operation to his hometown of Oxford, Michigan.[2]

Ray was the scion of C. N. "Cornelius" Ray, his grandfather and namesake, who founded United Fuel and Supply, the precursor to Ray Industries, Inc., in 1924. Four years later, he established a business relationship with American Aggregates Corporation in Oxford, Michigan, and began to focus primarily on sand and gravel mining. The elder Ray dropped the United Fuel and Supply name in 1936, officially adopting the Ray Industries, Inc., moniker.[3] Cornelius Ray's son, Charles Henry Ray, continued the family enterprise and tried his hand at several sideline business ventures over the decades, including the manufacturing of charcoal briquettes, though sand and gravel mining always remained the company's foundation. That changed, however, when grandson C. N. Ray graduated from college and decided to broaden the company's horizons.

Some might say Sea Ray was born of Ray's dissatisfaction with the charcoal business. In 1959, Ray decided that charcoal simply did not offer the kind of potential he sought in his business ventures. "I decided my ambitions in my business career exceeded those of this particular job," he explained.[4]

Ray found a company in Toronto interested in the charcoal business and agreed to sell them the entire charcoal operation for less than $200,000 in cash and stock. Prior to the sale, however, the buyer's stock, which had been thriving on the

---

Sea Ray founder C. N. Ray's distinctive signature graced the documents that finalized the Carr-Craft purchase in 1959.

Early Sea Ray boat designs, such as those in the 1960s, first began to take shape as drawings on a drafting board.

Toronto Stock Exchange, plummeted. Saving Ray from a terrible financial blow, the Canadian company's chairman of the board, Bob Armstrong,

immediately agreed to make up the difference in cash equal to the stock's earlier value.[5]

Armstrong's generosity was particularly important because, at the time, growth at the Ray family sand and gravel business was becoming stagnant, mostly because of limited product distribution. When its charcoal operations shut down, Ray lost a supplemental revenue stream. In addition, his friend and trusted business associate, Mehaffey, became unemployed.[6]

Ray and Mehaffey, who had been friends for many years, were also fraternity brothers at the University of California, Los Angeles (UCLA). After graduating in 1949, each had gone his own way—Ray to the family business of Ray Industries in Oxford, Michigan, and Mehaffey to a paper company sales department in Philadelphia. They kept in touch, however, and within a few years, Ray had hired Mehaffey to oversee the West Coast distribution for Ray Industries charcoal briquette business.[7]

So, with the seed money safely in hand from the sale of the charcoal business, Ray summoned Mehaffey back to Michigan, even though he was unsure of the business venture he would pursue.

**October 1959:** C. N. Ray purchases the assets of Carr-Craft, a small fiberglass boat manufacturer in Detroit. The new company is christened Sea Ray and is part of Ray Industries, Inc., the existing Ray family business.

**April 1960:** Sea Ray unveils its lineup at the first boat show on Lake Orion just outside of Oxford. Sea Ray introduces six models: the 200, 400, 500, 600, 700, and 800, ranging in length from nearly 13 feet to 17 feet. The new company receives its first boat orders from retail buyers.

**January 1960:** Ray moves the Sea Ray operation to his hometown of Oxford, Michigan. The company contracts with noted automobile design firm Harley Earl Associates to design innovative interior styling for some of its boats.
*(Graphic courtesy of Ford & Earl Associates, Inc.)*

He felt confident that he and Mehaffey could successfully collaborate on a prosperous enterprise.

**The Brainstorm**

Ray and Mehaffey worked well together as businessmen and friends. Mehaffey had studied business at UCLA, with a focus on accounting, while Ray had pursued marketing. Their respective strengths complemented each other, especially when the two men assessed the potential of various businesses in 1959. "I needed him to look at the balance sheets and the profit and loss that were supplied by companies that we were considering," Ray recalled.[8]

From the dozens of business ventures considered, Ray and Mehaffey visited one that particularly piqued their interest—Detroit-based fiberglass manufacturer Carr-Craft, which had molds for a few boat models, a golf cart, and a coffin. Ray had been around boats all his life and had even raced Pacific One Hydroplane Design (POHD) boats, manufactured in California in the 1930s, for fun while in college. "I didn't want anything to do with coffins, and I'm not much of a golfer, but the boat appealed to me," Ray said.[9]

Ray also believed in the viability of fiberglass as a building material for boats. Fiberglass was still relatively new to the boating industry and the general public at the time, but he believed it had potential. So, Ray and Mehaffey set out to educate themselves on boatbuilding and the pleasure-boat–manufacturing industry, visiting a handful of boat manufacturers and gleaning as much insight as possible. Among their findings were the encouraging facts that sales of outboard boats had doubled in the past decade and fiberglass boat sales were steadily increasing as a percentage of the overall boat market, accounting for about 30 percent of all boat sales in 1958.[10]

After completing their research, Ray and Mehaffey believed it was possible to find business success in the recreational boating industry but knew they would have to start small. Both also agreed that although the Carr-Craft operation offered an inexpensive entrée into the boating industry, it did not have prominent brand names or business relationships. Nonetheless, Ray decided to make an offer to Carr-Craft owner Ray Carr for the assets of his company.[11]

At the time, Carr was hard-pressed. He was not selling many boats; he had only a few existing

**1960:** Sea Ray shows off its 1961 lineup for the first time at the prestigious 1960 Chicago National Boat Show.

**Summer 1962:** Sea Ray introduces its model-year 1963 lineup. Inboard/outboard stern-drive motors are offered for the first time.

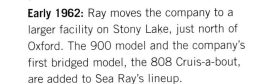

**Early 1962:** Ray moves the company to a larger facility on Stony Lake, just north of Oxford. The 900 model and the company's first bridged model, the 808 Cruis-a-bout, are added to Sea Ray's lineup.

Left: Sea Ray's 1961 brochure depicted a boat hull just removed from the mold, giving potential customers a glimpse behind the factory walls of fiberglass boat production.

Opposite page: Sea Ray's inaugural 1960 lineup ranged from the small catamaran 200 and tail-finned 600 to the Harley Earl showcase 700 and the large, offshore-capable 800 model. The influence of automobile styling was obvious in the tail fins of the Sea Ray 600, which was retired after this 1961 version. The 700 was the company's first entirely new model and the first Sea Ray to highlight the innovative interior treatments of Harley Earl Associates. The 800 was the largest boat in Sea Ray's 1961 fleet, though a redesign had taken about 7 inches in gunwale length from its 1960 version.

orders; his boat designs were minimal and not original; and he had a barely sufficient complement of tools and equipment. So Carr struck a deal with Ray, who purchased Carr-Craft's assets for about $50,000 on October 21, 1959.[12]

Ray wanted to move away from the Carr-Craft name, however, and put his own stamp on the product. Using his marketing expertise to create the company logo, he decided on a marine derivation of his own name coupled with a stylized representation of a stingray. Sea Ray Corporation had officially been launched.

**The First Sea Ray Show**

Ray was pleased to own Carr-Craft's material assets—even though they were meager, as he appreciated the human assets he gained even more. He hired Carr as director of manufacturing, along with the company's fiberglass specialist and designer Michalak, and another Carr-Craft employee, Art Johnson, to work along with Mehaffey and himself.[13] The original plan called for Ray to manage the overall operation, Mehaffey to handle sales, and the three-person Carr-Craft crew to design and build the boats.

Two months later, in January 1960, Ray moved the operation 40 miles north of the Motor City to Oxford, where he lived. He hired additional workers and set up shop in a small building on Indianwood Road that had previously served as a potato warehouse.[14] When Carr left the new enterprise after only a couple of months, Mehaffey found himself more involved in the design and production process. He recalled:[15]

*Carr lasted until about the first of the year, maybe a little longer, and C. N. let him go ... and so I sort of moved inside into the production plant. I tried to get the problems straightened out one way or another, which we did, mainly through Jerry and Art and through some material suppliers that we'd come to know in a very short time. They were very helpful.*[16]

The new Sea Ray team worked feverishly to produce models based on variations of the existing Carr-Craft molds, as well as one entirely new model for the 1960 summer season. They managed to design a line of six fiberglass models (or "fiber glass," as the company brochures of the time referred to them), all for outboard motors, ranging from 12 feet 8 inches to 17 feet 1 inch in overall length, and designated with the Sea Ray name and a number derived from the boat's approximate length. Sea Ray's first line included the 200, 400, 500, 600, 700, and 800 models. The 700 was brand-new. Though the 800 was larger, at more than 17 feet in overall length, the 700 was Sea Ray's ultimate luxury model and the one that really showcased the influence of Harley Earl Associates, the renowned auto body–design company hired by Ray to overhaul Sea Ray boat interiors. The 600 was the "sports car" of the group

# 1960 Sea Ray Boat Specifications

| | Length, overall | Length, gunwale | Beam, maximum | Beam, transom | Depth, maximum | Weight, approx. | Motors, maximum |
|---|---|---|---|---|---|---|---|
| **Sea Ray 200** | 12'8" | 14'6" | 80" | 72" | 26" | 420 lbs. | 2–40 hp |
| **Sea Ray 400** | 14'2" | 15'7" | 72" | 64" | 30" | 350 lbs. | 50 hp |
| **Sea Ray 500** | 14'9" | 15'9" | 70" | 61" | 33" | 425 lbs. | 60 hp |
| **Sea Ray 600** | 15'3" | 16'4" | 68" | 62" | 29" | 390 lbs. | 60 hp |
| **Sea Ray 700** | 15'6" | 16'10" | 79" | 70" | 35" | 575 lbs. | 80 hp |
| **Sea Ray 800** | 17'1" | 18'2" | 80" | 74" | 40" | 780 lbs. | 100 hp |

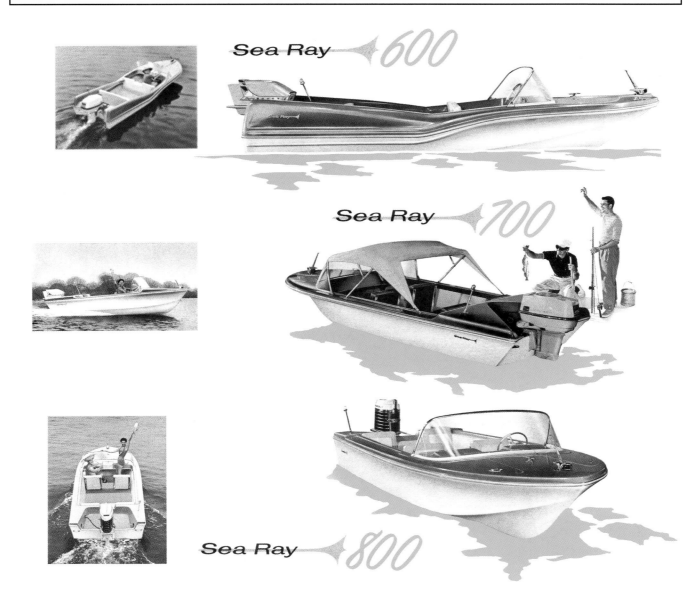

Sea Ray 600

Sea Ray 700

Sea Ray 800

# FINDING STRENGTH IN FIBERGLASS

TO EXAMINE THE ORIGIN OF FIBERGLASS boats, it is necessary to consider the concurrent development of fiberglass and plastic resins. Though commonly referred to as "fiberglass," the more precise designation is "fiberglass reinforced plastic" (FRP) as pleasure-boat manufacturers and the U.S. Coast Guard typically refer to such material.

Fiberglass is, not surprisingly, a fine fiber made of glass that is heated, pressurized, and elongated. While a crude form of glass fibers was mass-produced for use as insulation and for decorative purposes as early as the last third of the 19th century, it was not until 1932 that a young Corning Glass researcher named Russell Games Slayter discovered the direct precursor to today's fiberglass.[1] Meanwhile, another major U.S. corporation, Owens-Illinois, was also experimenting with glass fibers. In 1935, the two companies joined forces to produce the material, which was patented the following year.[2] Their new product was designed primarily as an insulation material, but its extraordinary properties would make it useful for many applications. Those properties include:

- High tensile strength
- High elasticity
- Dimensional stability
- Resistance to moisture absorbtion
- Flame resistance, with a high melting point
- Sunlight resistance[3]

The term "fiberglass" had an evolving etymology over the years. The substance was originally tagged "Fiberglas" (with one "s") by Owens-Illinois when the company patented it. Most references to the substance in the media and elsewhere used that spelling initially, sometimes with the capitalized "F," sometimes a lowercase "f." Eventually, the lowercase, two-word, double-"s" rendition, "fiber glass," became common. It would be sometime in the late 1960s before Sea Ray began using the now universally accepted one-word, double-"s" term, "fiberglass." Fiberglass has become the common term used to

with the most dramatic styling—a shallow-draft, high-speed planing hull that shouted "speedboat."

The 1960 Sea Rays also offered appealing, and appealingly named, deck colors—Bahama Blue, Desert Gold, Siesta Red, Beachwood Tan, and Alpine White, all complemented by an Alpine White hull. Though the upholstery on the seats of these early decks was colorful, all but the 700 lacked the full deck treatment that became available on every model the following year.

Standard equipment for even the largest of the 1960 Sea Ray models was limited to bow chocks, bow eye, aluminum cockpit trim and rub rails, deck cleat, hull drain plugs, stern handles, steering wheel, windshield, and upholstered seats. Within a couple of years, the standard equipment list doubled for the smaller boats and quadrupled for the larger ones.

The most conspicuous omission in any boat purchased in 1960 from Sea Ray or any other boat maker was, of course, a motor. All boats were designed for use with motors that had to be purchased separately from a marine products dealership. Fiberglass boat manufacturers were tooled up overwhelmingly for outboards in 1960—a situation that was soon changed by Volvo, Outboard Marine Corporation (OMC), and Mercury Marine.

With the new lineup ready and newly branded, Ray and Mehaffey arranged for Sea Ray's first public show, an all-Michigan affair that took place

refer to FRP applications as a construction material, omitting reference to the plastic component.

Plastic, the other FRP element, was also developed in the 19th century. Plastics can be defined as organic or synthetic materials capable of various stages of liquidity and of being molded.[4] Synthetic resins, viscous liquids capable of hardening, were regular and complementary components of such experimentation.[5] In 1936, the same year Owens-Illinois patented Fiberglas, Dupont researcher Carlton Ellis received a patent for a polyester resin that could be formed and cured into a thermo-setting plastic that remained hard even when heated. This was essentially what was needed to combine with fiberglass to make a high-quality FRP, but Dupont only produced the new material in small batches initially.[6] In 1942, American Cyanamid came up with a cold-setting polyester resin that made FRP viable for commercial products.[7]

**But Does It Float?**

A mechanical engineer and independent boatbuilder named Ray Greene had worked with fiberglass and plastic resins since the 1930s and produced a fiberglass rowboat reinforced with polyester resins generally acknowledged as the first FRP boat in 1942.[8]

In 1946, the U.S. Navy commissioned Trenton, New Jersey–based Winner Manufacturing Company to produce three 28-foot fiberglass personnel-carrier boats.[9] In 1947, Winner went on to produce the first mass-produced, series-built FRP recreational boat, a small runabout, with limited success.[10]

Meanwhile, Owens-Corning made a concerted effort to convince recreational boat manufacturers that fiberglass-reinforced plastic was the perfect material for manufacturing boats.[11] The boat industry at large was generally conservative and skeptical of this new, artificial product. Fiberglass was adopted gradually during the 1950s, initially with sailboats, dinghies, and small runabouts. It would be the second half of the decade before manufacturers were confident enough to use fiberglass on larger boats or to demonstrate a firm commitment to using the new building material.

The strength of fiberglass was demonstrated dramatically at the 1955 New York Boat Show when, for a televised demonstration of its sturdiness, Lone Star Boat Company dropped one of its 15-foot fiberglass runabouts from a forklift holding the boat 15 feet up. The boat bounced around before finally settling down. Examination showed that the fiberglass hull had not even cracked.[12]

During the 1950s, more and more boat manufacturers were won over by the advantages of FRP as a construction material. Sea Ray was among the first group of boatbuilders to embrace the new technology.

at Indianwood Country Club on Lake Orion outside of Oxford in April 1960. Ray had established a relationship with Peninsular Distributing, which had invited all of its Michigan dealers.

This first show provided Ray the opportunity to demonstrate his showmanship in a modest and effective way. The country club hosting the event had a large room that featured glass doors overlooking the lake, and Ray specifically requested that the drapes on the doors remain closed when the dealers entered. After the luncheon and a short informative talk, the drapes were opened dramatically at just the right moment, revealing five new Sea Ray boats (the 200, 400, 500, 600, and 800) on the water, gleaming in the sunlight. Sea Ray received its first orders that weekend.[17]

Response to Sea Ray boats during the rest of 1960 was encouraging. Despite the fact that the company's emerging distribution network extended no further than the Michigan state line, and that its production capacity was limited, growing sales encouraged Ray, Mehaffey, and Michalak to set their sights on the upcoming Chicago National Boat Show.

**Building the Sea Ray Way**

All major recreational boat manufacturers and boat retailers from around the country presented

Above: Sea Ray's 1961 brochure enticed prospective buyers with "enthusiasm" and some color in its duotone presentation. This was the last year that a long stingray tail crossed the company's name in marketing materials.

Below: C. N. Ray visited the Carr-Craft boat garage in 1959, the same year he purchased the fiberglass boat company's assets.

their products at the Chicago National Boat Show, which was considered a prestigious boat-industry event. As a premier marine manufacturing showcase, the event offered an unbeatable opportunity for Ray and company to introduce Sea Ray to a much larger audience, including the people who would actually sell Sea Ray boats—the dealers.

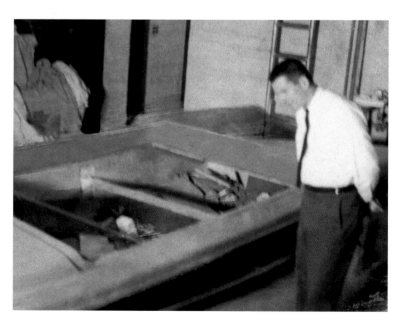

Again, Ray's marketing sensibilities played a key role in presenting Sea Ray's public face. The Chicago National Boat Show featured so many boats on display that it was difficult to stand out in the crowd. So Ray decided to generate enough buzz on the showroom floor to entice people to seek out the Sea Ray exhibit: He bought a holding tank for the event, delivered it to Sea Ray's allotted space, filled it with water, and placed a large stingray inside. The display of the sleek, whip-tailed fish captured the imagination of show attendees and word soon spread, capturing the attention of many people who also noticed the well-designed boats with their well-appointed interiors featured nearby. "They took a look at our boats and went bonkers," Ray said. "None of the other boats in that place looked anything as neat as ours did."[18]

Dozens of boat dealers at the Chicago event were soon interested in handling the Sea Ray line. Since Ray's business acumen proved as sharp as his marketing savvy, he had already decided to sell his boats in a manner not typical at the time. Most boat manufacturers in the 1960s believed the best way to sell boats was to provide them to as many dealers as possible, paying little heed to the quality of individual dealer operations or to the territorial dynamics of a dealer network. Ray, however, did not see it that way.

Ray believed that assigning hand-picked dealers the responsibility for a large, exclusive territory would prevent split sales among dealers in close proximity, which in turn would increase the likelihood of higher overall sales for each dealer, thus creating loyalty to Sea Ray.[19] Time would prove him right, as he later recalled:

*I personally knew all the dealers and became friends [with them] in a manner of speaking, and I was really pushing exclusivity. I wanted them to handle Sea Ray and no other competing boat line. I really got the message across to quite a few dealers, and they got more profitable.*[20]

Beyond these shrewd business incentives, Ray made a concerted effort to form substantive relationships with dealers. Besides boating, Ray, a U.S. Air Force veteran, was also passionate about airplanes. His twin-engine Aero Commander provided another tool for interacting with Sea Ray dealer applicants, whom Ray would sometimes take for a spin.[21] "I took a lot of dealers up in it, and they got their jollies sitting in the co-pilot seat," Ray recalled. "They loved it!"[22]

Ray was serious about carefully selecting the right dealers to handle the Sea Ray product line, spending considerable time observing each dealer's facilities before reaching a decision. With his efforts paying off, Sea Ray soon established a solid, growing network of quality dealerships.

The awareness of and enthusiasm for Sea Ray that had sparked at the 1960 Chicago National Boat Show energized the young company. That event had attracted many dealers and placed the company on the pleasure-boating map. In addition, the unusual dealer network philosophy that Ray put into effect during this critical period would help greatly with its future success.

**Inside and Out**

Right from the start, Ray somehow understood—better than many industry veterans—three critical aspects of the boat business: heavier can mean better, interiors matter, and arranging a dealer network carefully and in a way that allows dealers to make money increases the likelihood of increased sales and lasting loyalty. Most fiberglass-boat manufacturers of the time used as few layers of fiberglass and resin as possible to minimize expenses and to support the misguided notion that the minimum weight required for structural safety purposes was best. Boat manufacturers' limited funds and lack of imagination resulted in simple interiors, often with minimally finished decks. From the beginning, Sea Ray's vastly improved pleasure-boat building with respect to these aspects impressed attendees at the Chicago National Boat Show.

Michalak's hands-on experience with fiberglass had provided him with extensive knowledge about Sea Ray's materials, including the building of the prototype hull molds. Though the resin component was initially applied manually with brushes, the company soon shifted to using spray mechanisms and "chopper guns," spray-nozzle devices that introduced fiberglass cut into uniform short lengths into the resin spray, allowing for a faster and more even application.[23]

In 1960, Sea Ray attended the Chicago National Boat Show, a prestigious industry event that gave Sea Ray the opportunity to introduce its boat line to the public.

Sea Ray never limited its use of fiberglass in hull construction and consequently produced a boat that offered solid construction, evident from the satisfying sound and appearance that came with it. Just as automobile buyers listen for a comforting, solid thud when closing a car door as an indication of quality construction, a boat buyer is also reassured if a similarly solid sound comes from a strike on the side of a boat hull. Michalak explained:

*We didn't try to build our boats real thin. We weren't concerned if we ended up using a little bit more fiberglass. We were more concerned if we used less. We found structurally in a hull or a deck, you need to have the right amount of stiffness. Get the low percentage of resin to glass, and you got something that felt like a piece of tin.*

# THE HARLEY EARL CONNECTION

FROM THE INDUSTRIAL DESIGN STUDIOS OF HARLEY EARL ASSOCIATES

O F THE MANY UNIQUE features that made early Sea Ray boats one of a kind in the 1960s, their lavish interiors designed by Harley Earl Associates were especially important. The Earl name carried considerable cachet in 1960, when Sea Ray's first models were presented, even though Harley Earl had retired several years earlier.

Earl had made a name for himself in California, where he designed custom luxury auto bodies in the 1920s. He subsequently moved to Detroit and, for the next 30 years, worked on cars for General Motors (GM), where his innovative ideas flowed into the company's designs and design features. His automobile design concepts, first sketched as line drawings and then produced as clay models, were later transformed into such classics as the 1927 LaSalle and the 1930s Buick

"Y Job," widely recognized as the first "concept" car. The 1948 Cadillac introduced a modest version of an Earl brainchild—the tailfin. Two years later, it achieved much more dramatic expression in the 1950 LeSabre "dream car."[1]

According to Earl, the LeSabre's dramatic lines and graceful curves were inspired by a Lockheed P38 Lightning he had seen at Selfridge Air Force Base during World War II. The name had most likely been derived from another 1940s aircraft—North American Aviation's F-86 Sabrejet fighter—exemplifying how transportation design concept lineage was shared between airplanes, automobiles, and eventually boats.

In 1953, Earl initiated the design of a new sports car for GM that eventually became known as the Corvette. It was one of the first,

*You needed a certain amount of bulk thickness and also a certain amount of resin. If you go for the low end of something, you're going to get something that sounds like a tin can.*[24]

From early on, Sea Ray made a point of promoting the solid construction of its boats. At the early boat shows, Ray and company encouraged attendees to strike the boats with their hand to feel—and hear—the substantial heft.[25] The 1963 company brochure boasted of Sea Ray boat "hulls of durable, husky construction."[26] The 1964 brochure proudly proclaimed:

*We take great pride in pointing out the weight of our boats. Sea Ray boats are frequently as much as 30 to 40 percent heavier than compet-*

*itive boats of the same size. This extra weight gives today's Sea Ray buyer one of the strongest, safest, smoothest-riding glass boats ever made.*[27]

Perhaps the largest improvement and major selling point of the earliest Sea Ray boats was their striking interior. Most fiberglass boats at the time featured decidedly no-frills interiors—plain, vinyl-covered seats that sat atop a vinyl-covered and padded piece of plywood, as well as unattractive stucco floors and austere dashboards. Ray recognized the importance of interiors to automobile owners and believed boat owners would appreciate a similarly attractive and comfortable interior.

Ray knew fellow Michiganian Jim Earl, son of Harley Earl, the successful car designer whose sleek lines, tailfins, and plush interiors had revolu-

and certainly the most popular, full-production cars built with a fiberglass body.

By the time Earl retired in 1957, some 35 million cars featured his design concepts. Summing up his distinguished automobile-designing career, Earl offered a rather modest appraisal:

*My primary purpose has been to lengthen and lower the American automobile, at times in reality and always at least in appearance. Why? Because my sense of proportion tells me that oblongs are more attractive than squares, just as a ranch house is more attractive than a square, three-story, flat-roofed house or a greyhound is more graceful than an English bulldog.*[2]

Earl's design aesthetics greatly influenced the pleasure-boating industry. By the 1950s, many boat designers were taking their inspirational cues directly from Detroit. Fiberglass had given them a wonderfully malleable building material, while boat decks provided an open space for industrial-design expression.

With a long family and business history in Michigan, C. N. Ray was familiar with automobile design in general and Harley Earl's creations in particular, as were Arch Mehaffey and Jerry Michalak. The fresh and attractive designs that the Harley Earl Associates team created for Sea

Harley Earl was famous for creating numerous innovative car models, including the fiberglass Chevrolet Corvette. Sea Ray commissioned his son, Jim Earl, to design the interior of its inaugural 1960 lineup. *(Photo courtesy of General Motors Corp. Used with permission, GM Media Archives.)*

Ray played an important role in the successful launch of the Sea Ray brand. In addition, Sea Ray would prove the most adept of all boatbuilders in adopting suitable styling sensibilities from the automotive industry.

tionized automobile design many times since the 1920s. Jim Earl, who operated his father's design business after he retired, was also known as a first-rate designer in his own right, so Ray commissioned Harley Earl Associates to design an interior for his brand new Sea Ray line the year it debuted.[28] Later, he remembered how fast his impatience had turned to delight when he saw the final product:

*We took a deck and hull down to his facility, and I said, "Okay, I want you to come up with a [mind-boggling] interior." Well, I think it was after six weeks, I was getting a little impatient. So I called him up and said, "Well, what the hell's happening? Are you doing anything?" He says, "Yes, as a matter of fact, why don't you come*

*down tomorrow and take a look?" Arch and I went down, and it was spectacular!*[29]

Jim Earl and his team quickly impressed Ray with their work on the boat—they had incorporated stylish and colorfully upholstered seats (some two-tone) with chrome frames; colorfully upholstered side panels (some with practical, built-in pockets); an attractive, waterproof polypropylene carpet to cover the deck; and a handsome dashboard and steering wheel. All of these features were breathtakingly new for fiberglass boats in the early 1960s.

While the 1960 Sea Ray line offered only one or two models with Earl-designed interiors, every model of the 1961 line was available for purchase as a "custom" version featuring Earl's craftsmanship. The unveiling of Sea Ray interiors at the

Chicago National Boat Show in 1960 made an immediate impact on Sea Ray sales, and soon competing manufacturers were attempting to copy the innovations.[30]

Of course, Ray made sure the Harley Earl name and logo were prominently featured in Sea Ray's early marketing materials. The first Sea Ray brochure in 1960 mentioned Harley Earl Associates' styling, and the 1961 brochure truly honored their work.

It was 1962, however, before Sea Ray published a brochure that showed prospective buyers its stylish boats with the Earl-inspired interiors in their full-color glory. The pages featured enticing splashes of blue, tan, and red—the three interior color schemes, which offered appealing contrasts to the neutral tones of the hulls. Sea Ray began touting its boat interiors as the brand's primary value point the following year with a prominently featured tagline: "The compelling difference in Sea Ray is interior styling."[31]

**A Stern Introduction**

By the end of 1960, Ray had nearly exhausted Sea Ray's seed money and needed additional funding to expand into a larger facility to better manage incoming orders. To secure additional funding, Ray

visited the National Bank of Detroit early in 1962, where he and his father had done business for Ray Industries. Unfortunately, the bank did not express interest in funding a boat business and denied his application. Taken aback, Ray turned to his next-door neighbor, an attorney and friend, who loaned him $50,000.[32]

The new, if limited, funds were enough to support the company for the time being and allowed Ray to move the growing operation in 1962 into a suitable 28,800-square-foot building just north of Oxford on Stony Lake in Michigan.[33] The new plant stayed busy that year as a 19-foot boat and a new, bridged 18-foot Cruis-a-bout were added to the Sea Ray lineup.

While the early response to Sea Ray Boats was encouraging, the company was operating on minimal capital and had yet to turn a profit.[34] Still, the larger production facility gave Sea Ray workers some much-needed elbow room, while developments in marine-motor technology and

Above: Even though Sea Ray did not reproduce the 808 bridge model of 1963 the following year, the company reintroduced the style several years later.

Left: The 900 model, introduced in 1962, added nearly 2 feet and 200 pounds to the 800, which was previously Sea Ray's largest model.

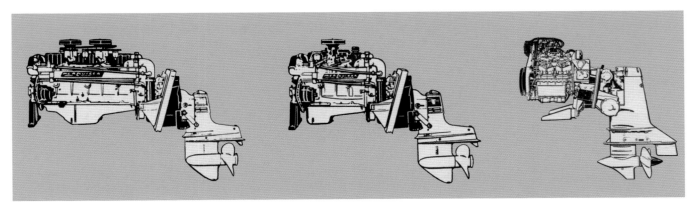

the resulting marriage of motors and boats soon provided the company, along with its competitors, some profitable breathing room.

Mehaffey remembered later how the development of the inboard/outboard and the prospect of selling a boat complete with motor changed the game. "The first time I got the idea that maybe there was something else in life was when OMC came out with their inboard/outboard version of their 90-horsepower, two-cycle engine, which sounded good, and we bought them and put them in our boats," Mehaffey said. "They never sold very well ... but they were better than outboards."[35]

OMC and Mercury Marine MerCruiser inboard/outboards were better not only because they allowed a larger engine size and a lower center of gravity than the straight outboards, but also because adding them as a package deal could significantly increase the gross profit on a sale.

Inboard/outboards (often shortened to I/Os) were also known as stern drives because the motor was mounted inboard in the stern of the boat and away from the motor's propeller-driven lower unit, which remained outboard. OMC and Mercury's versions, introduced to the industry in 1961, while not the first stern drives on the market, were the most popular early models.

Everyone at Sea Ray recognized the obvious performance and economic value of offering the stern drives with their boats, so the company began retooling its 16- to 19-footers to accommodate them. With the introduction of the 1963 line, Sea

The development of inboard/outboard stern-drive engines revolutionized the pleasure-boating industry. In 1963, Sea Ray offered one OMC stern drive and two Mercury MerCruiser stern drives. The sturdier and more powerful MerCruisers quickly proved the more popular brand.

Ray offered the 90-horsepower OMC stern drive and two MerCruiser stern drives—the 110 horsepower and the 140 horsepower. The OMC model allowed for a doubling of the gross profit gained on a sale of the boat alone. With the more powerful and sturdier MerCruisers, the equation was even better—the profit margin grew by another 50 percent.[36]

By the end of 1963, Sea Ray had sold 1,100 units, considerably more than in any of its first three production years. Higher-margin stern-drive options constituted a large portion of sales. For the first time, the company gained a modest profit.[37]

Sea Ray had motorboated far in only five years. By the end of 1963, in just four production years, the company had progressed from brainstorm to reality; from owning six boat models to eight; from selling only boats and outboard-motor models to selling some models complete with inboard/outboard stern drives; from one in-state distributor to a growing network of widely dispersed dealers; from a two-car garage operation to a 28,800-square-foot office/manufacturing facility; from an average player to the manufacturer of the "Cadillac" of pleasure boats; from unknown to well known and respected.

The buoy featured on the cover of Sea Ray's 1966 brochure indicated to prospective boat buyers that Sea Rays could handle deep and rough offshore waters as well as more shallow and calm inshore waterways.

## CHAPTER TWO

# SEA RAY STYLE

## 1964–1967

*One of the things I remember C. N. saying in the early days was, "If it has my name on it, it has to be the best."*

—Jerry Michalak, fiberglass specialist
and designer[1]

ALTHOUGH NEWS OF JOHN F. Kennedy's assassination in November 1963 shocked the world, drawing national sympathy and creating a defining moment in American history, the nation's engine of commercial enterprise continued to run smoothly. At Sea Ray, the year's strong sales spurred C. N. Ray to finance another expansion of the Sea Ray facility early the following year, once again doubling the size of the Oxford plant's production floor. The early to mid-1960s served as transitional years for the company, as it redesigned and rebuilt various models as stern drives, while continuing to offer outboards and the occasional straight inboard.

During its transitional phase, Sea Ray reduced the total number of models it was producing. The 600 was retired in 1963, and the 808 bridge model dropped from the 1964 lineup. As a result, Sea Ray offered one less model in 1964 than the previous year, and, with just seven models (two of which were simply stern-drive versions of existing outboard models), the company offered fewer models than it had started with in 1960. The reduction in models was temporary, however, as the company continued to grow, adapting to technological developments in the industry and becoming better acquainted with the market.

Aside from the demanding but welcome changes brought on by technological innovation and increased sales, Sea Ray had established a comfortable and increasingly efficient operation by 1964. Ray handled the company's overall business strategy and remained closely involved in expanding the dealer network, while Jerry Michalak focused on product development. The hiring of Tom Dugall as the general sales manager and Bill Offer as the finance administrator early on had allowed Arch Mehaffey to focus his attention more fully on the Oxford plant's operations as general manager.[2] Michalak recalled Mehaffey's role during the early Sea Ray days:

*Arch [Mehaffey] was more or less originally running the plant because he was there every day. He was the guy with the sharp pencil who would make projections on what we should do and pricing the boats.*[3]

From the onset, Sea Ray had been a high-quality manufacturer that offered superior craftsmanship and design features, and as such it was rightfully in the higher-priced tier of boat brands. Effective pric-

---

By the late 1960s, C. N. Ray had developed some additional business ventures that would have a significant impact on Sea Ray operations.

Sea Ray significantly increased the square footage of its Oxford, Michigan, plant every few years in the 1960s and 1970s.

ing strategy was crucial for not only recouping expenses and generating a reasonable profit without discouraging sales, but also for establishing the company's overall market niche. Despite the considerable flexibility in pricing in terms of profit margins, it was necessary to maintain an effective balance. Priced too high, Sea Ray sales would diminish and become a direct competitor's gain; priced too low, profits would diminish and consequently reduce revenue for innovation and expansion. Mehaffey had always considered the important responsibility of pricing the company's boats as part of his duties, and he was especially talented in this area.

Recalling Mehaffey's pricing prowess, veteran Sea Ray employee Jim Steffens, who started working for Sea Ray as a hole-cutter in 1967, said, "He [was] a wizard as far as pricing the boats."[4] Meanwhile, Ray had focused on developing the dealer network through a variety of creative approaches. For example, for one of the earlier dealer meetings, Sea Ray flew in all the dealers for a two-day tour of the Oxford, Michigan, plant. It also developed an incentive program in which dealers could have a percentage of their sales refunded to them if they reached certain sales benchmarks. Top-producing dealers even won cruises to sun-drenched locales such as Monaco and Acapulco.[5] Ray and the rest of the Sea Ray team

made sure the dealers knew the important role they played within the company, and by the mid-1960s, Sea Ray had dozens of dealerships carrying its line, most of them exclusively. "We had a lot of dealer programs set up," Michalak recalled. "Back then, we had only 100 or so dealers. It was more of a big family."[6]

**A Major Production**

In Sea Ray's first few years, as Ray and Mehaffey were novices in terms of boat production, Michalak's knowledge of boatbuilding was critical for Sea Ray's survival. The production team depended on Michalak for design ideas and leadership in the most crucial aspects of hands-on production work. However, Ray and Mehaffey quickly expanded their knowledge of boat production. Steffens remembered their involvement in the production process:

*Early on, C. N. [Ray] used to walk the plant, and Arch [Mehaffey] did too. They'd walk down with the general managers ... C. N. used to come through, or during model change, Arch would come through and physically look at the boats, and say, "I don't like this carpet. Put this carpet in. Take that carpet out." They seemed to be in touch with what we were doing.*[7]

In the 1960s, fiberglass boats were built essentially the same as they are today, though the details and technology have changed. A brand-new fiberglass boat model started out as a wooden prototype hull and deck—cut and shaped in a traditional way dating back decades, if not centuries, in terms of fundamentals. The process began with the cutting and shaping of a skeletal wooden boat frame, which was then covered with sheets of marine plywood, forming the prototype mold. It was at this stage that, over time, the process began to deviate from traditional boat-making techniques to accommodate the use of fiberglass as a building material. A wax or other type of release agent was applied to the wooden mold to facilitate the removal of the fiberglass hull and deck, which were applied to and shaped on the wooden base. The mold was then covered with a gel coat and, in the earliest days, several layers of long mats made of woven fiberglass strands. Each layer was then wetted down thoroughly with a polyester resin (a syrupy liquid that served as a glue and provided an outer coating for the fiberglass). As the 1960s progressed, manufacturers began to replace this process with use of the chopper gun, which allowed for the simultaneous application of fiberglass and resin.

After the fiberglass hull was formed and separated from its molded prototype, wooden support beams called "stringers"—also reinforced with fiberglass—were laid both lengthwise and across

This early SR 230 schematic shows the new model's ample seating, one of two small "vee" berths mounted along the forward cabin, and the lavatory (head). The SR 230 design defined Sea Ray's style for years to come.

the inside bottom to provide additional structural support and internal compartmentalization. A flat deck floor was then laid above the stringers. The entire unit, inside and out, was then coated liberally with the resin. The separate fiberglass deck was created in the same way, followed by hole-cutting in both components. The completed deck was then riveted with the hull. The joining of the hull and deck created the basic boat body, though a con-

**September 1964:** Sea Ray introduces model-year 1965 boats. The SRX 17 and the SRV 230 are the company's first "deep vee" hulls, built to handle deeper, rougher waters.

**September 1966:** Sea Ray introduces model-year 1967 boats, including the SRV 380, the company's first cathedral-hulled boat, along with the SRV 190 Sportsman and SRV 160.

**September 1965:** Sea Ray introduces model-year 1966 boats, which include three more deep vees—the SRV 170, 180, and 190, all in both outboard and inboard/outboard versions.

**September 1967:** Sea Ray introduces model-year 1968 boats, which include the SRV 370, SRV 240, and SRV 185.

siderable amount of additional materials and work were required to prepare a Sea Ray boat for the marketplace. This included running electrical wiring; installing engines (for stern drives and inboards), seating, and other mechanisms and components; and painting and polishing.[8]

In the early years, the Oxford plant had several production employees with boatbuilding experience, but Sea Ray also benefited from a local workforce with experience in other types of mechanical production, including the automobile industry, which was thriving in nearby Detroit. The Oxford plant's proximity to that city was generally an asset, but it also proved a detriment. Sea Ray paid its employees well, but the young company could not match the wage and benefits packages available at General Motors (GM) or other major automobile manufacturing companies, so Sea Ray would periodically lose skilled workers to the automobile industry.

Steffens remembers days when he would walk into the shop as the only one present from his department because the others had been hired at GM. "Everybody wanted to gravitate to General

Motors," he recalled. Steffens had also worked at GM for about two years before returning to Sea Ray. He recalled the factors that brought him back to the Oxford plant:

*At GM, you felt like you were a number—part of the union and a number. [At Sea Ray], you had a say on what you did and how you did it. They left it up to you to organize your own time. It wasn't something moving down the line every 30 seconds, and you slam a part on it and at the end of your shift, you go home. You had an ability to use your creativity and your brain as far as making things fit together and work.*[9]

**Collaborative Design**

Despite these occasional defections to Detroit, the production crew at Sea Ray successfully handled the difficult demands of the mid-1960s. By that time, a growing and increasingly experienced Sea Ray production team had been trained to work from the prototypes and spec sheets that Michalak produced for both new models and modifications of existing ones. Consequently, Michalak's constant presence on the production floor was no longer necessary, enabling him to devote more time to new product development.

Regardless of his growing expertise, Michalak had never been egotistical about the concept of boat design. Design had always been a collaborative effort at Sea Ray, and the company's primary designer regularly solicited input from a wide variety of employees. Steffens remembered Michalak's style:

*Jerry Michalak, early on, would give the design and get the input from employees on a mold. If you were an assembly person or an engine person, he would come to you and say, "What was good about a certain mold? What was bad about a certain mold? Do you have any input?"*[10]

While Michalak was unquestionably Sea Ray's principal product developer, the design aspect of the business allowed Mehaffey to demonstrate his handy knack for creating potential Sea Ray boat styles. Mehaffey continually took note of pleasure-boat style changes to share with Michalak; he also came up with his own ideas. It was not unusual for

Sea Ray's 1965 SRX 17 model was not successful, so its production ceased the following year as several other deep-vee versions were introduced. Here, C. N. Ray dismounts from his Morane–Saulnier MS 760 Paris jet, aboard which many early dealers experienced memorable rides.

The SRV 230 model, pictured above in the 1966 Sea Ray brochure, featured a popular deep-V hull. The model was available as a single-engine or twin-engine design.

Mehaffey to describe a style concept to Ray or Michalak and suddenly start sketching it on paper.[11]

One style idea that Mehaffey had suggested was the reverse sheer. A boat's sheer refers to the line of the gunwale, the upper edge of the boat side where the hull and deck meet, running the length of the boat. Gunwales of the time were either perfectly straight or had a sheer curved up toward the bow and stern. With a reverse sheer, the curve is turned down toward the bow or stern. Mehaffey's idea of a reverse sheer had originated while he observed the boats at the Chicago National Boat Show one year. "I came back and started to doodle and draw," he explained. "Whenever I drew a Sea Ray boat, I always drew it with the curved gunwale, and finally we started to get the boats to look like that."[12]

Michalak began designing boats with a slight reverse sheer for Sea Ray's mid-1960s deep-vee hulls (commonly referred to later as "deep V"). The reverse sheer became another of Sea Ray's signature style elements, and later models had a much more pronounced downward curve.

**Vee for Victory**

Two product development goals in particular had captured Ray, Mehaffey, and Michalak's collective attention in 1964. One was the desire to build a boat more than 20 feet long, while the other was to design and incorporate a deep-vee hull similar to those introduced by other offshore boat manufacturers. The deep-vee hull was characterized by a high deadrise, the angle between the bottom of a boat and its widest crossbeam. Designed for deeper, larger bodies of water, it provided a smoother ride and offered more storage and cabin space.

Sea Ray introduced two deep-vee models at the 1965 Marine Trade Exhibit and Conference (MTEC) at Chicago's McCormack Place in September 1964. The first "express" model, the SRX 17, was a sleek, sophisticated stern-drive–powered model that measured just over 17 feet at the centerline. However, it was the other deep-vee model introduced in Chicago that year, the stern drive SR 230, that met both of Sea Ray's goals and enthralled boat dealers. At 23 feet and 4 inches, the boat exuded power and grace, reflected in a deep-chested cutwater at the forward edge of its bow, which sliced through rough water with authority.

Chicago-based MTEC, which premiered in 1960, was considerably younger than the well-established Chicago National Boat Show, which had existed since 1929. Unlike its industry elder, MTEC was open only to marine industry professionals.[13]

# THE STERN DRIVE PACKAGE

CHARLES STRANG, AN AVID OUTBOARD boat-racing enthusiast, invented the modern and practical stern-drive inboard/outboard (I/O) motor in 1948, while attending graduate school at Massachusetts Institute of Technology (MIT).[1] His design concept separated the engine from the outboard's lower unit, which contained the propeller, placing it inboard in the stern while leaving only the lower unit outboard, then mechanically connecting the two under the deck with a drive shaft and a type of universal joint similar to those commonly used in cars.

The stern drive combined elements of the straight inboard and outboard motors in a hybrid that offered the best of each. This configuration allowed the use of a larger and more powerful boat motor and provided a lower center of gravity, like an inboard. It also maintained the maneuverability of the outboard, all while providing more interior room than possible with the straight inboard.

For personal reasons, Strang asked his friend Jim Wynne to patent the stern drive, and

Volvo introduced the first such I/O motor, called the Penta Aquamatic, the following year. Mercury and Outboard Marine Corporation (OMC) followed in 1961 with their own versions.[2]

The stern drive had a profound effect on the boating industry, mostly because it

PHOTO COURTESY OF CHARLES D. STRANG

Sea Ray's SR 230 was on display both in the event's exhibition hall and on Lake Michigan.[14] By the time Sea Ray distributed its 1966 brochure describing the boat's triumphant MTEC debut, the company had incorporated the "V" into the SR 230 name:

*Many competitive manufacturers familiar with the inhospitable waters of Lake Michigan shied away from on-the-water demonstrations. Not so with Sea Ray. We welcomed the opportunity of displaying the SRV 230 in her native habitat. Loaded with some of the most knowledgeable dealers in the Marine Industry, SRV 230, powered by twin 150-Merc I/Os [inboard/outboards], knifed through the choppy waters of Lake Michigan. From her maiden voyage on through her last voyage three days later, the com-*

*ments were: "she's a beauty"; "she sure can take it"; "no rattles or bangs"; "we were deeply impressed."*[15]

The 1965 SRV 230 sold out within six months of its Chicago debut.[16] Its deep-V hull produced undeniable performance enhancement, while its design (along with that of its 1968 revision, the SRV 240) defined much of the distinctive styling that remained a Sea Ray signature over the years—a high-deadrise, deep-V hull with gently curving handrails and a stripe along the center of the topsides (the outer-hull surface visible above the waterline). It also provided a perfect match for the company's renowned, well-appointed interiors.[17]

Sea Ray quickly capitalized on the popularity of the deep V by offering three smaller boats in

prompted boat manufacturers to package engines with their boats rather than sell only the boat, as had been customary. While that presented new capital outlays for manufacturers, it also allowed them to price their boats with an additional profit margin. Furthermore, the new stern drives gave the final customer an enhanced product. Ultimately, it proved a boon for everyone—engine manufacturers, boatbuilders, marine dealers, and boat owners.

Sea Ray introduced the new stern drives in its largest models in 1963, continuing to offer the straight outboard versions as well. The company gradually phased in

more stern drives and offered fewer outboards over the years. By 1968, there were just four straight outboard models left. Sea Ray intermittently offered outboards until 2000, when it started selling only stern-drive boats. In 2004, the company surprised most in the marine-manufacturing industry when it reintroduced an outboard, the 185 Sport Bow Rider.

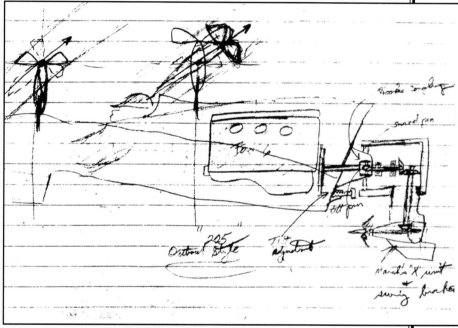

ILLUSTRATION COURTESY OF CHARLES D. STRANG

Left: Charles Strang, inventor of the modern stern drive, designed a Mercury Marine version with superior horsepower and performance that soon captured the majority of the stern-drive market, easily surpassing Volvo and OMC's initially underpowered effort.

Right: A portion of Strang's MIT inventions ledger for 1948 clearly shows the first depiction of the modern stern drive.

1966 with a full-bodied hull and the distinctive V-model styling features. While the SRV 230's size and price point limited its competitiveness outside the stern-drive market, the more modestly sized and priced SRV 170, SRV 180, and SRV 190 were also marketable as outboards. Sea Ray offered all three of these smaller deep Vs as both straight outboards and I/Os. These models generally sold well, particularly as I/Os.

With sales of deep Vs increasing, Sea Ray continued to convert more of its line to deep-V hull models for 1967, introducing a modification of the SRV 190 and another small version of the deep V, the SRV 160. The SRV 160 gave Sea Ray a new opening price point as a bargain outboard model 15 feet 3 inches at the centerline.

The SRV 190 Sportsman was the first Sea Ray boat with an official descriptive model name, as opposed to the typical combination of letters and numbers or "custom" and "deluxe" designations (other than the "Custom Skier" name used to designate no-frills versions of various models).

The Sportsman, a stern drive presented as an "offshore family sportsman model," was different from its 1966 predecessor because it sported a deeper V hull design that added 6 inches of molded depth.[18] The extra space created a more comfortable boat in terms of both its ride and lounging potential. While the 1966 SRV 190 had a small forward storage area, the new Sportsman had a true cabin, with upholstered interior, bunks, and a fair amount of head room.

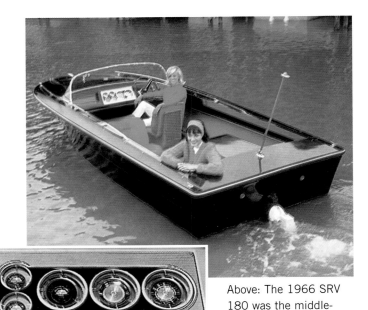

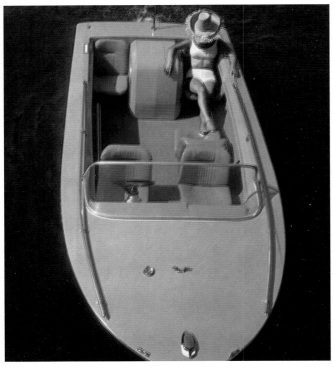

Another new Sea Ray model produced in 1967 was the SRV 380, a modified deep V with a cathedral, or tri-hull. As a stern drive with little more than 18 feet at the centerline, the SRV 380 was not nearly as long as its model number indicated and did not appear, at first glance, to have the sleek, curvy silhouette Sea Ray had been perfecting since the company's inception. In fact, the SRV 380, viewed from behind or above, looked extraordinarily ponderous—a floating rectangle with a smaller recessed rectangular storage area on top of the deck area just forward of the cockpit, and a slightly pointed prow in the front. A frontal view of the boat exposed the voluptuous swept-back curves of the cathedral hull. The SRV 380's hull design gave it added stability, while its 120- to 200-horsepower range provided plenty of power.

Stability, however, was not an attribute of the nation's psyche during the mid-1960s. The Vietnam War had begun to elicit massive protests, and civil rights demonstrations were taking place in many American cities. Some remained peaceful, while others exploded into full-blown riots. Sea Ray's home state of Michigan was not immune to the unrest.

Nevertheless, Sea Ray's strong business foundation withstood the social upheaval that

Above: The 1966 SRV 180 was the middle-sized of the three new V-hull models introduced that year. Along with the SRV 190, it featured a new aluminum instrument cluster (inset) as standard equipment.

Below: The smallest of the new 1966 deep-Vs, the SRV 170 (pictured here in the 1966 version of blue), was just 16 feet at the centerline.

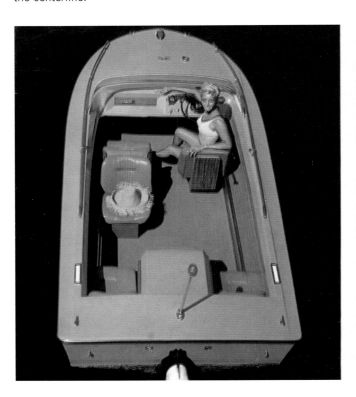

shook the nation, as the company's revenues grew at about 30 percent a year during the mid-1960s.[19] Sea Ray's first deep-V model, the SRV 230, had been an extraordinary success and became one of the most copied boats in the industry. It also helped establish Sea Ray's definitive style. As the company had significantly increased its business west of the Mississippi River, it opened a small branch office and warehouse in Inglewood, California, in 1966. By 1967, Sea Ray had become one of the top 10 fiberglas (as the company's 1967 brochure spelled it) boat builders in the country.[20]

While Sea Ray had prospered in Michigan by selling mostly to dealerships east of the Mississippi River, Ray's appetite for additional West Coast business and other blossoming business ventures was about to result in a surprising move. On the national scene, however, more social upheaval and tragic deaths were on the horizon.

Right and below: The photos featured in the 1967 SRV 380 marketing brochures did not thoroughly display the new boat's striking cathedral hull.

Sea Ray's 1968 SRV 240 Hardtop flagship offered the boat manufacturer's first covered cockpit, affording boaters some protection from the weather.

## CHAPTER THREE

# FULL SPEED AHEAD

## 1968 – 1972

*We were taught that from the time you came in, you either did it right or you didn't do it. We used a lot of the best materials money could buy. They didn't skimp on the hardware, the carpets, the vinyls, or any of the gauges and components. [C. N. Ray] wanted to make sure, even back then, that it was as trouble-free as possible, and [that] it was a good experience.*

—Jim Steffens, senior manufacturing advisor[1]

THE SOCIAL STRIFE THAT had defined much of the 1960s intensified in the latter years of the decade, with the number of protests against the Vietnam War and demonstrations in support of civil rights both increasing. Within a two-month period in 1968, both Martin Luther King, Jr., the powerful voice of peaceful resistance in the fight for civil rights, and Robert F. Kennedy, the popular New York senator and U.S. presidential candidate, were assassinated.

Violence and protest marked the following year as well, though spirits around the world soared as people witnessed an extraordinary event—man walking on the moon. The televised Apollo 11 and Apollo 12 lunar landings in July and November 1969 temporarily eased the world's tension as viewers witnessed the rockets blasting off into space from a location less than 15 miles away from where Sea Ray would establish a new production facility just a few years later.

While war, politically motivated violence, and moon landings were some of the most compelling events of the late 1960s in the United States, another peril was affecting many American citizens and businesses—runaway inflation. Although President Richard Nixon cut federal spending after being elected in 1968, and the Federal Reserve Board raised interest rates, the price of consumer goods, including boats, continued to rise quickly.

Nevertheless, Sea Ray products sold relatively well through the end of the decade, with the company undergoing significant expansion in the next few years.

### Phoenix Rising

While a considerable majority of Sea Ray's late 1960s business came from dealers east of the Mississippi River, the company had also made inroads into the western U.S. market, where substantial untapped opportunity for additional growth remained. So it seemed wise to build a Sea Ray facility at a location west of the Mississippi River.

Sea Ray also considered the West because of the pressure it was receiving from unions in Michigan. With Oxford approximately halfway between Flint and Detroit, two Michigan union strongholds, Ray " ... didn't want too many eggs in the Michigan plant," Mehaffey recalled. "In Oxford, you always had the union looking over your shoulder. Just about every two years, we had [an attempt by a union to be voted in]."[2]

At first, California seemed the logical place for Sea Ray to set up shop. As a large coastal state with

In 1969, Sea Ray's stylized stingray logo gave way to this colorful oval incorporating propeller and water symbols.

Sea Ray's world headquarters and production facility in Phoenix was completed in the spring of 1971. Though waterways are not plentiful in Arizona, nearby Saguaro Lake and Firebird Lake proved excellent boat-testing sites.

plenty of lakes and waterways, it housed a large population with considerable discretionary income for recreation. But further consideration of the Golden State's high real estate prices and worri-

some union environment persuaded Ray to consider alternative western locations.[3]

Meanwhile, Ray had purchased a citrus farm in Rainbow Valley, southwest of Phoenix, where he maintained a residence. He also owned a Learjet business with an office at Phoenix Sky Harbor International Airport. With California ruled out as a suitable state for a new operation, Arizona became the not-so-obvious choice. While lacking an abundance of waterways, Arizona nonetheless had a few substantial lakes and was well located as a general production and distribution point for the western United States.[4]

**September 1970:** Sea Ray introduces model-year 1971 boats. New models include specifically designed and designated SRV 240 Weekender and Cuddy Cabin versions, SRV 220 Cruiser and Cuddy Cabin versions, the SRV 193, and SRV 183.

**September 1968:** Sea Ray introduces model-year 1969 boats. New models include the SRV 210 and the SRX Pachanga, the company's first performance speedboat.

**September 1969:** Sea Ray introduces model-year 1970 boats, including the SRV 370, SRV 200, SRV 180, and SRV 150. The SRX Pachanga is offered with an innovative jet-power option, while the SRV 240 is available in a new hardtop version.

Jerry Michalak (standing) designed two of the most innovative and popular Sea Ray models in the late 1960s and early 1970s. Like C. N. Ray and Arch Mehaffey, he believed relocating to a larger manufacturing facility in the early years was key to business growth.

At first, Ray brought only Mehaffey to Arizona to help him find a building suitable for a product development facility, and they soon selected one in the Phoenix area. What had started as a rather tentative effort toward establishing a Sea Ray presence in the Grand Canyon State now became a full-fledged commitment.[5] As Ray recalled:

*[Mehaffey] moved his family out here, and then we rented a place principally for Jerry [Michalak] for design and development. Then we decided we were going to build some boats. And then the next thing you know, that was going good. We were getting more dealers set up in the West. So we built a plant— air-conditioned—to keep our workers happy.[6]*

Longtime Sea Ray employee Roger Giles began working for the company in accessory and parts sales in Phoenix shortly after Sea Ray opened its new production facility in 1971. Constructing a marine manufacturing facility in the dry desert environment of Arizona seemed reasonable to Giles:

*Everybody used to say, "Why a plant in Phoenix? There's no water around." I always answered, "Who cares? We're covering the western United*

**September 1971:** Sea Ray introduces model-year 1972 boats, including Hardtop and Sportbridge versions of the SRV 240 and the SRV 163.

**Summer 1972:** Sea Ray establishes a production facility for larger boats on Merritt Island in Florida, as well as a small design facility on the mainland nearby.

**May 1971:** Sea Ray's new corporate headquarters, including a production facility and a product development and engineering (PD&E) facility, opens in Phoenix, Arizona.

**September 1972:** Sea Ray introduces model-year 1973 boats. New models include the SRV 240 Sport Bridge II and the SRV 220 Overnighter. Swim platforms are introduced on the SRV 240 models.

# PHOENIX FLIGHTS

WHILE THERE WERE CONVINCING market and logistical reasons for bringing Sea Ray headquarters to Phoenix, Arizona, in 1968, the fact that founder C. N. Ray had settled in the area and established sideline businesses there most likely influenced the decision-making process. For example, Arizona Learjet Sales, one of Ray's businesses, operated out of Sky Harbor International Airport in Phoenix.[1]

Never a man to shy away from risky activity, as reflected in his founding a company in an unfamiliar industry, Ray's daredevil side beyond the business world was evident in his continuing penchant for flying.

Ray's flying career started after he graduated from high school and joined the U.S. Army Air Force in 1943, when he enlisted in the Aviation Cadet Program. He was commissioned as a Second Lieutenant in 1944 and piloted B-25 airplanes. After the atomic bombing of Hiroshima in 1945, he served as a First Lieutenant and flew B-29 aircraft.

Ray had long used his excellent flying skills to conduct Sea Ray business through the years. He loved piloting airplanes almost as much as boats and owned at least one of each from Sea

Ray's earliest days onward. As Sea Ray continued to grow and his Learjet operation expanded, the World War II Air Force veteran hired another pilot to help him meet the increasing demands.

Howard V. Mc Donald, or "Mac," had retired from the Air Force as a squadron commander of a jet tanker outfit in 1964. He first flew with Ray in the spring of 1966 on a short flight to Ray's citrus farm—another Phoenix-area business/pleasure project.

Over the years, Mc Donald transported top Sea Ray dealers to special dealer gatherings in Hawaii, Monaco, and Cozumel, Mexico. "I flew them all," Mc Donald recalled. "I'd fly the dealers down to Cozumel, Mexico, and then I'd go back and get another group, and I'd shuttle them back and forth. This was done almost every year until 1978."[2]

In the years after the Phoenix move, Ray owned several airplanes, including a Learjet 23, Learjet 25C, Learjet 35, Learjet 36, Cessna Citation 501, Falcon 50, and an Augusta 109 helicopter. While Mc Donald piloted the majority of Sea Ray's business flights in his almost 20-year association with the company, it was not uncom-

*States, and Phoenix is a central location. It doesn't matter if we sell a boat in Phoenix. It's a geographic issue."[7]*

While Sea Ray developed its Phoenix facility, the Oxford plant continued to produce boats at a fast rate. The company's 1967 line had been successful, including the SRV 230, which featured 22 feet 2 inches at the centerline and a molded depth of 55 inches. It boasted a full fiberglass inner liner with foam flotation chambers, upholstered cabin interior and bunks, teak step plates and trim, teak bulkhead doors, a sliding forward deck hatch, deluxe instrument cluster, mechanical steering, and two seating arrangement options, as well as other optional equipment.

Although it was a large, fine boat, sales of the SRV 230 had flagged slightly since its triumphal introduction a few years earlier. Michalak knew the boat reflected a fundamentally sound design, so instead of altering the style dramatically, he decided to enlarge, refine, and rename the boat, incorporating similar styling along with a new Sportsman model name. In 1968, Sea Ray replaced the SRV 230 with the SRV 240 Sportsman, the new "flagship of the Sea Ray fleet" that offered greater deck and cabin space.[8] The deck of the SRV 240 Sportsman did not differ much from its predecessor style-wise, but with more than a foot and a half added to the length and five more inches in molded hull depth, the boat's expanded dimensions and improved performance energized sales of the company's lone 20-plus–footer.

Boating and aviation have long been two of C. N. Ray's passions. Pictured here in front of Ray's Learjet 25C are, from left to right, chief pilot Howard Mc Donald, Ray, and Mehaffey, Sea Ray's executive vice president.

mon for Ray to pilot some of the aircraft as well. No matter which accomplished pilot was at the cockpit controls, however, mechanical failure and Mother Nature sometimes interfered.

Mc Donald, whom Ray referred to as "a really talented guy," recalled an aerial incident that occurred after Sea Ray had established its product development and engineering (PD&E) operation in Titusville, Florida.[3] Mc Donald and Ray had traveled from Phoenix to Titusville in a Learjet 25 with

no problems until their approach to the airport. As they began their gradual descent, Mc Donald attempted to transfer the aircraft's fuel into its wing tanks, a typical measure taken during landings. On approach to the airport, Mc Donald dropped the flaps and landing gear. Soon thereafter, one engine suddenly quit, and a moment later, the other did as well. He recalled:

*I sure didn't want to hit those approach lights lined up on the runway. So I slid off to the side of them, got over the fence [to the airport property], passed the approach lights, and I squeezed [the airplane] over to stick it on the runway, and we parked in front of the terminal.*[4]

To successfully bring the Learjet to the center of the runway without engine power proved a remarkable display of aerial prowess. Soon after landing, Mc Donald and Ray realized that someone had improperly set the switch used to transfer fuel to the wings, so the fuel had pumped *out* of the wings and back into the aircraft's fuselage tank. "We had about 1,000 pounds of fuel, but it was in the wrong place," Mc Donald explained.[5]

Logging a remarkable 18,000 flight hours, with a number of those during his Sea Ray days, Mc Donald always handled situations with a cool head and a steady hand. He piloted for Sea Ray until 1985.

The SRV 240 came with a fitted white vinyl standard top and refinements such as a wood-grained sport steering wheel, storage area with teak-covered flooring, and quilted vinyl side-paneling. By all accounts, the SRV was a high-performance beauty that proved extraordinarily popular with boat buyers. The 240 design served as the main template upon which Sea Ray would build for years to come.

In addition to the SRV 240, Sea Ray's 1968 line also introduced the SRV 185, which was nearly identical in size to the SRV 180 but featured slightly

Right: The SRV 240 replaced the SRV 230 as the flagship of the Sea Ray fleet in 1968. Pictured here are two 1970 boats— the basic model and the hartop version, the first stylistic variation produced from this important boat design, which featured a sporty fiberglass roof covering the cockpit area.

more molded depth and a walk-through wind-shield; an SRV 160 model, newly designated as DLX (deluxe) to accompany the basic Custom Skier; and the 16-foot-5-inch stern-drive, cathe-dral-hulled SRV 370, a slightly downsized version of the 18-foot-3-inch SRV 380 model, which also only lasted a single season.

### Happy Anniversary

As Sea Ray entered its 10th year in business, the company's line of boats was markedly different than that of its inaugural year. In 1959, Sea Ray's lineup included six boats—all outboard models—with the smallest boat measuring a mere 12 feet and the longest 18 feet. In 1969, Sea Ray's lineup included 10 boats, with the smallest boat at 16 feet and the longest at 24 feet, and two-thirds of the boats were stern-drive models. Furthermore, Sea Ray had made numerous refinements to its boats that offered not only stylistic élan but also functional improvements.

Sea Ray produced a special brochure for its 10th anniversary year of 1969 that featured com-mentary from all three of the company's original

Avocado was a popular color for boat interiors in the late 1960s and early 1970s, as this SRV 190 model shows.

principals—Ray, Mehaffey, and Michalak. Mehaffey elaborated on the quality construction of Sea Ray boats:

*Since the development of our first boat more than 10 years ago, Sea Ray has adhered to a very strict policy of using not only the best con-struction material available, but [also] enough material to ensure structural integrity second to none. Pound a Sea Ray with your fist. You will feel the difference. Ask your dealer to show you a cutout from another Sea Ray he has delivered.*

*Usually, prior to delivery, the installation of an accessory will require a deck, transom, or through-hull cutout. If that doesn't convince you, ... compare the weight of a Sea Ray with that of a comparable boat. Weight is, after all, a pretty good indicator of the amount of material used in a boat. Weight has a lot to do with how well a boat rides; how well the steering, windshield, seats, accessories hold up during continued use; how well the [core] value holds up, because a solidly built boat doesn't shake apart with vibra-tion and flexing; how well a Sea Ray will survive an accidental encounter with another boat, rock, or log. A sense of pride and security becomes quite important in the decision to buy a boat. Sea Ray provides both requirements.[9]*

In Sea Ray's 1969 brochure, Michalak also touted the company's commitment to designing excellence, its new product development and engineering (PD&E) facility, and the craftsmen who built the boats:

*Before the first Sea Ray was put on the drafting board, a firm commitment was made to design the most beautiful line of boats afloat. Having adhered to this basic policy, Sea Ray has continued to cre-ate boats that lead the field in styling and design. In our modern design and engineering facility in Phoenix, Arizona, Sea Rays are in a continual process of testing and evaluation for design, styling, and engineering improvements for the pre-sent and for the future. It is here that the original design is perfected and transformed into the pro-duction tooling to build a boat that will stand head and shoulders above the rest. After all, it is the ded-ication of craftsmen fiercely proud of their work-*

Above and left: The SRX Pachanga, introduced at Sea Ray's 10th anniversary in 1969, featured a radical departure in style for the boat manufacturer. The Pachanga was designed to satisfy the growing number of boaters who were attracted primarily to speed and less to size and amenities.

Right: The SRV 210's large walk-through windshield (inset) and long hatch offered cockpit ventilation and easy access to the foredeck.

*manship that results in superior performance. The Sea Rays of today tell that story well. Tomorrow is even more challenging.*[10]

A notable new design for Sea Ray in 1969 was the SRX Pachanga. The Pachanga was a boat built for speed, with a long, low profile. The name is Spanish for "a lively party" and was presented in the Sea Ray literature, invariably along with the word "Blast!" which associated the new boat with a common colloquialism for having fun—"having a blast." Pachanga had a nice ring to it, sounded energetic, and conjured images of exotic seaside locales, while "Blast!" encapsulated the excitement the boat offered.

Sea Ray's Pachanga lived up to its name. Offered with motors producing from 155 to 225 horsepower, the boat could exceed 50 miles per hour, with the low-profile making this speed feel even faster when on the water at full throttle. The boat's sleek standard equipment served to heighten

the sense of speed—rotating bucket seats, a recessed instrument panel, air intakes on the deck, louvered exhaust ventilators, and a prominent racing stripe. A low profile windshield with a rakish tilt was available as an option.

The SRX Pachanga was Sea Ray's new "sports car" model, harking back conceptually to the company's 600 from its original 1960 line. The Pachanga was longer and lacked the 600's tail fins and curvaceous styling but, nevertheless, had an appealing minimalist style of its own. With the 225-horsepower stern-drive motor and a lower center of gravity, it reached speeds unattainable in the earlier 600. At 18 feet long with no cabin, the SRX Pachanga was built more for speed than space.

The SRV 210 was also introduced in 1969. The deep-V 210 was a smaller version of the SRV 240, with fewer luxuries, but priced a little lower and designed to fit a particular market niche. Two inches narrower at the beam, four inches shallower in hull depth, and 600 pounds lighter, the new SRV 210 had a relatively deep-V hull that offered a smooth ride. The boat also had a walk-through windshield with a center-opening bow area (essen-

Standard equipment for all Sea Ray stern drives in 1970 included recessed instrumentation mounted in custom panels, welded windshield frames, an electric blower with separate ducting, natural teak trim, and heavy duty stainless steel bow and stern eyes, among other features.

tially an elongated hatch that opens all the way back to the cockpit area) that allowed easy access to the foredeck and a small, or "cuddy," cabin.

### Down and Out

Downsizing and outboards seemed to reflect the style guidelines for Sea Ray's 1970 line, partly in response to inflationary pressures in the economy that were forcing Sea Ray costs and prices upward. In 1970, the company introduced four new models (including one replacement model), which were essentially smaller versions of existing models; shortened the centerline length of one existing model; and offered three additional outboards.

The new SRV 200 was, like the SRV 210 introduced the previous year, shorter and more economical, featuring the same type of V hull as the SRV 240. The nearly 20-foot SRV 200 hull was similar but shallower than either of its predecessors, and its smaller size allowed only storage space in the bow rather than a true cabin. It also featured the same kind of walk-through windshield as the SRV 210.

The SRV 180, which replaced the SRV 185, was a full foot shorter with a few inches less depth in the bow, but with sleeker lines and a newly styled interior. Along with the new models, Sea Ray removed nearly a foot from its SRV 190.

One of Sea Ray's new outboards, the 16-foot-5-inch SRV 370, was a smaller version of the tri-hulled stern-drive SRV 380, which measured 18 feet 3 inches. Being nearly two feet shorter than the 380, the SRV 370 was presented as a more moderately priced family-oriented pleasure boat. The company also offered the 14-foot-6-inch SRV 150, a bargain boat with a lower opening price point for beginning or infrequent boaters. In addition to these new outboard models, Sea Ray also introduced an outboard 190 model. The cumulative effect was a Sea Ray line with double the outboards than the previous year.

Meanwhile, something entirely new was available with the SRX Pachanga. Sea Ray's sleek speedboat was available for purchase with "jet power," fitted with the Berkeley Packajet 455S option. The Packajet forced water out of a jet nozzle at the back of the boat.

It was also during this time that Ray was talking with Orin Edson, founder and chairman of Bayliner, an Arlington, Washington–based boat manufacturer, about the possibility of a merger between Sea Ray and Bayliner. Edson had been successful building boats analogous to the Chevrolets of the recreational boat industry, as compared to Sea Ray's Cadillacs. Ray recalled how close the two companies came to merging:

*We thought we'd put the Cadillac and Chevrolet concept together into a company we would call*

*Advance. We were going to blend the two products in the same dealership, and interface the management of both companies. Sea Ray even designed a boat for Bayliner.*[11]

**The Weekender Arrives**

The Phoenix plant, completed in May 1971, became Sea Ray corporate headquarters. It also provided 68,000 square feet of production space, the PD&E center, and produced the full Sea Ray line for the western United States, the western provinces of Canada, and South America.

By 1971, Michalak and Mehaffey, heeding customer feedback that indicated a strong market for larger boats despite spiraling inflation, began producing even larger models. The 1971 line included a larger SRV 240 model with six more inches at the centerline and a foot and a half more hull depth. The SRV 210 was enlarged to become the SRV 220, adding, in its largest version, a foot in length and a remarkable two feet in hull depth to its predecessor. The two smallest boats, including the SRV 150 introduced just the year before, were dropped. Mehaffey remembered the gradual transition:

Right and below: The 1971 SRV 240 Weekender cabin offered many comforts of home. The galley included a stove, icebox, sink with running water, cabinets, and bottle racks.

*Our customers wanted bigger Sea Rays. They also didn't like our outboards at all. The owners quit buying Sea Ray outboards, and our dealers quit buying Sea Ray outboards, and we quit making them.*[12]

Along with producing larger boats, Sea Ray gradually increased its use of more descriptive model names. The 1971 line included specifically designated Cuddy Cabin and Weekender versions of its SRV 240 as well as Cuddy Cabin and Cruiser versions of the SRV 220. The hardtop SRV 220 was placed on temporary hiatus.

Three years after its 1968 introduction, the 24-foot SRV 240s remained the largest and most desirable hull design in the Sea Ray fleet. The Cuddy Cabin version kept the model's popular basic design intact, along with its price point. The 240 Weekender of 1971 became Sea Ray's new premier model, designed for comfort and overnight accommodation—luxuries achieved in great measure by its extraordinarily spacious cabin and cozy cabin features.

The 240 Weekender provided 6-and-a-half feet of cabin depth, more than enough to allow almost anyone to comfortably stand up straight belowdecks, a first for any Sea Ray boat. The Weekender's spacious, lighted cabin came with a complete galley, including a small stove, icebox, sink with electric water pump, freshwater storage, and built-in cabinets. A dining table seated four and slid forward, out of the way, when not needed. Two 8-foot bunks provided space for lounging and berthing.

The similarly styled new SRV 220 was nearly 22 feet long and also came in relatively shallower and deeper-hulled versions, designated as the Cuddy Cabin and Cruiser models. The Cruiser hull was two feet shorter and deeper than the 240 Weekender and came with an alcohol stove, icebox, and sink, as well as the sliding four-seat table and two 7-foot bunks.

The other major change for the 1971 line was the alteration of its tri-hulled models. Sea Ray dropped the boxy SRV 380 and 370 in favor of slightly longer, lower-riding, and significantly sleeker models designated as the SRV 183 (16 feet 3 inches) and 193 (19 feet). The interiors of these cathedral models were upgraded, and both were offered as outboards as well as stern drives. The 1971 lineup

also included three more boats joining the Pachanga as models offering the jet-powered option.

**Florida Treasure Hunt**

While the Phoenix plant was proving valuable for delivery to western distributors, Ray and company were setting their sights on Florida as the perfect place for constructing larger boats. Intending to design and build a 30-foot boat, Michalak had already designed a 30-foot hull in Phoenix, though it was still in the early stages of development.[13]

"The customers kept asking the dealer when Sea Ray would build a bigger boat," Ray recalled. "That's one of the reasons we moved to Florida. We had to build bigger boats."[14]

Florida, located between the Atlantic Ocean and the Gulf of Mexico and teaming with lakes, rivers, and boaters, was an obvious choice considered by Sea Ray principals for years. Now that a commitment had been made to produce boats measuring 30 feet or longer, the time seemed right to establish a production facility in the Sunshine State.

In early 1972, Ray and Mehaffey began scouting locations to build a new production plant in Florida. They decided on an advantageous spot on Merritt Island, a peninsula located inland of Cocoa Beach and Cape Canaveral.[15] Michalak arrived soon thereafter and established a small design facility in Titusville on the mainland, approximately 15 miles away. Boat production on Merritt Island began early the following year.[16]

Meanwhile, the Oxford plant remained Sea Ray's primary production facility, having expanded to 120,000 square feet by 1972. Sea Ray offered customers four distinct 240 models that year. The Hardtop was revived after its one-year hiatus, and the company added the SRV 240 Sportbridge model to its existing Cuddy Cabin and Weekender.

The 240 Sportbridge was Sea Ray's first attempt at a bridged boat since the unsuccessful 808 Cruis-a-bout of 1962, which lasted only two years on the market. The two models were decidedly different. The 808 was a small boat with a slim mid-deck bridge, raised just slightly from the deck, which added little to its functionality. Meanwhile, the 240 Sportbridge was a larger boat model with a far more substantial foredeck bridge raised high above the deck floor, offering a favorable perch for piloting and all the weather protection of the Hardtop underneath. In fact, this original Sportbridge was essentially a Hardtop model ingeniously designed with the cockpit positioned on top of the hardtop.

As its tri-hulls continued to sell well, Sea Ray added the 16-foot SRV 163 to the line in 1972. The 163 only lasted one year, however, and it would be many years before the company offered another model that small.

The late 1960s and early 1970s Sea Ray lines demonstrated the company's growing disenchantment toward small boats and outboard models. In 1968, when the SRV 240 debuted, Sea Ray had only four outboard models, two of which were basic and deluxe versions of the same boat. The next year, the company had one less outboard model, though there were six in 1970. By 1971, Sea Ray was back down to three outboard models as it began offering distinctive variations of the larger, and more popular, 240.

Rapid inflation remained a troublesome factor in the early 1970s, as the price of wages and consumer goods increased. Sea Ray was not immune to effects of the general economic trend. In 1970, the U.S. Congress had taken the unusual step of passing a law that gave President Nixon power to regulate wages and prices. Nixon initiated a 90-day wage and price "freeze" during the summer of 1971, and after the freeze ended, he established a federal commission with power to regulate wages and prices. The freeze did not check inflation entirely, but it did slow its growth.

The extraordinary measures taken to control the economy were one important factor in the sharp rise in boat sales for 1972. While industry-wide annual boat sales rose a mere 11,000 units from 1970 to 1971, they increased by more than 183,000 units in 1972. In terms of dollars, industry-wide sales rose nearly 25 percent—from less

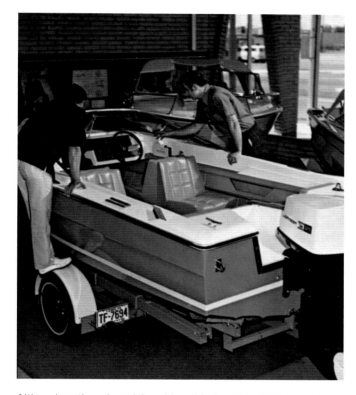

Although outboard models sold well industry-wide in 1972, Sea Ray heeded its own sales statistics and customer feedback and gradually dropped the number of outboard models it offered.

than $1 billion in 1971 to more than $1.245 billion in 1972.[17]

Unfortunately, the U.S. economy was approaching a more serious slump that would stifle the pleasure-boating industry within the next few years. Still, as 1972 ended, Sea Ray was getting close to offering boats 30 feet long for the first time. It was also on the verge of producing an innovative masterpiece that would revolutionize boating design while generating great revenue and creative momentum for the company.

To its credit, Sea Ray weathered the economic storm of the mid-1970s, as company marketers continued to entice prospective retail customers with the romance of boat ownership.

## CHAPTER FOUR

# SUNDANCER SENSATION

## 1973–1978

*We changed every three years. We didn't want to just keep building a
boat that looked like somebody else's boat.*

—Jerry Michalak[1]

POLITICAL AND ECONOMIC turmoil continued to mar the U.S. landscape as Sea Ray settled into its new Merritt Island facility in 1973. Newly reelected President Nixon ended his wage price controls for most industries that year, while also calling for continued voluntary restraint. The strategy was unsuccessful, however, as inflation soared to its highest levels in 20 years. Meanwhile, the Watergate scandal that would eventually lead to Nixon's resignation began to unfold.

Events overseas also brought harmful fallout to Sea Ray. In October 1973, fighting broke out between Arabs and Israelis, forcing the Organization of Petroleum Exporting Countries (OPEC) to issue an oil embargo against the United States and other nations in retaliation of their support of Israel. With one-third of its oil supply cut off, the United States suffered serious displacements in energy availability. When OPEC resumed oil shipments in April 1974, the emboldened organization had nearly quadrupled the crucial product's price. The high oil prices increased Sea Ray's production costs, which in turn affected customers.

### Settling on Merritt Island

Sea Ray had a strong sales year in 1972, even though the 1970s were presenting a challenging eco-

nomic environment. After committing to a new location, Sea Ray took its time to fully establish the Merritt Island facility. C. N. Ray had already purchased a home near Fort Lauderdale, and though Jerry Michalak had set up the design and development department in Florida in 1972, it would be two years before the department was established at the Merritt Island facility. Meanwhile, Arch Mehaffey remained in Phoenix but made biweekly trips down to the Sunshine State. Gradually, other key Sea Ray employees were brought to the Southeast.

The Merritt Island facility initially produced 240s and 220s, the largest boats in the Sea Ray fleet at the time. Meanwhile, Michalak, Mehaffey, and Sea Ray engineers worked diligently on several projects. The Sea Ray team continued to develop refinements for existing boat models, smoothing out any wrinkles in the new 30-foot designs, which included an Expresscruiser version. Ray also directed Michalak and Mehaffey to develop ideas for reconfiguring the interior space of the SRV 240.

---

Sea Ray owner's manuals offered everything from nautical flag instruction and a primer on buoys to trailering and winterizing tips. The 1970s-era owner's manuals were illustrated with the company's blue and green oval logo.

In 1973, Sea Ray introduced the SRV 240 Sport Bridge II, which had a reshaped bridge covered with a fabric bimini top and mounted on a metal frame. Michalak and crew also introduced a functional design feature to all the 240 models—a teak swim platform on the back of the boat. The handsome wood platforms offered Sea Ray owners a safe, convenient boat extension to facilitate diving, swimming, skiing, and fishing.

Sea Ray also added a custom hardtop to the SRV 220 Cruiser and rechristened it the SRV 220

Sea Ray's Merritt Island plant began production in 1973. It was the first of several plants the company would open in Florida. *(Photo by Bill Kilborn.)*

Overnighter in 1973. Within a few years, there would be an additional hardtop model of the sporty mid-size boat.

The SRV 240 Sundowner entered the lineup the following year. This boat featured a three-quarters enclosed, raised helm incorporated into the Weekender design, marking the fifth version of Sea Ray's popular 24-foot boats.

### Birth of the Sundancer

National recreational boat shipment statistics for 1974 and 1975 clearly reflected the negative effects of the late 1973 Arab oil embargo and early 1974 price increases within the pleasure-boating industry. Following many years of consistently increasing sales, total domestic recreational boat shipments for 1974 had grown to 729,000. That

**September 1973:** Sea Ray introduces model-year 1974 boats, including the SRV 240 Sundowner.

**September 1974:** Sea Ray introduces model-year 1975 boats. New models include the SRV 240 Sundancer and the SRV 200 Amberjack.

**Early 1973:** Merritt Island plant begins production. Jerry Michalak's design operation is moved to the completed Merritt Island facility.

**September 1975:** Sea Ray introduces model-year 1976 boats, including the company's first 30-foot boats. New models include the SRV 300 Sedan and SRV 300 Sedan Bridge, along with 30-foot versions of existing Weekender, Hardtop, and Sportbridge styles. Also introduced is the SRV 195.

figure plummeted to less than 600,000 the following year.[2]

Nevertheless, these years would prove especially important for Sea Ray as Michalak and Mehaffey's efforts at reconfiguring the below-deck space of the SRV 240 came to fruition. Sea Ray's 1975 model year introduced the SRV 240 Sundancer in the company's brochure with remarkably little fanfare. At first glance, the Sundancer seemed rather similar to the 240 Weekender, reflecting the same exterior in the same dimensions. But thoughtful

Sea Ray started using the tagline "Ask the Man Who Owns One" in 1973, when the SRV 240 Sport Bridge II was introduced. The boat featured teak swim platforms.

design changes made all the difference to customers, and such was the case with Sea Ray's new 24-foot model.

Introducing innovative styling belowdecks, Sea Ray's design team had ingeniously shifted the popular 240 mid-cabin hull's layout to include an extra sleeping area. Therefore, the Sundancer offered additional accommodation for adult guests or children, which made an important difference for Sundancer owners. This adjustment eventually led to strong, consistent sales for Sea Ray Sundancers and the establishment of the boat as the new Sea Ray standard-bearer. With characteristic modesty, Michalak acknowledged Mehaffey's contribution to the Sundancer design:

*The Sundancer was as much Arch's [Mehaffey] thinking [as mine]. After going to all the different*

**September 1976:** Sea Ray introduces model-year 1977 boats. New models include the SRV 300 Sunbridge, SRV 240 Sedancruiser, SRV Sedan Bridge, SRV 200 Sunrunner, the open-bow SRV 197 and SRV 187, and the SRV 185.

**August 1978:** Sea Ray's new Pickel Island production facility begins producing runabouts.

**September 1978:** Sea Ray introduces model-year 1979 boats, including the SRV 225 Expresscruiser, SRV 190, and SRV 192.

**September 1977:** Sea Ray introduces model-year 1978 boats. New models include the SRV 300 Expresscruiser and the SRV 260 Sundancer.

**April 26, 1978:** Sea Ray purchases Pickel Island in the Tennessee River in Knoxville, Tennessee, and starts building a production facility.

The SRV 240 Sundancer, introduced in 1974, featured an innovative design that provided maximum use of limited space.

*[boat] shows, we finally came to the conclusion that, beyond an express boat, it would be nice to have a space and make use of that space and also create a raised helm position. [It] just made a super all-around boat.*[3]

Sea Ray also introduced the SRV 200 Amberjack in 1975. While the Sportbridge model had been designed specifically for fishing purposes, the Amberjack, named after a popular game fish common to Florida coastal waters, offered a stylish and well-designed alternative. The 20-foot Amberjack featured an open foredeck, full walk-around cockpit, large bow-floor storage compartments, and a fish box beneath the helmsman's seat, as well as fishing rod storage space and built-in rod holders.

### 30 Feet Deep

While building 30-foot boats had been a primary objective in the establishment of the Florida plant, Ray, Mehaffey, and Michalak were nonetheless apprehensive about developing the larger and more expensive Sea Rays. Despite the fact that many dealers clamored for larger boats, it was a gamble, given the success of the existing line. According to Michalak:

*We didn't want the dealers to tie a lot of their money up with buying one or two bigger boats and then not be able to sell them. We'd rather keep busy the plants that are building smaller boats, and by which [Sea Ray] was making money.*[4]

Unfortunately, Sea Ray had made a resource commitment to manufacturing its largest and, therefore, least fuel-efficient, boats back in 1972, just before OPEC initiated its crippling oil embargo, followed by the organization's steep price increase. These unforeseeable developments made the mid-1970s perhaps the worst time to introduce the larger 30-foot boats to the market, but Michalak and crew had already developed the designs, and the Merritt Island plant was ready for production. So, Sea Ray proceeded with its plan as scheduled.

Sea Ray's 1976 line introduced two brand-new 30-foot models, the SRV 300 Sedan and Sedan Bridge, along with three new 30-foot versions developed from existing Weekender, Hardtop, and Sportbridge styles. All were large, handsome, and smooth-running boats.

Adding more than five inches of length to a fiberglass boat, along with the attendant accoutrements, was a major undertaking with considerable weight consequences. With additional cabin and cockpit features and nearly twice the fuel capacity, the 300-model Weekender, Hardtop, and Sportbridge, ranging from 9,000 to 9,800 pounds, were actually more than double the weight of their 24-foot 240 counterparts. The SRV 300 Sedan and Sedan Bridge were even heavier, each weighing more than 10,000 pounds.[5]

Michalak's initial 30-footers featured weight toward the back of the boat and were designed for inboard and stern-drive propulsion.[6] A 350-horsepower inboard was available as well as twin inboard 233- or 260-horsepower engines. The new Weekender, Hardtop, and Sportbridge came with these same power options as well as twin stern-drive options of 188 to 280 horsepower.[7] The basic SRV 300 models with the smallest available motor had a maximum speed of 35 miles per hour—fast enough for many owners but not everyone.[8]

Whether it was the weight of the boat (and the consequent loss of speed), the expensive price tag, the exorbitant price of fuel, or some other factor, Sea Ray's new 30-footers did not sell well at first. Many 1976 300 models languished on dealer showroom floors, reflecting the worst-case scenario that Sea Ray principals had feared. "They hardly moved," Michalak recalled.[9]

A different design strategy was implemented in 1976 on the opposite side of the Sea Ray fleet-size spectrum, as the company introduced the SRV 195, a runabout slightly longer than the 190 and of sim-

---

At more than 10,000 pounds, Sea Ray's new SRV 300 Sedan and Sedan Bridge models introduced in 1976 were more than 13 times heavier than the largest model from the company's inaugural 1960 line.

ilar style. An open-bow version called the SRV 197 followed the next year. In 1977, the SRV 185 and 187, shorter models with similar open and closed bows, were also introduced. These models replaced the slightly smaller closed-bow SRV 180 and 190.

Meanwhile, Jimmy Carter was elected president of the United States in 1976, the nation's bicentennial celebration year. Double-digit inflation continued during the Carter years, accompanied by a stagnant economy, producing an ugly economic phenomenon dubbed "stagflation." Interest rates rose even higher, as did the nation's deficit spending, a practice with negative economic consequences.

With sales of its 300 models unsuccessful, and having spent considerable funds on major innova-

American flag decals became common on Sea Ray boats during America's bicentennial year (1976), as shown here on an SRV 300 Weekender, a model introduced that year.

tions during the previous two years, Sea Ray's 1977 line brought more modest, though hardly inconsequential, changes. That year, the company introduced the Sunbridge version of the SRV 300, which featured a 5-foot bridge extension and two additional, portable chairs; SRV 240 Sedancruiser and Sedan Bridge models that offered the same style and substance of the 300 Sedans in a smaller model; and the SRV 200 Sunrunner, a sportier version of the SRV 200, which continued in production.

**A Smile or a Frown**

As Sea Ray worked through a challenging second decade, the company still maintained the service mentality and dealer relationships that Ray and Mehaffey had been so careful to nurture since the beginning. All manufacturers, including Sea Ray, have two customers to keep happy—the retailer (or dealer) and the customer, who purchases the product from the dealer. In these early

# PICKEL ISLAND

IN 1978, SEA RAY PUR-chased Pickel Island, an 82-acre island just a few miles southeast of Knoxville, Tennessee, situated near the confluence of the French Broad River and the Holston River, which together form the Tennessee River.[1] The island is named after the Pickel family, long-time area residents who had owned the island and additional nearby acreage throughout the 19th and 20th centuries.[2]

Sea Ray's Pickel Island home is an ideal site for a boat manufacturer. Sea Ray engineers test every manufactured boat on the river behind the facility. As part of the Forks-of-the-River Industrial Park, the island is connected to the eastern riverbank by a short bridge.

Knox County's original 1966 plans for developing the Forks-of-the-River area as an industrial site called for Pickel Island to be used as an industrial airstrip to accommodate the air traffic that would generate from any businesses relocating to the area.[3] As it turned out, the island was not included in the 800 acres initially prepared for development at Forks-of-the-River in 1967. It would be about 10 years before Pickel Island was established as an integral part of the expanding industrial park.

Ray and Mehaffey were delighted to purchase Pickel Island in 1977. The island's name came from the longtime Knoxville-area family that had settled there in the 19th century.

---

years, Ray developed an effective strategy to ensure that Sea Ray dealers would remember his commitment to retail customer service. As customers returned their warranty cards to Sea Ray headquarters, Ray would write them a pleasant (or apologetic) letter and pass a copy along to the pertinent dealer with a little smile or a frown drawn, as each case warranted. Ray commented on his approach:

*I just wanted to be the best and really take care of all the tiny details that add up to the big score. It isn't two or three things. It's everyday attention to the customer's needs. I think I instilled that kind of philosophy.[10]*

The reputation Sea Ray earned for customer service spread " ... up and down the docks," according to Ray, and remained strong in the difficult 1970s.[11] Jim Steffens, who worked in sev-

eral departments during his 37 years as a full-time Sea Ray employee, echoed Ray's perspective on the importance of customer service:

*I think if Sea Ray is known for anything, it's that if you do get a poor-quality product, you bring it to someone's attention, and we'll bring it back to the plant and either make it right ... or have the dealers fix it. They'll stand behind it. If it's a manufacturing defect, we've replaced hulls on them.[12]*

### Pickel Island Paradise

With solid service playing a crucial role during any tough economic time, Sea Ray's sound service reputation played a crucial role in helping Sea Ray dealers build a customer base for the company's 30-foot boats. Despite the annual price increases necessitated by inflation, sales of the 30-footers had picked up enough by 1977 to encourage the company to design a new one. In 1978, the company introduced the SRV 300 Expresscruiser that featured above- and below-deck seating arrangements different from other 300 models. The SRV 300 Expresscruiser was well received.

In another acknowledgement of the 300 models' growing popularity, Sea Ray began offering three different floor plans for its SRV 300 Sedan and Sedan Bridge in 1978. The company's increasingly sophisticated production methods made it a relatively simple matter to replace the necessary Sedan model cabin features as dictated by sales, thus offering customers a level of customization.

The solid performing Sundancer also received some refinements. Sea Ray added a couple of feet

By the late 1970s, many marine safety patrols in Michigan used Sea Ray runabouts. Pictured here is the Oakland County Sheriff's Department. Sea Ray's Oxford, Michigan, plant was located in Oakland County.

and several other adjustments to the 24-foot model, introducing the new SRV 260 Sundancer in 1978.

Sea Ray's continued success, particularly with the new Sundancers, pushed Ray to consider adding another production facility. A real estate broker informed him of an ideal available site in Tennessee. It was situated on the outskirts of Knoxville, near the confluence of the French Broad River and the Holston River, which together form the Tennessee River. The site offered extraordinarily convenient access to a major waterway in a state with relatively low business costs and limited union influence. It was also geographically well positioned for distribution throughout the entire eastern United States.[13]

Ray and Mehaffey visited the site, and both were immediately struck by its suitability for Sea Ray operations. They purchased the 82-acre island, known as Pickel Island, on April 26, 1978, for $215,000 and began manufacturing runabouts there in August. Sea Ray began construction on a second facility at the Pickel Island site, and that was completed the following year.[14]

The SRV 300 Expresscruiser marked Sea Ray's seventh model that measured more than 30 feet in length.

For Sea Ray, the counterproductive economic climate of the 1970s had inevitably necessitated layoffs and other protective measures. Still, the company's innovative new products and solid reputation had allowed it to prosper far more than most marine manufacturers, and the decade proved a time of significant creativity and expansion for Sea Ray.

As 1978 drew to a close, further changes for Sea Ray were on the near horizon. Founder Ray was closing in on a momentous personal decision that would mark the end of an era, while Sea Ray's continuing need for expansion would keep company executives focused on the South.

'79 Sea Ray®

One of the most dramatic changes in Sea Ray history occurred in 1979, the company's 20th anniversary year.

## CHAPTER FIVE

# SOUTHERN HEADING

## 1979–1985

*We were really gunning when we moved the whole operation to Knoxville.*
*That was a great decision, and I'm really proud of that one. Everyone*
*was happy with it.*

—C. N. Ray[1]

AS SEA RAY BEGAN ITS THIRD decade of operation in 1979, the U.S. recreational boating industry had yet to manage two consecutive years of increased boat shipments since the dramatic drop in 1975, though inflation and the increased manufacturing of larger boats had kept boat shipment dollars rising modestly. The stagflation that had been vexing the American economy for years prompted Paul Volcker, chairman of the Federal Reserve Board, to initiate tight-money policies in an attempt to check the rise in inflation.[2]

Late in 1979, the shocking abduction of Americans at the U.S. Embassy in Iran added to the nation's woes. Though the U.S. presidential election would not take place for another year, then President Jimmy Carter's struggle with the Iranian hostage crisis, along with the nation's ongoing economic turmoil, made it clear that the former Georgia governor would not return to the White House after the upcoming election.

Meanwhile, another president was also stepping down, as C. N. Ray turned over the Sea Ray presidency to longtime friend and business partner Arch Mehaffey in 1979. Retaining the position of chairman, Ray remained peripherally involved with the company, but moved on to other business and recreational interests he had developed over the years. He retained the position of chairman and remained involved with Sea Ray, particularly in the area of

international expansion, but he was no longer a constant participant in the company's operations.

Maintaining his passion and hands-on involvement with Sea Ray through the 1970s, Ray's vision and business acumen had steered the company from its humble beginnings in Oxford, Michigan, to a position as the nation's second-largest boatbuilder. His professional edicts for high-quality construction and exemplary customer service, as well as his efforts at establishing a dealer network that provided retailers with abundant territory and earning potential, had successfully permeated the Sea Ray organization.

By the time Ray relinquished his presidency, Sea Ray had firmly established itself as a marine manufacturer of premier quality. It had four manufacturing facilities across the United States, and its international business was growing rapidly. The company's design and engineering talent regularly created new models, while also refining existing ones. Sea Ray's 1979 line of boats was far broader than its inaugural 1959 line, with models ranging from relatively inexpensive 17-foot runabouts to an impressive array of mid-size cruisers,

---

A commemorative 25th anniversary logo accompanied all Sea Ray promotional materials in 1984.

Sea Ray founder and president C. N. Ray took the company from a modest operation in the 1950s to its position as the nation's second-largest recreational boat manufacturer by 1979.

including the ever-popular Sundancer and four 30-foot SRV 300 models.

Rob Parmentier, executive vice president, who started on the Merritt Island assembly line and subsequently worked in the sales department, remembered how inspirational it was to work for Sea Ray's founder:

*Nobody really wanted to see C. N. leave. I remember we would have meetings, and C. N. would be there. At every meeting you went with him, you had to bring something besides your usual report about how the line or plant was doing. He'd say, "I want something that will be a difference-maker today." I remember [when] you'd work all week to think of something that was a game changer to please him.*[3]

**Summer 1979:** C. N. Ray steps down as Sea Ray president and Arch Mehaffey is promoted to the top position.

**September 1979:** Sea Ray introduces model-year 1980 boats. New boats include the SRV 270 Sedan Bridge, SRV 245 Sundancer, SRV 225 Sundowner Hardtop, SRV 210 Cuddy Cabin, and SRV 207.

**September 1980:** Sea Ray introduces model-year 1981 boats. The new Vanguard designs debut, including the SRV 360 Vanguard Sedan SF, SRV 310 Vanguard Sundancer, 310 Vanguard Sportbridge, the twin-inboard SRV 310 Vanguard Express, SRV 260 Vanguard XL, and SRV 225 Vanguard XL. Also introduced are the SRV 360 Express Cruiser, SRV 255 Sedan Bridge, SRV 255 Amberjack, SRV 245 Sedan Bridge, SXL 197, SXL 195, SRV 172, and SRV 170.

**September 1981:** Sea Ray introduces model-year 1982 boats. New boats include the 355T Sedan, the company's first trawler-style boat; the SRV 270 Sundancer; SRV 245 Cuddy Fisherman; and SRV 210 Cuddy Fisherman.

**Early 1983:** Sea Ray opens a new plant designed to build small runabouts at Tellico Lake near Knoxville.

**September 1982:** Sea Ray introduces model-year 1983 boats. The 18-foot Seville series debuts in open-bow, closed-bow, and cuddy cabin versions. Other new boats include the SRV 390 Sedan SF, SR 355T Aft Cabin, SRV 340 Sedan Bridge, and SRV 245 Cuddy Cruiser.

Mehaffey took charge of Sea Ray at a time when, despite the difficult conditions of the American economy and, more specifically, the recreational-boating industry, Sea Ray was operating efficiently and profitably. The corporation had matured, developing more effective strategies and methods for manufacturing and responding to the marketplace. The company had firmly established its reputation in the domestic marketplace and had made great strides internationally. Sea Rays were being sold on six continents, with Merritt Island producing 30-foot models prodigiously in response to the hundreds of boats Sea Ray dealers sold each year. Furthermore, the company had just completed construction of a new administrative building at its Forks-of-the-River facility.[4]

### International Expansion

Sea Ray was able to maintain profitability during the difficult years of the 1970s in part by aggressively pursuing international business. The company secured the services of several individuals who served as freelance sales agents and attempted to penetrate the European, Asian, and South American markets. One such person, well-established European boat dealer Ekkehard Baensch, generated about $2 million in revenue representing Sea Ray from his home base in Germany. Baensch worked with his international contacts and sold Sea Rays to select dealerships in several European countries. Another sales agent, Steve Helwig, an export management representative who operated out of New Orleans, had started handling Sea Ray products on a limited basis in 1977, primarily focused on South America and the Middle East.

By 1979, Sea Ray's determination to become more involved in the European market encouraged Ray, Mehaffey, Jerry Michalak, and John Keim, Sea Ray vice president of sales, to attend the Genoa Boat Show in Italy. The logistical difficulties and lack of access and sales success encountered during the European trip prompted Ray and Mehaffey to offer Helwig a position as vice president of international sales in 1980. Helwig proudly took the position:

**September 1983:** Sea Ray introduces model-year 1984 boats. New boats include the SRV 340 Sundancer, Express Cruiser, Sedan Bridge, and Sport Fisherman; the SRV 390 Express Cruiser; SR 360 Aft Cabin; SRV 270 Seadancer; and the Monaco series of runabouts.

**August 1984:** Sea Ray introduces model-year 1985 boats. New boats include the new SRV 250, 260, 270, and 300 Sundancers; SRV 230, 260, and 300 Weekenders; SRV 230 and 250 Cuddy Cruisers; and the 300 Sedan Bridge.

**August 1985:** Sea Ray introduces model-year 1986 boats. New boats include the 460 Express Cruiser, 390 Sedan Sport Fisherman, 270 Amberjack, 250 Fishing Cockpit, 230 Fishing Cockpit, Pachanga II, and the Seville II series. The Pachanga II offers a swim platform molded into the stern of the boat rather than as an external attachment, the first mass-produced model with such a feature.

**Summer 1984:** C. N. Ray returns to take over as Sea Ray president again. Mehaffey continues in a consultant role. Ray initiates a major company reorganization.

**Late 1984:** Sea Ray opens its Palm Coast, Florida, plant designed for production of the company's largest sport yachts.

**Late 1985:** Sea Ray establishes headquarters at its Pickel Island site in Knoxville.

*I was the only hired gun, as John [Keim] used to call me, brought in from the outside, because C. N. really made a strong effort to promote from within. That was the commitment he had to the employees, even to the extent of the exclusion of family members. He never got into nepotism. So I came to an agreement. Joined the company as a vice president, which was a proud moment for me.*[5]

Helwig truly understood the intricacies of international sales and was the first person at Sea Ray with widespread international contacts. He immediately set about raising the company's international profile, arranging meetings with potential Sea Ray dealers for Ray and Keim in Europe, timed to coincide with the Paris Boat Show.

Helwig introduced Sea Ray executives during this important market-building trip to several key European businessmen who helped the company penetrate the European market. The first people Helwig introduced were David Lewis and his wife, Alexis, who were long-established Riva boat distributors operating in London.

Helwig recalled Ray's positive impression of the Lewis family:

*[Ray] looks me in the eye and says, "I'll tell you what: The quality of those people [the Lewis family] … What pleasant people! If the rest of this tour is going to be like this, I'm looking forward to it."*[6]

Next, the team journeyed to the Paris Boat Show where they met with Arie and Alex DeBoom—father and son—who ran a large network of marinas and dealerships throughout the Netherlands, along with operations at two large ports in France. "The DeBooms basically solved my territorial issues for both Holland and France in one fell swoop," said Helwig. The Dutch boat dealers would play a prominent role for Sea Ray in 1986 when the Knoxville-based boatbuilder established its first European manufacturing facility. After the Paris show, Helwig took Ray and Keim to Barcelona to meet brothers

Lars and Göran Sundberg, enterprising Swedes who had migrated to the South of Spain and established Marina Marbella SA, a prospering multinational dealership network.[7]

Delighted with Helwig's resourcefulness, Ray encouraged him to formalize agreements with these European boat dealers and map out a strategy for the rest of Europe, including Germany. Ray felt obligated, however, to honor his original agreement with Baensch, who had been Sea Ray's sole distributor on the continent until that point. It was an indication of the founder's strong ethics. Helwig remembered the way the new arrangement was handled:

*He could have sent him a letter and told him what was going on, but we went and visited Mr. Baensch, and [C. N.] said, "… here's the plan, Ekkehard, but I want you in on it. What do I need to do to let us do this [so] you're happy and we're happy?" C. N. didn't have to do it … but [Sea Ray] paid him for three years on every [European] sale we made. It was the right thing to do because he had worked and helped put that brand into the Europeans' minds.*[8]

Helwig eventually split Germany into four quadrants, with Baensch continuing as a dealer. Sea Ray's international presence continued to grow in the next few years. Jurgen Feichtner would be awarded an Austrian dealership. Mario Vassena, owner of Motomar Yachting at the time, became a valuable Italian dealer.

### Model Expansion

Sea Ray created some interesting new models and refinements in its boat line during the first few years of Mehaffey's presidency. In 1979, the 22-and-a-half-foot SRV 225 Express Cruiser was created to complement the 30-foot version. The SRV 185 and 187 open- and closed-bow runabouts were retired, and the slightly longer 190 and 192 models took their place.

Several other models were elongated and refined over the next few years. In 1980, Sea Ray lengthened the popular SRV 240 Sundancer by a few inches, modified its bow entry so the boat would rise on plane faster on less horsepower, and refined the cabin interior. The new design became known as the SRV 245, with the original 240 model offered only as a Weekender or Cuddy Cruiser. The latter style was also offered in 22-and-a-half-foot and 20-foot versions, with the Sundowner reemerging that year as a hardtop model.[9]

Sea Ray's 1981 line featured the company's first 36-foot boats, including the SRV 360 Vanguard Sedan SF and the SRV 360 Express Cruiser. The year also marked the introduction of the Vanguard models, attributed to six Sea Ray designs. Little expense was spared on the Vanguards, which included the stern drive SRV 225 Vanguard XL (Express Luxury) and SRV 260 Vanguard XL, the twin-inboard SRV 310 Vanguard Express, 310 Vanguard Sportbridge, SRV 310 Vanguard Sundancer, and SRV 360 Vanguard Sedan SF. Sea Ray loaded the Vanguards with many of the extras normally available only as options and priced the new versions accordingly.

Above: The SRV 360 Vanguard Expresscruiser, one of Sea Ray's 36-foot boats (also called the 360 T-Top), was introduced in 1981.

Below: Sea Ray's new 1981 Vanguard models, like this impressive SRV 310 Vanguard Sedan Bridge, were extraordinarily luxurious, even by Sea Ray standards.

The SRV 360 Vanguard Sedan SF designation illustrated the evolving nomenclature Sea Ray used for naming its boats. The SRV had long been used to designate a Sea Ray deep-V hull. As always, the number (in this case "360") referred to the boat's approximate length at the centerline (here, 36 feet). The Vanguard name was introduced to indicate spaciousness and luxury appointments.

The new 36-foot Sport Fish featured an enlarged rear cockpit to accommodate maximum deep-water fishing capability, as well as a high-sitting cabin bridge with a forward helm for an optimal view of the best fishing spots. As a Vanguard, the new boat had many luxuries, including a teak plank cockpit deck and all-teak trim; tinted glass windows; aft sliding doors that offered a 360-degree view; a mirrored forward stateroom; suede cabin seat fabric; woven-wood drapes; a mirrored vanity with studio lighting; imported Italian throttle and shift controls; and aircraft-style toggle control switches.

While grandly accentuating its largest boats in 1981, Sea Ray also made some changes to its smallest models. The company produced sporty new SXL (Sport Express Luxury) versions of the SRV 195 and 197, and built a new 17-foot model that utilized the open- and closed-bow options common to the company's smallest models, providing a lower opening price point for the Sea Ray line. Overall, the 1981 Sea Ray line included an unprecedented 31 models.

Sea Ray continued its daring design innovations the following year by producing a trawler-type 36-foot boat known as the 355T Sedan. The boat's relatively flat hull ensured stability, while its 304-gallon fuel capacity provided a great cruising range. A trawler-style recreational boat looks similar to a commercial fishing trawler

Introduced in 1982, the 355T Sedan's trawler style featured a deadrise of only 9 degrees instead of the 20–22 degrees common to Sea Ray deep-V hull boats. A lower deadrise added greater stability. The deadrise refers to the angle of the upward slant from the keel, the structural member running along the boat hull bottom from stern to stem. A perfectly flat-bottomed boat has a deadrise of 0 degrees.

above the water, but has a flatter hull bottom. A trawler has what is known as a displacement (non-planing) hull, which is designed to displace the same weight in water that the boat itself weighs. The boat is designed to merely float rather than skim across the surface of the water like Sea Ray's other hull designs. Trawlers are known more for their sturdiness, cruising range, comfortable and spacious accommodations, and economical operation than for speed or style.[10]

The 1982 line also marked the launch of a longer Sundancer, the 27-foot 7-inch SRV 270, and two new models designed for fishing—the SRV 210 and SRV 245 Cuddy Fisherman. At this point, the Vanguard name was still reserved for sport yachts longer than 30 feet.

**Tellico Lake and Palm Coast**

Sea Ray was doing well and expanding in the early 1980s, but the American economy remained sluggish. Newly elected president Ronald Reagan maintained the recently enacted federal tight-money policies, which had sent interest rates soaring. This had a pronounced effect on the recreational boating industry as many boat buyers relied on borrowed money for their boat purchases. In fact, the recreational boating industry saw boat shipments drop the first three years of the decade.[11]

By 1983, Reagan's economic policies, partially characterized by lowered tax rates designed to encourage investment and consumer spending, along with significantly increased military expen-

ditures, began to stimulate the economy. Inflation began to finally slow down and by 1984 dropped to about 4 percent. Consequently, tight-money policies were loosened, interest rates went down, and the economy began to grow. Boating industry numbers and Sea Ray sales rose considerably for 1983 and 1984.[12]

Even before the market upturn, Sea Ray's strongest sales were reflected in its largest, most luxurious yachts and its smaller, entry-level boats. In response to increased sales in these two market segments, Sea Ray built two new plants. In 1983, a relatively small plant was built at Tellico Lake, located about 40 miles downriver from Knoxville, for production of the company's new, economical Sevilles and other 18- to

Above: Sea Ray's success in the early 1980s resulted in the construction of new plants in Tellico Lake and Palm Coast, adding a total of 238,000 square feet of production space within two years.

Below: The Seville line, available in closed- and open-bow (or bow-rider) versions, debuted in 1983 and provided Sea Ray with a new European-inspired opening price-point series.

25-foot runabouts. Less than a year later, Sea Ray began construction on a much larger facility in Palm Coast, Florida, for the manufacture of its largest sport yachts, such as the 390s and the 460 Express Cruiser, a new design in the developmental stage, several years from being available on the market. Working in production at the Merritt Island plant at the time, Parmentier remembered helping set up the new Florida facility:

*Many of us went up there on the weekends to help get the plant started. Mike [Meyer, Sea Ray vice president and general manager at the Merritt Island facility who became vice president of product development and engineering in 1983] would take all of his supervisors, and we'd all go up there and help set up the assembly line. ... It was a swamp. Nothing was in Palm Coast back then. Literally, we backfilled a swamp and built one of our largest plants. Everybody just chipped in. You did anything you had to do, and you were proud of it. There was a passion for the company.*[13]

When Sea Ray opened the Palm Coast plant, Bruce Thompson was named quality control man-

ager. He had started working for Sea Ray in 1978 in the mold repair shop and made a reputation for himself by elevating the quality of work done there.

"The company had a great reputation for the quality of its products and for a good work environment," said Thompson. "I loved the work because I loved the boats and the designs that Jerry Michalak was producing. They were awesome, and we were making history."[14]

Thompson would later become a group senior vice president for product development and engineering (PD&E) at Merritt Island and preside over the conception and birth of many Sea Ray boats.

The Palm Coast plant, more than twice the size of the Tellico Lake facility, was completed late in 1984, the company's 25th anniversary year. Sea Ray now operated six production facilities. Merritt Island was the largest, with 225,000 square feet. The original Oxford, Michigan, plant was next at

---

Sea Ray designers expressed themselves most colorfully with the SXL runabout packages, as featured here on these 1983 SRV 190 and 192 models.

# THE MEANING OF "YACHT"

IN THE 1960s AND 1970s, SEA RAY DID not categorize any of its boats as "yachts." It would not be until the mid-1980s that Sea Ray began using the term as a collective categorization, and then only with a qualifier. By that time, the company had developed several boats longer than 30 feet, replete with well-appointed cabins that housed full galleys, comfortable heads (lavatories), and ample sleeping arrangement, complemented by plush amenities. In 1984, Sea Ray began categorizing these larger, luxurious boats as "sport yachts," and presented them in a separate brochure from its smaller boats.

Sea Ray was reticent in referring to its boats as "yachts," even with the "sport" prefix, mainly due to the evolving meaning of the term. The word "yacht," which has been in use for several centuries, is derived from the obsolete Norwegian term "jagt" and Middle Low German "jacht" (short for "jachtschip"). The word's roots are "jagon," meaning "to chase," and "schip," or ship. A yacht is, or was, literally a good "chase ship," the kind often employed in the pursuit of pirates.[1]

Over the years, the term gradually became associated with pleasure boating. According to the American Heritage dictionary, a yacht simply refers to "any of various relatively small sailing or motor-driven vessels, generally with smart graceful lines, used for pleasure cruises or racing." Further explanations in this dictionary definition specify that a yacht is used for pleasure, and it is not as large as a ship (but "relatively small").[2]

Today, a "yacht" usually refers to a larger and more luxurious boat. Yachts usually feature master and guest staterooms with queen-size beds and cedar-lined lockers; heads with showers and vanities; galleys with three-burner stoves and freezers; cabins with a washer and dryer, flat-screen TVs, and stereo systems; and cockpits equipped with the highest-tech radar/GPS Chartplotter and Sea Ray Navigator III systems (all standard on the Sea Ray 60 Sundancer).

In the 21st century, Sea Ray refers to boats between 36 and 49 feet as sport yachts, while its top-of-the-line boats more than 50 feet long are known simply as yachts.

---

At Sea Ray's 25th anniversary in 1984, the company specifically categorized its 30-foot or longer boats as sport yachts, while smaller boats were considered runabouts or cruisers. Sport yachts were presented in a separate brochure.

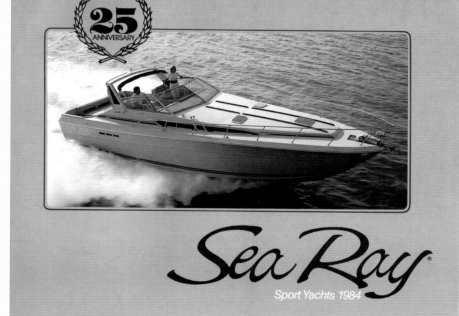

# THE MERCRUISER CONNECTION

MERCURY MARINE ENGINES, OR "power plants" as they are often called within the industry, played an important role in Sea Ray's success. Ever since C. N. Ray and Arch Mehaffey decided to include the early 110- and 140-horsepower MerCruiser I and II stern drives in several 1960 Sea Ray models, the two marine manufacturers enjoyed a mutually beneficial relationship. Sea Ray purchased motors from Mercury, which enhanced Sea Ray boats and ensured that both companies sold more products.

Although Sea Ray used power plants from other manufacturers over the years, including Johnson, Outboard Marine Corporation (OMC), and Crusader Marine Engines, no other marine engine manufacturer had an impact as significant as Mercury. Roger Patterson, then accounting supervisor at Mercury Marine who later served as president of the U.S. Marine Division of Brunswick Corporation, noted that by the early 1970s, Mercury's marketing strategy was designed to integrate the image of "a Sea Ray–style boat with outboards or stern drives, and families enjoying what they were doing."[1]

By the mid-1980s, Sea Ray used mostly Mercury Marine and Crusader Marine as its power plant manufacturers. But Mercury had the greater percentage of Sea Ray's business. "Mercury had the finances to come up with new product development ideas, and it was always a year ahead of whatever Crusader was doing," explained Sea Ray's Rob Parmentier.[2]

Sea Ray advertised its use of Mercury motors in the mid-1980s. Both manufacturers were recognized for high-quality products.

210,000 square feet. The new Palm Coast facility had 166,000 square feet; Knoxville, 144,000 (the other Knoxville facility was a nonproduction plant); Phoenix, 125,000; and Tellico Lake, 72,000.

### The Long and Short of It

In response to market conditions in 1983, Sea Ray introduced a new economy model called the Seville, a European-inspired runabout whose size designations were measured in meters. The Seville 5.6 M series, offered in closed-bow, bow-rider, and cuddy cabin models, were all approximately 18 feet long. Meanwhile, all of Sea Ray's other 1983 runabouts, except the four smallest (SRV 170/172, 190/192, 195/197, and 200/207), offered SXL renditions that sported vibrant new colors and prominent stylish striping to complement the basic versions.

Sea Ray also took advantage of opportunities at the other end of the size spectrum. Michalak, Meyer, and the rest of the PD&E team continued to design and build increasingly longer yachts. While Tellico Lake produced the small, simple Sevilles, the Palm Coast team added three feet to the previous year's flagship to create the SRV 390 Sedan SF, Sea Ray's first 39-foot boat. Sea Ray produced other large models as well. A new 34-foot Sedan Bridge debuted in 1983. The 355T Sedan, introduced the previous year, received an SR prefix in 1983 and was also offered in an SR 355T Aft Cabin version. The trawlers, known for their low speeds and low fuel consumption, were designed to address the high fuel costs and generally tough economic climate of the early 1980s.

Sea Ray built one SR 355T with a "single" Perkins diesel engine. The company had never before, and has never since, built a sport yacht with a single engine. It was dropped from the Sea Ray lineup, however, in 1984.

Although efforts during this time were primarily focused on the smallest and largest boats, Sea Ray did not neglect its mid-sized offerings. The SRV 225 Express Cruiser was revamped and a new 24-and-a-half-foot Cuddy Cruiser, the SRV 245, debuted that year as well. The company also dropped the Vanguard name in 1983, essentially returning to the strategy of offering the most luxurious appointments and exceptional features as options rather than standard items on high-end models.

In keeping with its increasing international focus, Sea Ray named its newly lengthened and styled 1984 runabout series Monaco, though the company continued to offer the SXL option package.

As Sea Ray introduced boats produced at the new Palm Coast facility in the company's silver anniversary year of 1984, it also began publishing two marketing brochures—one for runabouts and cruisers and the other for sport yachts. The sport yacht publication featured boats longer than 30 feet, including 1984's new 34-foot SRV 340 in Sundancer, Express Cruiser, Sedan Bridge, and Sport Fish models, along with an SR 360 Aft Cabin and an Express Cruiser version of the SRV 390. The 1984 runabouts and cruisers brochure offered newly revamped open- and closed-bow runabouts, all given the Monaco model name, and it also introduced the SRV 270 Seadancer, a twin-inboard 27-foot model. The new 27-foot SRV's inboard engines, positioned underneath near the center of the boat, as opposed to the outside at the stern as in outboard models, gave it a lower center of gravity and better balance fore and aft.

Following healthy sales in 1983 and 1984, Sea Ray offered some impressive new editions in 1985. The company manufactured Sundancers in new 250, 260, 270 (replacing the Seadancer), and 300 sizes.

The Sea Ray product development and engineering (PD&E) department presented Arch Mehaffey with this exquisitely detailed model of the 460 Express Cruiser on his birthday in 1988. It was the last boat Mehaffey helped Jerry Michalak develop.

The Weekender, which had been on hiatus, was brought back in 23-, 26-, and 30-foot versions that year. Also, Sea Ray modified and lengthened the hulls of its Cuddy Cruisers, producing new 230 and 250 models, each offered with a fishing cockpit option. A new 30-foot Sedan Bridge sport yacht also debuted, as did the 20-and-a-half-foot Seville 6.3 M series.

### Ray's Return and Reorganization

By 1984, Mehaffey had been steering Sea Ray as president for five years through challenging but exciting times. That year's final numbers showed that the marine industry experienced its highest level of growth since Mehaffey's inaugural year as Sea Ray president, with industry sales at nearly $4 billion.[15] Overall, the boating industry had experienced a 40 percent increase in business over the five-year period, with Sea Ray securing its share of the industry's success.

Still, significant changes were on the horizon. Ray and Mehaffey naturally remained in close contact after Ray retired, and Mehaffey, like Ray in his late 50s, had Sea Ray's future on his mind. Over lunch one day in early 1984, Mehaffey off-handedly broached the subject of the corporation's eventual presidential succession. He remembered the conversation:

*I said, "We aren't going to last forever. I know I'm not going to, and we need to at least sit down and start working with somebody as our designated [successor]." C. N. took that to heart and in a couple of months, he had come up with a whole new organization. On my 60th birthday, he said, "You are now a consultant. You can name your own terms."*[16]

Ray knew not to worry about the "name-your-own-terms" offer he made to his longtime friend and business associate. The two amicably worked out a reasonable arrangement, where Mehaffey worked as a consultant for another five years before finally retiring on March 31, 1989, which was also his 65th birthday.

During his 25-year full-time management tenure, Mehaffey had worked on the frontline with Ray, playing an important role in Sea Ray's transformation over the years. He had diligently overseen day-to-day operations in the company's various production facilities, contributed many design ideas, and encouraged optimal pricing and accounting practices. During his presidency, Sea Ray had also added two additional production facilities. Meanwhile, production of the company's 30-foot and longer sport yachts had doubled, including the introduction of two 39-foot luxury boats.

After assigning Mehaffey the consulting responsibility, Ray returned to the position of Sea Ray president and immediately began implementing a reorganization of the corporation. Despite Sea Ray's continued success, Ray knew it was necessary to develop a more sophisticated approach to corporate financial practices. Without a chief financial officer, the company had depended upon several key managers with accounting experience, including Mehaffey, as well as several bookkeepers, to make good use of its computerized accounting system. The company also received financial guidance from Arthur Andersen, one of the industry's most prestigious accounting firms at the time.

Ray and Sea Ray Executive Vice President John Hedberg soon added much needed financial horsepower to the corporation's structure. William ("Bill") Barrington, a partner in the prominent accounting firm of Peat Marwick, was hired as senior vice president of finance in 1985.[17] Just a couple of months later, Hedberg hired Rick Stone, an audit manager for Arthur Andersen, as vice president–controller under the executive vice president. Stone had han-

dled Arthur Andersen's Sea Ray account since 1977 and was thoroughly familiar with the company's impressive financial statements.[18]

### Hometown Knoxville

Beyond securing new financial expertise, Ray realized that Sea Ray needed to consolidate its crucial company-wide financial operations, which had become widely dispersed over the years. While the company's computer accounting department was based in Oxford, Michigan, Phoenix still served as the company's headquarters, where certain high-level administrative tasks were being conducted. But with two plants on Pickel Island, the Tellico Lake facility close by, and significant growth in Florida, Knoxville had become the logical locale for corporate consolidation. So, in the spring of 1985, Sea Ray's corporate staff moved to temporary offices in Knoxville, and by the end of the year, they relocated to the official corporate headquarters. Ray established all company-wide accounting, administrative, and management information systems (MIS) at that location. He recalled:

*When we moved to Knoxville, the company had really reached maturity. We were feeling our oats, and our international business was booming. I was having an absolute ball! I'd get in that Falcon 50 and fly to the London boat show and the Paris boat show and Barcelona and Düsseldorf and Genoa.*[19]

As new Sea Ray officers, Barrington, Stone, and then Senior Vice President and Corporate Attorney John Cronkhite began planning important changes in the company's financial and accounting practices under Ray and Hedberg's direction. Meanwhile, events were unfolding behind the scenes that would set the stage for another round of radical developments. The approaching changes would prove even more significant than Sea Ray founder Ray's initial, albeit short-lived, retirement.

The tuna tower, a high platform for spotting fish, was an impressive feature of the 1987 Sea Ray 460 Convertible.

## CHAPTER SIX

# BRUNSWICK AND IRISH STEW

## 1986–1988

*My biggest job was to hire people who were smarter than me and give them the opportunity to shine. That really was very gratifying to me because the company was successful that way.*

—C. N. Ray[1]

**B**Y 1986, SEA RAY HAD BEEN growing at a robust rate of 30 percent a year for several years and was regularly expanding its production capacity and product line.[2] The company had grown sixfold since the late 1970s, building more than 15,000 boats in 1985.[3] Even with such success, however, Sea Ray Founder and President C. N. Ray continued to implement reorganization efforts to fine-tune the operation and maximize efficiency to adapt to the changing industry.

The recreational boating industry had reached its high-water mark in 1974 in terms of domestic boat unit shipments, and boat dollar shipments had continued to rise steadily throughout the rest of the decade and into the 1980s. The total number of boats owned in the United States and the total retail expenditures for the industry had also steadily increased.[4]

The industry's leading manufacturers, including Sea Ray, had successfully countered the overall drop in boat shipments with increasingly efficient manufacturing methods that allowed for more affordable retail pricing, while still maintaining sensible profit margins across the entire lineup. Designers like Jerry Michalak had consistently created innovative products that enticed prospective buyers. While most boating enthusiasts purchased smaller, inexpensive models, an important purchasing trend was occur-

ring for mid-size and larger cruisers and yachts, which were becoming popular as family recreation vehicles. Sea Ray was a favored manufacturer due to its broad lineup and ample price-point choices.

With the recreational boating industry maturing in the 1980s and improving its overall efficiency, challenges were inevitable. A wave of consolidations swept through the industry as larger companies sought to acquire various boat manufacturers going out of business. Minneapolis businessman and investment strategist Irwin Jacobs gradually grew Genmar Industries in the early 1980s by buying small or bankrupt boatbuilders. By 1985, Genmar had acquired several prominent boat manufacturers, including Hatteras Yachts and Wellcraft.

The most significant consolidations were initiated from the marine engine side of the industry. Mercury and Outboard Marine Corporation (OMC), the two largest engine manufacturers for the boating industry, were selling an increasing number of bulk orders to large boat manufacturers such as

---

Sea Ray established its first overseas production facility when the company opened its plant near Cork, Ireland, in the summer of 1986. The plant started out building the Monaco series, including the 207 Bow Rider.

Sea Ray. Coupled with the highly competitive nature of the engine business, this increase in high-volume orders allowed boatbuilders to demand and receive considerably lower prices, which inevitably translated to shrinking profit margins.[5]

Mercury's parent company, Brunswick Corporation, decided to acquire several boat manufacturers, providing a captive market for the conglomerate's Mercury engines. Owning Sea Ray would allow Brunswick President and CEO Jack Reichert to implement the Boat, Motor, Trailer (BMT) concept, first championed by Orin Edson of Bayliner, in which all three boat elements were sold as one package. With the recreational boating industry enjoying a growth spurt, it was likely that Brunswick would recoup its investment relatively fast and end up with profitable new revenue streams.

After all, Brunswick was a larger corporate entity than the boat manufacturers, including Sea Ray, so it made sense in terms of the company's scope and size for the marine engine manufacturer to continue acquiring businesses. Brunswick had ownership interests in eight primary business sectors, from medical supplies and transportation control systems to bowling and engines, and its net sales and net earnings for 1985 were approximately $1.55 billion and $100.3 million, respectively.[6]

### Priming the Pump

When Vice President of Finance Bill Barrington and Vice President–Controller Rick Stone joined Sea Ray in mid-1985, the company's growing number of facilities were managed on a decentralized basis, with each plant essentially treated as a separate business. Stone believed it was important for plant managers to have a solid grasp of the accounting aspects of their respective operations, so he replaced each plant's bookkeepers with certified public accountants (CPAs). He recalled:

*I set the accounting policies, and they implemented them. They reported to me. I also made it sort of a requirement that they don't spend a lot of time in their offices but spend time out in the plant and become part of the management team in each of the facilities—an important part. [They would be] not just the person who is responsible*

**Early 1986:** Sea Ray opens its Cherokee Cove plant across from the company's existing facility on Tellico Lake in Tennessee.

**July 1986:** Sea Ray opens its first overseas plant in Cork, Ireland. A commissioning office in Hellevoetsluis, Netherlands, is also established.

**November 1986:** Brunswick Corporation acquires Ray Industries, Inc. (Sea Ray), for $350 million.

A **BRUNSWICK**MARINE Company

**August 1986:** New model-year 1987 boats are introduced, including the 460 Convertible; 410 Aft Cabin; 270 Hardtop; 270 Sport Fish; Sorrento 24XL, 24, 23XL, 23, 21XL, 21, 19XL, and 19; Seville 21 Bow Rider; and Pachanga 32 and 19.

**July 1987:** Sea Ray opens a plant near Fort Mill, South Carolina.

*for processing payroll and paying the bills but also someone the department heads [relied on] to manage their areas from a financial standpoint.*[7]

One of the accountants Stone first hired in 1986 at the Oxford, Michigan, plant was Robert VanNorman, now vice president of manufacturing operations for Sea Ray. Not entirely familiar with the boatbuilding business, VanNorman decided to research the company. He recalled:

*I certainly wanted to see what kind of company I was getting into. In Michigan, you can pull a company's financials at year-end, and I pulled [Sea Ray's]. It was just in great shape: little debt and great cash flow.*[8]

Another initiative Sea Ray undertook in 1986 was the founding of the Creative Learning Center for Dealer Development. Tim Harrington, a boating industry veteran, was hired as its marketing manager and director. He coined the still-popular catch phrase: "If it's not a Sea Ray, you missed the boat!"[9] To facilitate optimal dealer and end-customer support, Sea Ray had also established the Sea Ray National Customer Service Department at Knoxville headquarters the previous year, with Jim Carpinelli as manager. Carpinelli had come up through the ranks at Sea Ray, starting out as a laborer for the company in Michigan in 1975.

These new administrative creations continued Sea Ray's long-standing commitment of offering the best in customer service. Such considerations showed that even in an industry with a notoriously high dealer turnover rate, nearly one-third of Sea Ray's 1986 dealers had sold and serviced Sea Ray boats for more than 20 years.[10]

After its move to Knoxville, Sea Ray implemented several changes in its production flow to increase efficiency and overall quality. Although high-tech production processes were used, low-tech measures often proved effective as well. Phil Felice, senior vice president of operations, and Mike Morrison, vice president and assistant operations manager, helped simplify the production process in an effort to diminish the learning curve on the production floor. Describing these efforts, Morrison compared boatbuilding to making pizza, another "production" busi-

**August 1987:** Model-year 1988 boats are introduced, including the 430 Convertible, 345 Sedan Bridge, 305 Sedan Bridge, Sorrento 25DA, Laguna 23 Outboard, Seville 20 Cuddy Cabin, Seville 20 Bow Rider, Seville 18 Closed Bow (stern drive and outboard), Seville 18 Bow Rider (stern drive and outboard), Seville 16 Closed Bow (outboard), and Seville 16 Bow Rider (outboard).

**August 1988:** New model-year 1989 boats are introduced, including the 500 Sedan Bridge; 440 Convertible; 440 Aft Cabin; 380 Aft Cabin; 340 Sedan Bridge; 300 Sedan Bridge; 280 Sundancer; 260 Overnighter; 260 Cuddy Cabin; 250 Sundancer; 220 Sundancer; 230 Cuddy Cabin; 220 Cuddy Cabin; 210 Bow Rider; 200 Cuddy Cabin; 200 Bow Rider; 190 Closed Bow; 190 Bow Rider; 180 Bow Rider; 180 Outboard; 160 Outboard; Laguna 20; Laguna 17; and Pachanga 32, 27, and 22.

**August 1988:** Sea Ray Founder and President C. N. Ray steps down and becomes chairman of the company. Senior Vice President of Administration John Hedberg is named president.

**April 1988:** Sea Ray opens Riverview plant.

ness that demanded extremely fast and efficient production to remain viable:

> *You go in there [to a pizza restaurant] and what you see are full-color pictures that are either 100 percent scale or bigger. They give examples on how to make that pizza. Well, we did that in boatbuilding. In other words ... in those days, we used aluminum gunwale molding. It was a two-person job. You'd literally hold it up against the boat, and one guy drills through the molding, right in through the deck and hull joint, and then there would be a pop rivet and [you would] seal it. Well, we had an example board of a good drilling and a bad drilling—a straight one and an angled on—and examples of literally how to put a screw or a nut or a bolt in: "Here's the good one. Here's the bad one." Every station where they did that, we would put examples up of what was right or what was wrong. Those kinds of techniques worked. Our quality was high. Our warranty went way down.*

With a dry weight of just 2,900 pounds, the Pachanga 22 easily reached speeds of 60 miles per hour.

> *Our materials shrinkage went way down for all kinds of reasons having to do with building the product.*[11]

In early 1986, Sea Ray had opened a 72,000-square-foot production plant just across from the company's existing facility on Tellico Lake. The new plant, called Cherokee Cove, sat on a 57-acre tract the company purchased for $230,000 the previous year and was designed as a manufacturing site for the newly reintroduced Pachanga series. Sea Ray's expansion investment in the plant totaled $2.5 million, and plans called for a second building of similar size to be added at the site. Ken Hall, production manager at the original Tellico Lake facility, was named the plant manager at Cherokee Cove, while Gary Parisi continued as plant manager at Tellico Lake.[12]

### 460-Large and Pachanga-Fast

Sea Ray's 1986 lineup debuted two particularly noteworthy models, the 460 Express Cruiser and the Pachanga II, which was "fast, flashy, and fuel-efficient," as noted in *Boating* magazine's March 1986 boat test write-up. Michalak, who designed the

Pachanga II almost entirely anew, worked closely with Mercury Marine to develop the right engine for the speedboat—the 260-horsepower MerCruiser stern drive, as the 260 SX-15 was dubbed during its developmental stage, which was eventually offered in a version as large as the MerCruiser 350 Magnum.[13]

Aside from remarkable power, Michalak had incorporated many speed-conscious features into the design of the Pachanga II, one of which flouted Sea Ray's time-honored tradition of favoring heavy construction. Michalak's prominent use of advanced composite materials and innovative design allowed for minor sacrifices in durability in the 22-foot boat, which weighed hundreds of pounds less than its closest competitor. Furthermore, Michalak's design included six unusually wide, full-length lifting strakes (special planing surfaces running the length of the boat) that allowed the boat to rise out of the water (plane) quickly.[14] This resulted in a boat with quick pickup that could plane at slightly more than 18 miles per hour (mph) and then consistently hit 60 mph at full throttle.[15]

Sea Ray's new Pachanga II also offered another innovation—a swim platform molded into the stern of the boat rather than attached externally. Sea Ray

Above: Jerry Michalak was responsible for creating dozens of innovative boat designs for Sea Ray. He continued to design boats until 1996.

Below: One of the new Pachanga's exceptional design features was an innovative muffler system that achieved considerable noise reduction without significantly sacrificing engine performance.

was the first manufacturer to offer mass distribution of this feature.[16] Overall, the Pachanga II represented an impressive reentry by Sea Ray into the high-performance boat market.

The Pachanga II was not the only "level II" sport-boat version that Sea Ray offered in 1986, but it was the only true redesign. The Seville II was also marketed that year as an upgraded model of the existing Seville in terms of accessories. The Seville II added power steering, AM/FM stereo, and higher-quality gel-coat colors and accents than those used in the basic Seville model.

If the Pachanga II was the lightest of Sea Ray's 1986 models, the heaviest was the 460 Express Cruiser, the company's first sport yacht more than 40 feet in length. It was nearly 46 feet at the centerline and almost 15 feet at the beam, which marked the boat's breadth at its widest point. The luxury cruiser had forward and starboard staterooms, each with separate heads and enclosed showers, a large salon, and a full galley with par-

---

The 460 Express Cruiser was Sea Ray's first boat longer than 40 feet. The European influence that had developed in Sea Ray styling by the mid-1980s was reflected in the 460's forward-slanted radar arch, among other design features.

quet flooring. The yacht was powered by twin diesel engines and weighed in at 24,500 pounds.

With respect to size and luxury, Sea Ray had taken an important step in its lineup with the introduction of the 460 Express Cruiser. It had also achieved a milestone in high-end pricing. At a suggested list price of approximately $300,000, the "460-large" was $166,000 more than the 390 Express Cruiser, Sea Ray's next most expensive model.[17] This was the largest price gap ever between two Sea Ray models, including the lowest- and highest-end products in the company's lineup.

Sea Ray also offered a new model in its smaller sport yacht category that year, a new 268 Sundancer that filled the niche between the 250 and 270 models and was easy to trailer. The 268 Sundancer was more than one-and-a-half-feet longer and a half-foot wider than the 250 Sundancer. A Weekender version appeared the following year.

Also in 1986, Sea Ray began offering special Fishing Cockpit versions of two of its most popularly sized Cuddy Cabin models to accommodate the increasing number of boaters devoted to river and lake fishing. These specially appointed 23- and 25-foot versions typically included swivel helm seats, a substantial fish well to hold the catch, and rod racks and holders.

### Sea Ray's First International Plant

Sea Ray's international business had received increased attention during the first half of the 1980s as sales overseas grew steadily, with sales efforts managed by Murray Shektman, senior vice president of sales and marketing, and Steve Helwig, vice president of international sales. By the middle of the decade, pressure by international dealers for additional product prompted the company to build a plant in Ireland. Roger Giles, who was chosen to manage it, remembers how the scouting team had selected that location:

*The [Irish] government made it easy. The Irish Development Authority [IDA] was really proactive in guiding you right through the process. We had traveled through Switzerland, Austria, Spain, England, and even Northern Ireland, and there was so much bureaucracy that we could see it would be forever by the time you got through and got water access*

*and so on. But Ireland—it could happen. In fact, it did. A water location was available. There was a vacant building that had never been occupied that we could ... just step into.*[18]

Characteristically, once Ray decided to open a factory in Ireland, he quickly made it a reality. Giles recalled Sea Ray's efficiency in carrying out Ray's decision: "[We] made our first trip just looking for a place in January, a follow-up in March, decision in April, team in May, 25 guys hired and in training back [in Knoxville] in June, and back [to Ireland] July 1. We started producing the first boat July 4, 1986."[19]

Located on the River Lee at Little Island near Cork, in the southern part of the nation, the plant was installed in a vacant 75,000-square-foot building that was built to serve as a factory for ceramic tile. The purchase included 31 acres surrounding the building.[20]

Sea Ray had hired 25 new employees from the Cork area and brought them to Knoxville in June. They were trained mostly at the Tellico plant, where Sea Ray built the Monaco runabout series (the company planned to phase out the Monaco in the United States and move its construction and sales to Cork).[21] The Monaco had been displaced by the Sorrento

Above: Sea Ray had just enough production and office space at its Ireland plant to facilitate limited operations when production began in July 1986. In November, when this photo was taken, the facility was fully renovated and all 75,000 square feet became available.

Below: Sea Ray top management pictured in the 1986 Brunswick Corporation Annual Report included (left to right): John Hedberg, senior vice president of administration; C. N. Ray, division president; Murray Shektman, senior vice president of sales and marketing; and Michael Meyer, senior vice president of product development and engineering (PD&E).

Roger Giles (far left), the first plant manager at the Cork, Ireland, facility, led Sea Ray's Irish trainees on an outing in Tennessee's beautiful Smoky Mountains when they were in Knoxville for training in June 1986.

series in the United States and seemed well suited to the requirements of an opening model in Europe. The first finished boat came off the Cork assembly line on August 13, 1986,[22] and the plant shipped its first million dollars' worth of boats by December 10, 1986.[23]

When Sea Ray built its plant in Cork, the new European venture was legally established as Sea Ray Boats Europe B.V. in Hellevoetsluis, a small town in the western Netherlands. The Hellevoetsluis location was preferable as the official corporate address for several business-related reasons, including that it was near the home operation of Arie and Alex DeBoom, the father–son marine dealer team who were already representing Sea Ray in Europe. Furthermore, boats manufactured in Cork were shipped to the large port at Rotterdam, Netherlands, and then trucked to their respective dealerships on mainland Europe.[24]

Once Sea Ray's European operations were established, the company launched a massive marketing and advertising campaign on the continent. As Sea Ray had never relied much on advertising in the United States, the new campaign was unlike any other endeavor the company had undertaken. As marketing materials and advertisements flooded Europe, Ray, Shektman, Helwig, and others maintained a "hectic round of dealer and boat show visits."[25] By the fall of 1986, Sea Ray had seven new dealers in Europe, bringing the total to 21.[26]

### Summertime and the Living Is Easy

At the July 1986 Sea Ray dealers' meeting in Knoxville, C. N. Ray made several exciting announcements that went beyond the typical introduction of new additions to the Sea Ray model lineup. Business had been good, and the company had sold more than 15,000 boats for sales exceeding $288 million.[27] Ray announced that Sea Ray had a 12 percent market share, an impressive percentage considering the fragmented state of the recreational boating industry at the time.[28] In fact, Sea Ray had grown to become the second-largest recreational boat manufacturer in the nation.[29]

Ray shared further good news at the dealer meeting, announcing that Sea Ray and OMC had recently reached an agreement for the production of new stern-drive engines bearing a Sea Ray logo.[30] The OMC agreement had resulted from the efforts of OMC CEO Charles Strang, inventor of the stern-drive engine, who enticed Ray to use more OMC engines in Sea Ray boats. Ray recalled how Strang surprised him with OMC's new creation:

> He called and said, "C. N., I want you to come out to Waukegan [Illinois, where OMC is based]. I've got something I want to show you." So I went up there, and he had this big thing all covered up, and he pulled the cover off, and here was a stern drive—a really beautiful stern drive—much better looking than the old OMC round ones. And it had a "Sea Ray" [emblem] on it.[31]

OMC had built a prototype Sea Ray engine using a customized OMC Cobra stern drive that sported a Sea Ray emblem. Enthusiastic about the idea, Ray had signed a one-year agreement with OMC for the production of the engines.[32] As Shektman said at the time, "Introduction of this Sea Ray stern-drive model for 1987 marks the first step in the ongoing program through which OMC will eventually manufacture a broad line of marine propulsion equipment for Sea Ray."[33]

Besides finalizing their business agreement, Ray and Strang had also discussed the possibility of a corporate consolidation. Keeping in mind that 80 percent of Sea Ray dealers carried Mercury engines, Ray knew an acquisition by OMC would upset many important business relationships he had already established.[34] In an effort to protect these relationships, Ray soon turned his attention to Reichert, CEO of Mercury's parent company, Brunswick Corporation.

### The Brunswick Buyout

Mercury Marine's shrinking profit margin, the lure of a captive Mercury engine buyer, Sea Ray's continuing success, and Ray's receptiveness were all factors that encouraged Brunswick to begin acquisition negotiations with Ray early in 1986. While Sea Ray was not using outboards at all by the mid-1980s, it was Brunswick's single largest buyer of stern-drive engines.[35]

Several developments occurred during the course of the year to make an agreement likely before year's end. Brunswick executives quickly noticed when Sea Ray and Bayliner Marine Corporation of Arlington, Washington, both signed new deals in the summer with rival OMC for the purchase of stern drives. Such deals naturally catalyzed Brunswick's acquisition efforts. In fact, the company completed a deal on December 8, 1986, to acquire Bayliner for approximately $425 million.[36]

Another important factor in the acquisition process was the Tax Reform Act of 1986 passed by U.S. Congress in October and scheduled for enactment on January 1, 1987. The new tax legislation included a capital gains tax rate increase of 8 percent, providing an incentive for Ray and other corporate executives to sell their company by the end of the year. Brunswick executives, already primed for a major marine industry acquisition, knew it was a propitious time to make an offer. Furthermore, Reichert knew that OMC was pursuing the same type of acquisition strategy as Brunswick and had expressed an interest in Sea Ray.

Just a few weeks after the Bayliner acquisition, and just two days before the new Tax Reform Act would take effect, Brunswick and Sea Ray finally

Jack Reichert, then Brunswick CEO, was credited with initiating the BMT approach in which boats, motors, and trailers were sold to consumers as a package.

# A *BRUNSWICK MARINE* Company

reached an agreement. Brunswick purchased Ray Industries, Inc., for approximately $350 million on December 30, 1986, with only $50 million of the purchase price in stock.[37] Ray stayed on as president and was named to Brunswick's board of directors. Sea Ray's other top management also remained in place after the merger, keeping Sea Ray's successful distribution network intact. Brunswick grew by almost 40 percent with the Bayliner and Sea Ray deals and would now derive some two-thirds of its revenues and nearly three-quarters of its profits from marine engines and boats.[38]

Brunswick established a Sea Ray Division and a U.S. Marine Division (U.S. Marine was Bayliner's parent company) following the acquisition. With Brunswick now owning the top two recreational boat manufacturers in the United States, Reichert described the company's two new additions as distinct, but complementary, lines. "Bayliner is typically described—using an automobile analogy—as being in the Chevrolet–Pontiac end of the field," he noted. "Sea Ray is perceived to be in the Cadillac end of the business."[39]

While Brunswick's Bayliner acquisition had not surprised industry insiders, the Sea Ray deal had not been expected. In an interview with news media, Shektman shared his thoughts about consolidation in the industry:

*We feel, and have felt, that the industry was going to head in the direction of having fewer builders than you do today. And they would more or less have to be aligned to a power source. It's something we saw on the horizon. We definitely felt ... that at some point ... the boat and the engine [builders] would have to come together. For years we talked about it. Now, you're seeing it happen.[40]*

### Employee Ownership's Rich Rewards

From its earliest days in business, Sea Ray had offered its employees a healthy benefit package. A few years after the company turned a rea-

sonable profit in the early 1960s, a fixed-benefit retirement plan was also established. When Sea Ray moved to Phoenix, a profit-sharing plan was added to complement the fixed-benefit package. The plan was eventually amended to become a true employee stock-ownership plan (ESOP) in the 1970s.[41]

Arch Mehaffey, Ray's longtime Sea Ray partner, noted the distinction between the profit-sharing plan and the ESOP:

*The only thing that was different about them is that the profit-sharing plan could not invest in the company stock, and of course the stock-ownership plan was basically an investment in company stock. The company continued to make all the contributions, which started out very minimal ... less than $50,000 a year ... and grew.[42]*

When Ray established the ESOP for Sea Ray, few at the time imagined the incredible benefits the plan would reap in the case of a buyout. Such was the case with Brunswick's acquisition of Sea Ray, which suddenly and substantially raised the net worth of many Sea Ray employees, from executives and managers to production workers and office personnel. According to *Forbes* magazine, the transaction made multimillionaires of eight Sea Ray executives and millionaires of six others.[43] The net worth of many other employees rose by sizable amounts as well. Ray recalled the situation:

*That probably is the highlight in terms of my personal gratification with Sea Ray. It's great that the company built beautiful boats and everybody loved our boats, and we grew and grew. But the employees who built the boat—to give them the opportunity to become millionaires or earn $500,000 ... I thought that was really super.[44]*

The ESOP had invested employees directly in the success of Sea Ray and given them an additional sense of pride in their work for the com-

# SEA RAY SUCCESS FOR BRUNSWICK

WHILE BRUNSWICK'S 1986 PURCHASE of Sea Ray and Bayliner presented a captive market for Mercury Marine engines, the acquisition required Brunswick to honor both boat manufacturers' purchase contracts with Mercury rivals. As a result, Brunswick purchased $40 million in OMC engines for Sea Ray through May 1987.[1]

Beyond unavoidable contract obligations, Brunswick faced certain structural market risks implicit in its Boat, Motor, Trailer (BMT) packages. These potential risks received considerable media attention in the weeks following Brunswick's multiple acquisitions.

Even before the Sea Ray purchase, a Bear, Stearns & Company analyst had reacted to Brunswick's Bayliner acquisition by speculating: "[Some] of those other boat makers may now see themselves as Brunswick's competitors and buy their engines elsewhere."[2] Brian Bremner of *Chicago Business* asserted that boat manufacturers—other than those acquired by Brunswick—would now be reluctant to purchase Mercury engines, suggesting that the acquisition could end up "costing Brunswick some market loss to OMC."[3] He also raised the question of product overlap between Sea Ray and Bayliner. Brunswick CEO Jack Reichert responded with a question: "Do you think Chevrolet and Pontiac compete with Cadillac?"[4]

Nevertheless, the BMT concept eventually proved a success in the marketplace, with Brunswick implementing it well at the manufacturing level. Rival OMC, the largest engine manufacturer in the nation when Brunswick acquired Sea Ray, would declare bankruptcy in late 2000 after attempting to follow Brunswick's lead by purchasing five smaller boat manufacturers.

Meanwhile, dealers and consumers at all levels became comfortable with the convenience of buying boats, motors, and in many cases, trailers, as a package. As of 2008, Brunswick's Mercury Marine is the world's leading manufacturer of marine propulsion, and Sea Ray is its most prominent boat manufacturer.

pany. Over the years, Ray's personal generosity also affected company staff, including Giles, who had worked for Sea Ray in various capacities since 1971 and appreciated the bonuses given to him even when business was slow. He recalled:

*There were years where we really had to cut back. ... I remember when the Phoenix plant was down to 10 boats a week, and it was probably a 50-boat-a-week plant that could be up as high as 80, [but] there was still some kind of bonus paid. On top of that, there was always a Christmas check for $25 that didn't have anything deducted from it. It was kind of an extra C. N. [Ray] gift, you know, because that was the limit you could give without making any deductions. Anyway, he was very goodhearted in that way.*[45]

### The Big Tuna and Sorrento

Sea Ray offered more than 50 models in 1987, marketed in three categories, each with its own brochure. Sport boats, designed primarily for speed and casual daytime fun, included the Seville, Monaco, and Pachanga models, as well as the new Sorrento series. The Sorrentos were novel, small- to mid-sized sport boats designed to fit the niche between the smallest, inexpensive opening line (Seville) and the quickest, high-performance speedboat (Pachanga). Although Sea Ray's sport boats generally ranged from 17 to 24 feet, the new Pachanga 32 (originally dubbed Pachanga III) powerboat was also classified in this category. Sea Ray's sport cruisers were newly presented in a separate brochure for 1987, ranging from 23 to 30 feet and designed for overnight comfort or serious fishing. The sport cruisers included various renditions of the popular Sundancers, Weekenders, and several fishing models. The sport yacht designation was now reserved for luxury boats longer than 30 feet, extending out to the newest 46-foot boats.

Two 1987 models in particular, one at each end of the size spectrum, displayed Sea Ray's creativity and volition for risk, which was high thanks to Sea Ray's extraordinary success in recent years. The company had been growing at about 30 percent a year, and 1986 revenues had been nearly $450 million.[46]

The most ambitious of Sea Ray's new models for 1987 was the 460 Convertible, which was presented as the new Sea Ray flagship.[47] This luxurious behemoth was a long-range, all-weather, bridged, deep-sea fishing, hardtop yacht that featured an impressive multi-tiered fishing superstructure above the hardtop (sometimes referred to as a "tuna tower," leading to the 460's "Big Tuna" moniker). It offered European styling; the latest electronic marvels, such as state-of-the-art color video radar and satellite navigation; and

Powered by a V-8 stern-drive engine, the new Sorrento 21 was featured on the front cover of Sea Ray's 1987 *Sport Boats* brochure.

far more luxury than was typical for offshore fishing vessels. Its voluminous 700-gallon fuel capacity, approximately 45 percent more than the similarly sized 460 Express Cruiser, allowed for exceptional range. At a suggested list price of about $345,000, it was also more expensive than the Express Cruiser.[48]

The other prominent new line of boats introduced in 1987 was the Sorrento. The boats in this series were slightly wider and more upscale than the Sevilles but included the molded-in swim platform featured on the Pachangas. They were also offered in open- and closed-bow, basic and SXL, and 19- to 24-foot versions, like the Seville. Since the Sorrento series was not as drastically different as the 460 Convertible, or nearly as expensive, they did not present a serious business gamble compared to the company's new flagship. Nevertheless, refining existing sport-boat design features and rebranding the results in a new eight-model series certainly carried some degree of risk.

That year, Sea Ray also offered a new sport yacht and sport cruiser. The 41-foot 410 Aft Cabin sport yacht featured a raised helm; a large, enclosed aft cabin; and a nicely appointed salon. The 270 Sport Fisherman sport cruiser was a new mid-size fishing boat. Other changes in Sea Ray's 1987 models mainly reflected new designations for specific boats and series rather than new designs. The Sevilles were no longer named according to their measurement in meters, while various Cuddy Cruisers were renamed Cuddy Cabins, and Fishing Cockpits became Cuddy Fishermans.

Meanwhile, all Monaco production was moved to the new Cork plant in Ireland. The Monaco 210 and 210 SXL were marketed in the United States during their transitional model year of 1987, and many of the earliest Monacos produced in Ireland were shipped for sale in the United States to supplement the Sorrento runabout production. By the following year, however, Monaco products were offered only in Europe, and the entire series was dropped from Sea Ray's North American brochures.

### Adjusting to Change

Manufacturing companies, particularly successful companies like Sea Ray, are rarely acquired without some initial difficulties. Sea Ray employees at higher levels had to adjust their perspective. "There was a lot of friction to begin with," recalled Bill Barrington, vice president of finance at the time. "Here comes this big, bad parent company that has all [these] procedures, and forms, and ways to do things."[49]

Barrington gave a lot of credit to Brunswick CEO Reichert, however, for his management of the early stage of the transition. "He really did run a decentralized company," explained Barrington. "He allowed [Sea Ray's] vision to be just about as autonomous as you could possibly imagine."[50]

Sea Ray's first post-acquisition dealers meeting took place in Knoxville just eight months after the new arrangement had been formed. Reichert and Ray took the opportunity to proclaim the value of Sea Ray for its new parent company. Proud of his company and dealer network, Ray delivered a strong endorsement in the Sea Ray headquarters auditorium:

*I remember he was sitting in the third row, and all the dealers were there, and I said to him, "Jack, I have to say this in front of all of my dealers. I think you're going to be very proud of the fact that you bought this company because it's going to do well. You're sitting among the very finest dealers in the world, among the people who build the very best product in the world. You're going to be proud because it's going to continue to grow and help make Brunswick what you want it to be."*[51]

Ray had many reasons to feel proud. Sea Ray's fortunes had continued to blossom throughout 1987, and its 51 percent sales increase for the year had been 15 to 25 percent higher than most other boat manufacturers. In addition, the company's international network had never been stronger.[52]

Although Sea Ray operations experienced inevitable changes as a result of Brunswick's acquisition, business continued as usual, with the company continuing its projects already under development. Sea Ray executives also began their search for yet another suitable production site for the manufacture of two new models—the Laguna 23 and a new 16-foot Bow Rider outboard model. Focusing their search in the southeastern United States, Sea Ray soon discovered an appealing facility that had previously housed a textile machinery and parts distribution business on a 90-acre site in Lancaster County, South Carolina, near the town of Fort Mill. Lancaster County offered an appealing package of financing and tax incentives.[53]

Sea Ray's new 95,000-square-foot Fort Mill plant began operations in July 1987 with Carpinelli as

The Laguna series generated considerable excitement when it debuted at the 1987 Chicago Boat, Sports, and RV Show. The Laguna 23 was introduced in model-year 1988.

# POPPING THE CORK

CORK, IRELAND, THE SITE FOR SEA RAY'S first international manufacturing facility, offered many advantages for its new tenant, including a waterside location on River Lee and a building that would require minimal rehabilitation. Beyond that, the Irish Industrial Developmental Authority (IDA) worked closely with Sea Ray executives to ensure a smooth transition.

As the first major American recreational boat manufacturer to own a full manufacturing facility in Europe, Sea Ray faced some challenges as it switched to the continent's electrical standards, adopted certain style preferences, and established business relationships with local and regional materials suppliers. The company also had to meet new codified requirements for construction, manufacturing, and sales.[1]

For Roger Giles, the first plant manager of the Cork facility (or managing director, as the position was called in Ireland), it was an extraordinary administrative challenge, but also an exciting

undertaking. "It was a great adventure, and I have nothing but fond memories, but it was a lot of work," Giles said. "You're going from ground up trying to get a plant running."[2]

Although the plant had produced its first boats by August 1986 and Giles had admirably dealt with the production and administrative difficulties that inevitably accompanied a startup outside of the United States, the facility was not profitable its first year. Back in Knoxville, Jim Steffens asked C. N. Ray for his permission to take the Irish plant to a higher production level. Having worked his way up through Sea Ray production operations to his current position as production manager, Steffens had ample experience for the job. Ray offered Steffens the Cork plant manager position, asking him for a two-year commitment.[3] Steffens responded with a counteroffer:

*I basically told him, "I'll commit to you that in six months, if I can't go there, build boats, make*

plant manager. One drawback to the new site, however, soon became evident. As Lancaster County had never been home to a boat manufacturer, the area lacked a workforce with experience. The lack of experience caused problems, particularly in building the 23-foot Laguna. When the plant lost money during its first six months, Carpinelli was forced to lay off 20 of the plant's 160 workers. He pleaded with Sea Ray executives to move production of the Laguna away from the Fort Mill facility:

*Our biggest problem starting up was that we bit off more than we could chew. We were here with people who didn't know how to build boats trying to build a very sophisticated boat. But we realized that and said, "Hey, we're choking. Give us something simpler."*[54]

Sea Ray management obliged, and the Laguna was eliminated from Fort Mill's production run,

leaving only the company's smallest and most basic model, the 160 Bow Rider, manufactured at the site. The facility began to operate more efficiently.

After getting Fort Mill up and running, Sea Ray management quickly turned its collective attention to securing a place to produce its new 305 Sedan Bridge and the 340 Express Cruiser. The month after Fort Mill began operation, Sea Ray purchased a 58-acre tract for $900,000 in the Forks-of-the-River Industrial Park just a mile and a half upriver from its Knoxville plant headquarters. The company immediately began construction of a new $8 million manufacturing and distribution facility.[55] The new Sea Ray facility included three buildings—two 70,000-square-foot facilities (one for fiberglass molding and the other for the production assembly line), and a third, 40,000-square-foot building that housed the company's transportation department.[56] At the time, Sea Ray had a 54-truck Peterbilt fleet that operated under a full-service lease agreement through a national lessor.[57]

*money, and train somebody, then you can fire me." I knew the players already. It wasn't that big of a gamble for me.*[4]

Ray accepted his offer, and in April 1987, Steffens was named the new plant manager at Cork. He immediately initiated various operational changes in the plant's production processes to improve productivity, including the plant's use of fiberglass and gel coatings. Steffens had discovered that the coatings purchased locally were inconsistent, so he shipped the materials straight from Knoxville instead.

Steffens remained involved with the facility's operations for almost a year and increased the plant's production significantly.[5] "We went from one boat a day to seven boats a day and started making money," said Steffens.

He also helped establish the Riverview plant when the facility opened. He was then sent to the Oxford, Michigan, facility, which had started to lose money by the late 1980s.[6] As one of Sea Ray's most highly regarded production experts, Steffens often analyzed production operations and helped under-producing plants achieve higher production levels and profits.

When Sea Ray established its plant in Ireland, the 11-year deal had secured substantial tax credits for the company.[7] Sea Ray closed the Cork facility in 1997 after meeting that contractual agreement.[8]

In 1987, Sea Ray participated in the St. Patrick's Day parade in Cork, Ireland, hauling several boats down the city's main street during the festivities.

The Riverview plant, as the new facility was named, opened in April 1988, and veteran boatbuilder and administrator Mike Mitchell was named the first plant manager. Many employees from the Knoxville plant were relocated to Riverview, as production of the facilities' two new boats began.[58] The plant employed nearly 500 workers, mostly Sea Ray veterans, increasing the total number of Sea Ray employees in the Knoxville area to approximately 2,000.[59] Riverview was Sea Ray's third new manufacturing plant in less than three years and its fifth in six years.

Meanwhile, Barrington and Stone had observed some of Bayliner's centralized purchasing procedures and decided to implement a similar system at Sea Ray in an effort to increase efficiency and cut costs. Stone brought in Mike Myers in December 1987 as vice president of sourcing and material control to set up a new centralized purchasing program. Myers, who had been in materials and purchasing

management with General Electric, oversaw the creation of a computerized material requirements planning (MRP) system to centralize materials purchasing across all Sea Ray operations. The MRP would help Sea Ray achieve a more efficient purchasing apparatus, receive the most favorable volume and seasonal discounts on materials purchased, and afford easy analysis of purchasing data. "We made more money as a result of it because we had better data to go talk to our suppliers about, and there was a huge working capital improvement," Stone said.[60]

### Return of the Outboard Models

It had been many years since Sea Ray had produced an outboard model, but that changed in model-year 1988, when the smallest of the Seville series (the 16) and both sizes of the new Laguna series were offered exclusively as outboards. In Sea Ray's brochures, all boat model names were

printed in bold, capital letters, while model names on the boats themselves were rendered in darker, larger, eye-catching fonts.

The new Sevilles that were smaller than 20 feet featured 90-, 100-, or 135-horsepower outboard motors. The previous year's 17-foot model was elongated one foot, and the resulting 18-foot model was offered as both an outboard and stern drive. The new Seville 20 was a Cuddy Cabin version powered by a stern drive.

The Laguna was a 1988 Sea Ray model powered by outboard engines, offered with either twin or single 135-horsepower or single 175-horsepower outboards. This new Sea Ray was a fishing boat built in 20- and 23-foot versions, featuring a minimally sized but rugged and highly functional center console that afforded maximum open deck space for fishing ease.

Above: Sea Ray returned to manufacturing outboard models in 1988 with the introduction of the smaller Seville series. A 135-horsepower engine powered the Seville 18 Bow Rider.

Below left: Opening in March 1988, Sea Ray's Riverview complex cost approximately $8 million to establish.

Two sedan bridge models also debuted in 1988—a sport cruiser and a sport yacht. The 345 Sedan Bridge replaced the 340 Sedan Bridge and offered a wider beam and increased fuel capacity, while the new 305 Sedan Bridge was a shorter version with inboard engines.

Sea Ray also introduced a nearly 24-foot-long hybrid sport cruiser that year, the Sorrento 25 Sundancer, which offered European-influenced styling on the popular Sundancer mold. The company also unveiled the 430 Convertible, a smaller version of the flagship 460 Convertible.

### Ray's Final Farewell

The second half of the 1980s was developing as a time of dramatic change in the pleasure-boating industry. Unit shipments rose steadily from 1986 to 1988—23,626 boats for nearly $518 million—reaching a mark not registered since the all-time high of 1974.[61] During the same period, the total number of boats owned in the United States had grown to an

# If it isn't a *Sea Ray*, you've missed the boat.

estimated 15 million, a healthy increase of more than 36 percent, or approximately 5.5 million boats.[62]

After nearly two years of post-Brunswick Sea Ray presidency, Ray realized it was time to step down from his position. He explained:

*When I landed my helicopter and walked into my office, I didn't have that sprightly step. I didn't own [the company] any more. I finally said to Jack [Brunswick CEO], "I'm not doing the company any good any more, so you have to replace me." And he said, "Okay, but on one condition. You stay on as chairman, and you pick the guy you want to run the company."* [63]

With Reichert insisting that Ray choose his own replacement, Ray soon selected John Hedberg, an attorney who had served as outside counsel for Sea Ray in the mid-1970s while the company was headquartered in Phoenix.[64] By 1978, Hedberg had joined Sea Ray as a corporate attorney. He was instrumental in the reorganization of the company when Ray returned in 1985 and was promoted to vice president

of administration that same year.[65] He subsequently became senior vice president of administration and was named president of Sea Ray in August 1988.[66]

After relinquishing his presidency, Ray accepted the position of Sea Ray chairman and signed a one-year consulting contract.[67] The Sea Ray founder continued to maintain a presence in his corporate creation, but his participation was minimal after Hedberg succeeded him. This time, unlike in 1979, Ray's departure from day-to-day operations was final.

Although Ray no longer guided the company, Sea Ray's future looked bright as 1988 drew to a close. Hedberg had proven an excellent administrator, production teams continued to manufacture high-quality boats worthy of the Sea Ray name, the skillful PD&E operation was intact and working with the latest technology, the company had the extraordinary assets of Brunswick Corporation, and the recreational-boating market continued to strengthen. Although the situation appeared exceptionally promising, there would be more challenges to overcome.

Sea Ray began offering a few models as BMT (boat, motor, trailer) packages during the late 1980s and early 1990s, including the Laguna.

## CHAPTER SEVEN

# BATTEN DOWN THE HATCHES

## 1989–1994

*It was like somebody just turned the faucets off. You just couldn't cut enough in time, and that's when we started closing plants and laying off people and doing everything else that we had to do to catch up to this dramatic drop-off in business. It was the "Great Boating Depression." It was not a fun time.*

—Bill Barrington,
Sea Ray president and CEO, 1989–2001[1]

T HERE WAS PLENTY OF room for optimism as Sea Ray introduced its new 1989 lineup in August 1988. Even though the Knoxville-based company no longer received the day-to-day attention of C. N. Ray or Arch Mehaffey, Sea Ray had prospered for three decades and was eager to continue its success. In celebration of the company's 30th anniversary, Sea Ray brochures included a six-page introduction entitled, "Sea Ray—Three Decades Strong," which offered an informative overview of the boatbuilder's history and culture of high-quality manufacturing. In addition, the tagline "The Sea Ray Way" was abundant in marketing materials for that year.[2]

Sea Ray initiated several significant changes in model designation of its smallest boats for 1989. The changes brought the sport boat designations more in line with the nomenclature long used for larger models. The Sorrento name and metered sizing was dropped entirely, while the Seville joined the Monaco in a group of model names that would be used for only a few basic models sold in Europe. The Sorrento and Seville series were replaced in the domestic market with numerical designations for similar, but refined, styles. For example, the new 160, 180, 190, 200, and 210 Bow Riders of 1989 reflected the same hull and essentially the same deck style as those used with the 1988 Seville series, but incorporated higher-quality appointments. The new 230 and 220 Cuddy Cabins featured Sorrento-type hulls.

Meanwhile, very few of the 1989 sport cruisers were altered, other than the sport yachts, which underwent significant change. Sea Ray's most prominent development was its new flagship and first 50-foot boat, the impressive 500 Sedan Bridge. The boat's bridge was exceptionally well suited for navigation, and its large, aft cockpit, as well as its sumptuous salon and three spacious staterooms, afforded plenty of space for entertainment. Twin 550-horsepower Detroit Diesel engines were offered as standard features, with 650s as an option.[3] Jerry Michalak remembered Sea Ray's first 50-foot boat as one of his personal favorites and as the "perfect size" for combining large scale with convenient one-person operation.[4] He recalled:

*One person can handle that boat because of the layout. You're high enough on the helm position. You have good enough control of the boat. You can go back and grab dock lines ... you don't have to have somebody else on the boat.*[5]

Sea Ray adopted a new logo in 1987 that featured the company name with its stylized initials rendered in a suitably fluid text style and color scheme.

While the Sedan Bridge had sold successfully at several different sizes, the boats in the Convertible series that Sea Ray debuted with much fanfare in model-year 1987 had been pared down to only one—the 440 Convertible—by 1989. The large, impressive-looking tournament fishing boats with an optional tuna tower—a high platform for spotting fish—had not sold nearly as well as forecasted.

The 415 Aft Cabin sport yacht, however, had sold well, so Sea Ray added 38-foot and 44-foot versions (the 380 and 440, respectively) for 1989. Sea Ray also introduced its largest Sundancer, the 420, that year. All Sea Ray sport yachts included an impressive list of standard features, including full swim platforms, self-bailing cockpits, double-wide helm seats and companion seats, full galleys, and 12-volt directional lighting.[6]

Since Brunswick acquired Sea Ray in 1986, the number of boats sold in the recreational boating industry had increased three years in a row. John Hedberg, who served first as senior vice president of administration and then as president between 1987 and 1988, had focused on managing the inevitable policy and administration adjustments that accompanied the acquisition. While Brunswick had not interfered with Sea Ray operations, new programs and paperwork resulted in some changes. Rob Parmentier, who by this time had moved to Sea Ray's sales department and accepted the position of sales manager for sport yachts and yachts, remembered how Hedberg handled the situation:

*Hedberg was a brilliant man. He kept our team grounded in a very stressful time. John [Hedberg] was a calming presence and tried to work through the period in which Brunswick was now asking a lot of us in terms of reports and financial information that you would expect when you've just been purchased.*[7]

Meanwhile, Sea Ray's first employee and former president Arch Mehaffey retired on March 31, 1989—his 65th birthday. He had served as a consultant to Sea Ray for the previous five years, and his retirement marked the first time that a founding member was no longer affiliated with the company.

**March 1989:** Former president Arch Mehaffey retires.

**June 1989:** Executive Vice President of Finance William (Bill) Barrington is promoted to president and CEO after John Hedberg retires.

**May 1989:** Sea Ray shuts down its domestic manufacturing plants for a weeklong "production adjustment."

**September 1989:** The Fort Mill, South Carolina, plant shuts down.

**Late 1989:** The Cherokee Cove plant in Tennessee is closed.

**August 1989:** Sea Ray introduces most of its model-year 1990 boats, including the 480 Sundancer, 370 Sun Sport, 350 Express Cruiser, 350 Sundancer, 310 Express Cruiser, 310 Sundancer, 270 Sundancer, and 250 Weekender.

As the 1989 model-year progressed, sales had started out relatively well, running slightly higher from August 1988 through March 1989 compared to the same period the previous model-year.[8] Sales plummeted, however, in April 1989. As April, May, and June were generally crucial months for recreational boatbuilders, with retail customers purchasing boats in preparation for the summer and dealers clearing space on their showroom floors to allow room for the next year's models, April's sudden drop in sales was unusual and alarming.

Sea Ray executives blamed rising interest rates and gasoline prices as well as colder weather for the sluggish sales as the company publicly announced a weeklong "production adjustment" shutdown to begin May 29, 1989.[9] Sea Ray also announced that about 390 employees from the company's 10 plants would be laid off,[10] although each person affected would receive their full bonuses, earned and unearned vacation pay, and extended coverage on the company's medical and dental plan.[11]

William (Bill) Barrington stepped into this challenging environment in June 1989, when Hedberg retired, becoming Sea Ray's new president and CEO.[12] Ray had agreed to remain Sea Ray chairman and extend his consulting contract through 1990.

Barrington had been promoted from senior vice president of finance to executive vice president of finance when Hedberg was promoted to president in 1988. Brunswick had then sent Barrington to the Advanced Management Program at Harvard Business School, a prestigious three-month, in-residence course (often used by corporations to help groom executives for ascension to a CEO position).[13]

Barrington accepted Sea Ray's top position just as the market was falling drastically. "When I took over, product was starting to stack up in the field, and it had been such a long period of growth that nobody wanted to admit that something might be going awry," remembered Barrington. "So I didn't have an opportunity to enjoy the good times very long before the industry took a nosedive."[14]

After Barrington was named president and CEO, Rick Stone was promoted to senior vice president

**Early 1990:** New second-half 1990 boats are introduced, including the 370 and 330 Sedan Bridges.

**April 1990:** A sales office in Frankfurt, Germany, is opened.

**August 1990:** New first-half model-year 1991 boats include the 280 Weekender, 225 Bow Rider, 200 Overnighter and OV LTD, 200 SR, 200 Bow Rider, 185 SR, 185 Bow Rider, 170 Bow Rider and Closed Bow, and 170 LTD versions.

**Early 1990:** PACE Process pilot program is initiated at the Tellico plant in Tennessee.

**Late 1990:** The Sykes Creek facility is opened on Merritt Island in Florida.

and chief financial officer. He understood Brunswick's choice for the Sea Ray top position. "Brunswick was smart enough, quite frankly, to put somebody in the role who knew something about the business and had the most critical piece that you need—a relationship with the dealers," Stone recalled. "Bill had that because of his involvement as vice president of finance."[15]

Upon both financial experts' respective promotions in 1989, Stone took over some of Barrington's responsibilities, adding budgeting, strategic planning, and dealer credit financing duties to the accounting, purchasing, and information technology oversight he had already been handling as controller.

As the new management team struggled to deal with the market's drastic downturn, Sea Ray laid off approximately 960 employees from the company's domestic plants on July 27, 1989.[16] The situation continued to worsen, however, forcing Sea Ray to shut down several plants. Fort Mill closed first, followed by the Cherokee Cove and Riverview plants, all within a two-year period.

## Sundancers and Sun Sports

As part of the stringent measures implemented in response to the decline in the recreational boating market, Sea Ray held back some boats from its 1990 model-year lineup during the August 1989 product release, reserving delivery of several models until the second half of the model-year in 1990. By this time, the company was selling more boats 26 feet and longer than any other manufacturer.[17] The new offerings—eight boats longer than 26 feet, including five at the beginning of the model-year in August and three in early 1990—would help Sea Ray retain that distinction.

Sea Ray's most prominent new models in August of that year were the Sundancers. As this standard-bearer remained consistently popular, the company introduced four newly sized and upgraded models—the 270, 310, 350, and 480—the largest Sundancer yet. At nearly 48 feet long, the 480 Sundancer was powered by twin 485-horsepower diesel V-drive inboard engines. It was, of course, luxuriously appointed, and it featured a

**January 1991:** The Oxford, Michigan, plant is shut down. It had been Sea Ray's first bona fide manufacturing facility.

**March 1991:** Sea Ray implements the PACE (People Achieving Customer Expectations) quality management program throughout its facilities.

**August 1992:** New 1993 model-year boats include Sea Ray's first 65-foot boat, the 650 Cockpit Motor Yacht. Also introduced are the 630 Hardtop, 550 Sport Fish, 440 Express Bridge, and 250 Express Cruiser, along with the Laguna 29 and 21 Walkarounds, Laguna 16 Side Console, 190 Ski Ray Sportster, and 185 Ski Ray Spitfire.

**Early 1991:** New second-half 1991 models are introduced, including Sea Ray's first 60-foot yacht, the 600 Super Sun Sport; the 290 Sun Sport; and the 190 Ski Ray, the company's first tournament ski boat.

**August 1991:** New 1992 boats are introduced, including Sea Ray's first 63-foot boat, the 630 Super Sun Sport. Also introduced are the 550 Sedan Bridge, 350 Express Bridge, 310 Sport Bridge, 310 Amberjack, 270 Sundancer, 240 Overnighter, 230 Sundancer LTD, and 160 Outboard LTD, along with the 24, 21, and 18 Laguna Center Consoles and the 24 Laguna Flush Deck Cuddy.

The 480 Sundancer was the largest of the series when it debuted in model-year 1990. Some of the attractive features on the luxurious yacht included the boat's high helm and wrap-around dash.

wraparound control console and wraparound cockpit seating.

Another compelling 1990 debut was the 370 Sun Sport, whose sleek, low profile and curved-wrap windshield offered a striking silhouette, even from a distance. The most captivating feature of this new Sea Ray series was its cockpit, which featured a dramatic, circular seating arrangement and salon. The Sun Sport also reflected Michalak's growing preference for rounded designs. Michalak recalled:

*We were doing very rounded curvature. It's probably harder for the plants to [manufacture], but everything had a flow to it. The interiors were very creative.*[18]

The Sun Sport was a notable addition to the Sea Ray lineup and the first example of the design team's new use of rounded features, a creative new trend that continued to grow over the next few years. Other models debuting in August 1991 were the 250 Weekender and the 310 and 350 Express Cruisers, all larger and more refined than the existing models.

Despite such extraordinary product offerings, Sea Ray's 1990 model-year did not start out par-

**November 1992:** The Cork, Ireland, plant is awarded ISO 9002 certification by the Irish Standards Authority.

**August 1994:** New 1995-model boats include the 630 Sundancer and the redesigned 370, 330, and 250 Sundancers; Select versions of the 200 Overnighter and Bow Rider; refinements of the 195 and 175 Bow Rider; and the Sea Rayder F-16 and Sea Rayder Select.

**July 1993:** The Frankfurt, Germany, office is closed.

**August 1993:** The Sea Rayder debuts. In addition, 1994 model-year boats offer refinements to 270, 290, and 300 Sundancers; 180 and 200 Bow Riders; and Select versions of the 220 Bow Rider and Overnighter. Most of Sea Ray's boats in the sport boat category are now designated as the *Signature* series.

**Summer 1993:** The Riverview plant is reopened for production of the new Sea Rayder model.

# HIGH-TECH BOATBUILDING

DURING THE 1980s AND 1990s, MAJOR technological developments occurred in industrial design, including boatbuilding, due to the growing influence of computers in the manufacturing process. Developed in 1983, computer-assisted design (CAD) software was combined with computer-assisted manufacturing (CAM) systems to facilitate CAD–CAM design technology. CAD systems incorporated the requisite mathematical calculations and other project data into the design and engineering process, illustrating the end product through vivid two- and three-dimensional visual representations. In terms of efficiency, this new design tool surpassed traditional methods (use of a calculator and hand-drawings) by allowing for faster and more precise rendering of prototypes. CAD was integrated with various CAM systems that facilitated certain preset and precise manufacturing functions, such as drilling and cutting. During the same period, computer numerical control (CNC) machining, which allowed greater accuracy in cutting and forming parts, became more affordable, thus streamlining the manufacturing process. Computer-automated systems also

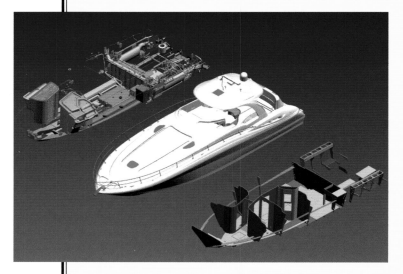

Left and opposite: Boat manufacturers greatly benefited from the development of CAD–CAM technology in the 1980s. Mike Meyer, Sea Ray's vice president of product development and engineering (PD&E) at the time, was instrumental in introducing the new technology to Sea Ray.

ticularly well. By October 1989, two months into the 1990 model-year, Sea Ray sales had improved slightly from the spring quarter's dismal numbers, but were still down 16 percent from the same period a year earlier.[19] By this time, the lackluster conditions in the recreational-boating industry were exacerbated by a serious national recession.

By the end of 1989, about 1,300 Sea Ray employees had been laid off, with about 800 eventually recalled.[20] It was even worse for many other boat manufacturers, as shipments industry-wide plummeted by nearly 100,000 units for calendar-year 1989.[21]

Still, Sea Ray executives were optimistic when the boat models for the second half of the 1990 model-year became available early in 1990. Two new versions of the Sedan Bridges were offered at 37 and 33 feet. The new 370 and 330 Sedan Bridges were similar to the 500 Sedan Bridge in styling but had different sizes and price points.

As the crucial spring season arrived in 1990, Sea Ray executives tried to stimulate sales overseas to make up for the domestic downturn. In April, the company established a sales and service office in Frankfurt, Germany, staffed by John Cronkhite and Roger Giles.[22] Cronkhite was a senior vice president and general counsel at Sea Ray, handling legal matters and also human resources, while Giles served as Sea Ray vice president, overseeing dealer and consumer services. Once assigned to the overseas office, each kept their respective positions as vice president, although Cronkhite added "European operations" to his title, and Giles added "European sales."

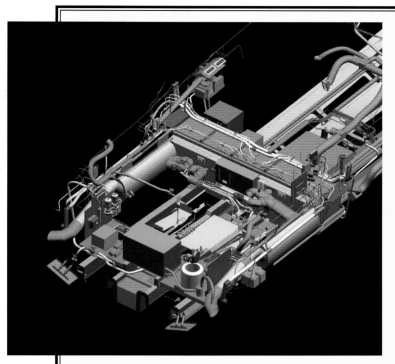

helped maximize efficiency in other business processes, such as purchasing operations and administrative tasks.

This fertile period of technological development coincided with C. N. Ray's return to the company presidency and his extraordinary modernization and reorganization efforts. While Sea Ray had always embraced new technology, it increased its focus more on expanding its use

of high-tech devices during this period. For instance, when efficient and affordable facsimile (fax) machines were becoming popular in the mid-1980s, Ray personally advocated their use and successfully overcame some initial dealer resistance to the new technology. Determined to incorporate fax systems throughout the dealer network, he even offered special in-house financing to facilitate the installation of this new means of communication.

Meanwhile, Mike Meyer, Sea Ray's vice president of product development and engineering (PD&E) at the time, was instrumental in introducing the new CAD–CAM technology to the company. Meyer, a former Sea Ray dealer, had served as plant manager at the Merritt Island facility before establishing Sea Ray's new research and development facility at the plant in 1983, along with Jerry Michalak.[1]

Thanks to CAD–CAM, by 1990, Sea Ray had developed a large database of "time-proven, proprietary formulas for determining the optimum combination of hull weight, shape, length, number of strakes, horsepower, gear ratio, propeller size, shaft angle, position of engine, and other factors influencing performance, ride, and the amount of useable interior space in the boat."[2] While the company never lost its appreciation for handcraftsmanship, it recognized the flexibility and precision afforded by computer applications.

Unfortunately, the domestic recreational-boat market continued to deteriorate. When the fiscal year ended on June 30, Sea Ray had experienced a drop of more than 40 percent in the number of boats it sold, totaling less than 10,000, its lowest product output in many years.[23] While international sales were more stable, they were not strong enough to make up the difference. By July 1990, Sea Ray was forced to lay off about 250 employees company-wide.[24]

Undeterred by diminishing sales, however, Sea Ray continued to move forward, opening a new plant in 1990 on Merritt Island at Sykes Creek, which would handle additional production of the 500 Sedan Bridge. The island now had three facilities—the main Merritt Island plant, the new Sykes Creek facility, and the product development and engineering (PD&E) site.

### Ski Rays, Bow Riders, and the 60-foot Mark

As Sea Ray prepared its new 1991 lineup in 1990, it used the Tellico plant as the pilot site for a new quality management program called the PACE Process. PACE (People Achieving Customer Expectations) was designed to help Sea Ray employees achieve maximum efficiency and quality in virtually all areas of operation.[25] It adopted the criteria used for the Malcolm Baldridge National Quality Award, a nationally recognized, public–private total quality management (TQM) initiative designed to help American manufacturers meet growing challenges abroad.

Despite sinking market conditions, Sea Ray continued to dramatically expand its August 1990 array

Sea Ray initiated its People Achieving Customer Expectations (PACE) Process in 1990. PACE was a quality control and customer service program that offered various forms of training and assessment.

of new models for the 1991 lineup. While the previous model-year's new offerings had included only sport cruisers and yachts, for model-year 1991, the company focused more on smaller boats, offering 13 new sport boat versions. Although the new models did not feature brand-new hulls or decks, they marked the beginning of a broadly based rethinking of Sea Ray's smallest models. Sport boats offered two different cockpit seating arrangements for most of the smaller stern drives, and customers could select either two bucket seats and an aft seat with sun pads, or two back-to-back seats with conventional rear seats and a fiberglass motor box.

Among the new boats Sea Ray presented for 1991 were the "trailerable" (as per the boat, motor, trailer, or BMT, concept) and non-trailerable versions of the 17-foot Bow Rider and Closed Bow Limited models. The 180 Bow Rider stern drive was replaced with the longer 185 Bow Rider and a 200 Bow Rider. Three other 20-foot sport boats were offered as well— a Closed Bow 200 Sea Runner, a 200 Overnighter, and a 200 Overnighter Limited. Two other newly refined Closed Bow runabouts were introduced as the 185 Sun Runner and 225 Sun Runner.

In the sport cruiser group, Sea Ray introduced a 280 Weekender to complement the 28-foot Sundancer, as well as a Limited version of the 220 Sundancer.

As Sea Ray's lineup expanded, its marketing efforts increased as well. The company complemented the brochures on its three major boat categories—sport boats, sport cruisers, and sport yachts—with a small, general product-line brochure. Separate brochures were published for the Laguna series, the 500 Sedan Bridge, and the 600 Super Sun Sport, which debuted in early 1991. A new tagline was also used: "Sea Ray ... Worth More from the Very Start."

While Sea Ray battled market lethargy with product innovation and marketing savvy, the U.S. Congress added to the company's market woes in late 1990. The Omnibus Budget Reconciliation Act (OBRA) passed in Congress and signed into law by President George H. W. Bush on November 5, 1990, implemented a 10-percent tax on recreational boats costing more than $100,000. The tax legislation, designed as a deficit-reduction measure, would take effect in January 1991. The luxury tax seemed ominous to the recreational boat industry, especially boatbuilders like Sea Ray, whose lineup included high-end luxury yachts.

A few weeks after the new tax legislation was signed, Brunswick announced the imminent closing of its Oxford, Michigan, plant, scheduled for early 1991.[26] Established in 1962, it had been one of Sea Ray's oldest and largest facilities, producing at least 100,000 boats over the years.[27] Right before the plant closed, only 15 boats were being built each week.[28] Jim Steffens, who had served as vice president and general manager of the facility, explained why it was necessary to shut it down:

*The Knoxville facility was facing another drop, and it was kind of crazy to keep [the Oxford plant] operating at 15 boats a week and have [the Knoxville plant] operate at 10 because they'd lose money at both facilities. It wasn't a matter of closing the plant because it wasn't making money or the quality was bad or it was inefficient. They did it because it wasn't economically feasible to keep the two locations open, and you wouldn't shut a newer location to keep an older location open.[29]*

The Oxford plant ceased operations on January 20, 1991.

As the spring of 1991 approached, Sea Ray's second group of 1991 boats arrived at dealers' showroom floors. The company reached another milestone with the introduction of its new 60-plus-foot model, the 600 Super Sun Sport, which maintained the circular styling of the 370 Sun Sport with semi-circular recesses, wraparound seating arrangements, round tables, sun pads, and other items. While the rounded features of the more modest 370 Sun Sport were eye-catching, they made an even larger impact on the striking 600 Super Sun Sport, which offered the ultimate in luxury with lavishly appointed staterooms, salons, dinette areas, and galleys. Twin 735-horsepower diesel inboard motors propelled the large yacht.

Sea Ray designer Jerry Michalak, whose official title had changed to senior vice president of PD&E (versus "product design and development"), remembered the stark contrast between the original prototype of the 600 Super Sun Sport, which was built with simple materials, and the final, luxury version:

*[The original] was built of wood, and we built it like you [would] build a wood boat. We'd just scale out our drawings, build the ribs, gunwale, [and] keel, and set them up on a level platform. Then ... you sighted everything in, and you established your chine [the line of intersection between the side and bottom of a boat], covered it with plywood, and ... put a layer of fiberglass. [Then] we'd actually put an engine in and run it.*[30]

Another sport boat that was introduced early in 1991 was the 290 Sun Sport, an elegant hybrid of a sport boat and well-appointed cruiser. With essentially the same sleek silhouette as the much grander 600 Super Sun Sport, the 290 Sun Sport was smaller but nonetheless featured impressive amenities not usually found on this type of boat.

The other Sea Ray that debuted in the second half of the 1991 model-year was the 190 Ski Ray outboard, which was designed with input from Water Ski Hall of Famer Ricky McCormick and women's slalom world record–holder Suzi Graham.[31] The result was a quick, highly maneuverable 19-foot ski boat in bowrider and closed-bow versions, powered with a 175-horsepower

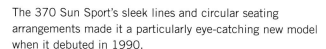

The 370 Sun Sport's sleek lines and circular seating arrangements made it a particularly eye-catching new model when it debuted in 1990.

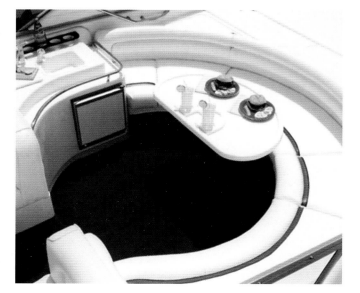

Mercury outboard. The 190 Ski Ray provided Sea Ray with a strong entry in the tournament ski market, as well as a welcome niche addition at the smaller end of Sea Ray's line. The boat received considerable attention thanks to three one-hour specials that aired on U.S. television in the spring of that same year, showing Ski Rays in action.[32] The American Water Ski Association quickly awarded the boat competition eligible certification, a distinction that was not easily earned.[33]

### Setting the PACE

To alleviate the effect of poor market conditions in the early 1990s, Sea Ray implemented the PACE Process throughout its operations, encouraging better employee attendance, cross-training, and employee feedback, among other aspects. Barrington believed it was a crucially important development in Sea Ray operations:

*It was basically an employee involvement program. We got the employees involved in their jobs and how [to perform them] more efficiently, and how the company can save money. I think it brought [Sea Ray] back to the employees. ... We brought the employees back into the whole scheme of running the company and trying to make sure that the employees understood what kind of value they bring to their jobs.[34]*

Sea Ray's PACE measures laid the groundwork for an even more formal and rigorous program specifically designed for International Standard Organization (ISO) certification, which was implemented in 1991 at the Cork plant. As the world's largest developer and publisher of international standards for quality management systems, the ISO requires companies to meet several prerequisites before gaining certification. These include developing a manufacturing protocol manual with strict, high-quality standards for most aspects of operation; developing a carefully conceived plan for achieving those goals; implementing the plan company-wide; and meticulously monitoring, measuring, and analyzing data to implement necessary adjustments and ensure

---

Introduced with the 190 Ski Ray in 1991, a Limited version of the 16-foot 160 Ski Ray added another outboard to the series in 1992.

the highest-quality system is developed and maintained.[35] The prestigious ISO certification was not easily achieved, according to Barrington:

*You ... document everything you do and lay out a menu for your employees. It's a very heavy documentation process. We really spent a lot of time at the plant level getting through the entire process. It was a mighty effort.*[36]

### Sedan Bridges, Limiteds, and the 63-foot Mark

Although the recreational-boating industry was floundering and Sea Ray's profits were decreasing, the company continued to manufacture an impressive number of new boats. As Barrington believed that one of the most important ways to reenergize Sea Ray sales was to stimulate the boat-buying public with new product and features, he maintained high levels of monetary support for Sea Ray's PD&E efforts. Chief Financial Officer Rick Stone acknowledged Barrington's contributions to Sea Ray's success during the turbulent marketplace of the 1990s:

*Bill [Barrington] understood that the industry runs on new product—a lot of new product and innovative product. When he got the reins, we started to throw a lot of money into PD&E. So, you give Bill a lot of credit for that.*[37]

With direction from Barrington, Sea Ray began including more variations on its mainstream models while continuing to introduce brand-new models. The company's increasingly versatile production techniques made it easier to retool for new or revised product, allowing Sea Ray to achieve greater flexibility with its production runs. It was no longer prohibitively expensive to offer special-edition versions of a select number of models. Limited versions of boats became a staple in the Sea Ray lineup in the early 1990s, and in any given year, the company offered several existing models in a carefully conceived luxury Limited version.

Another factor that allowed Sea Ray to offer a continuous stream of refinements was the extraordinary growth in technology during the 1990s. Features like exceptional sound systems and Global Positioning System (GPS) navigation instruments that

Sea Ray's Cork plant employees worked diligently to achieve ISO 9002 certification in 1992. The plant was the first fiberglass boat manufacturing facility in the world to achieve this distinction.

had once been expensive were now fairly reasonable additions that offered extra value to boaters.

Sea Ray created a number of new models and refinements on existing boats for the 1992 model-year, introduced in August 1991. The 630 Super Sun Sport designator reflected a 3-foot change (in designation only) to the previous year's 600 model, establishing a new and larger Sea Ray flagship. Sea Ray also added the 550 Sedan Bridge to complement the 500 Sedan Bridge, and added two other new bridge boats, the 350 Express Bridge and 310 Sedan Bridge. A *Sea Magazine* boat reviewer called the 550 Sedan Bridge a "well–thought-out and attractive motor yacht

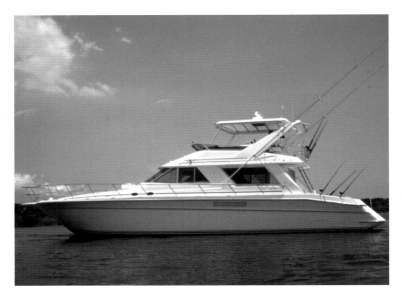

Above: Sea Ray added three bridged boats to its 1992 lineup, with the 550 Sedan Bridge sport yacht the largest of the trio.

Below: Sea Ray's newfound penchant for round features reached new levels in the company's magnificent new 63-foot flagship, the 600 Super Sun Sport, which debuted in 1991.

that makes optimum use of the space available" and "lives up to its owners' high expectations of quality, luxury, and performance."[38]

Sundancers also experienced some adjustments in 1992. The 500 superseded the 480 (in model-designator nomenclature only). The 440 Sundancer replaced the 440 Aft Cabin, as Sea Ray took the rearward-cabin style off the market for a few years while it was refined. The 270 Sundancer was also introduced, as Sea Ray attempted to fill every size niche with the popular family cruiser, and a Limited version of the 230 Sundancer made the already appealing sport version even more attractive.

Sea Ray also offered another cruiser in its 1992 lineup by adding four feet to the 270 Amberjack fishing boat, resulting in the 310 Amberjack. Sea Ray also refined a number of its smaller sport boats, including the 160 Outboard and 200 Overnighter, which received Limited treatment. A new 240 Overnighter was also introduced.

The Laguna sport boat series was also in full force, with 18, 21, and 24 Center Console versions

Above and right: The 500 Sundancer was Sea Ray's largest sport yacht in 1992 and was moved to the yacht category in 1993. The wide beam allowed for a larger salon that included a 21-foot wraparound sofa, among other luxurious features.

and a new 24 Flush Deck Cuddy that offered a closed bow, a fuller console, and a cuddy cabin that was flush with the deck rather than below it. The Lagunas received additional promotional support when Sea Ray placed Laguna ads in major fishing publications. The line was also featured in the company's sponsorship of ESPN's *Mark Sosin's Saltwater Journal* and in 30-second commercials that Sea Ray offered to dealers for use in their local markets.[39]

The most notable omission from the 1992 brochures, however, was the Pachanga. Sea Ray's perennial speedboat had once again been put on hiatus.

As Sea Ray's new lineup was distributed to dealers across the nation, the company secured a prominent new agreement in December 1991 with Walt Disney Company. Sea Ray would pro-

vide Disney theme parks with ski boats, patrol boats, and executive yachts, while Ski Rays would be featured in a regularly scheduled ski show presented at Epcot Center in Orlando. Lagunas would be used as patrol and rescue boats at both locations, and various Sea Ray yachts would be available for VIP use in Walt Disney Company's headquarters region of Southern California.[40]

The new 1991 version of the 200 Overnighter offered two cockpit seating plans and more horsepower than previous versions.

### Spitfires, Sportsters, and the 65-foot Mark

Despite the challenging times, Sea Ray continued to build even larger yachts. The 650 Cockpit Motor Yacht, which debuted in August 1992 for model-year 1993, marked yet another new flagship for the company's growing fleet. The 650 Cockpit Motor Yacht was almost 65 feet long, with an 18-foot-wide beam. It had a dry weight of 67,000 pounds and a 1,000-gallon fuel capacity. The massive yacht came with twin 900-horsepower diesel engines and a luxurious deck and interior.

Two other yachts Sea Ray produced during the same period included a hardtop version of the 630 and a special Sport Fish version of the 550, which became the company's largest fishing yacht.

In the sport yacht category, Sea Ray's 1993 line debuted the luxurious 440 Express Bridge, which offered a walk-through flybridge (the open deck above the pilot house), sleeping accommodations for six, and a fully appointed galley, among many other appealing features. Another model-year 1993 boat, the 290 Sport Fly Bridge cruiser, also made good use of its upper deck and incorporated design features specifically aimed toward success in the Japanese market.

Sea Ray also focused considerable attention on its small sport boats, which included two new tournament ski models. The 185 Spitfire Ski Ray was 18-and-a-half feet long, with clean, simple lines, and a powerful 260-horsepower Mercury inboard engine. The 190 Sportster and 190 Sportster Bow Rider each boasted MerCruiser 350-Magnum Tournament Ski engines with approximately 270 horsepower. These powerful new models considerably augmented Sea Ray's Ski Ray line.

Sea Ray also offered two new versions of the Laguna, the company's entry-level fishing boat. The Laguna 16 Side Console had its console on the starboard side of the deck rather than the center. The sport boat's small size and minimalist styling allowed for an appealing price tag for boaters more interested in casual fishing than tournament fishing, speedboating, or luxury. Sea Ray also offered larger Lagunas that featured a much more substantial console, while still allowing boaters to walk completely around the deck for maximum fishing utility. Both the Laguna 21 and the larger 29 Walkaround were stern drives.

The 1993 model-year also marked the initiation of a trimester model-year for all purchases. Dealers were offered three separate purchase windows throughout the year.

### Keeping the PACE

Sea Ray began developing its PACE program for dealers as well as its trucking and shipping suppliers in the fall of 1992.[41] The company had brought its other suppliers into the program the previous year and had already provided customer service training through its PACE program for every employee, totaling more than 6,000 training hours. Brunswick recognized Sea Ray's innovative program by awarding it the President's Award for Quality.

Late in 1992, Sea Ray's concerted efforts at achieving higher efficiency and quality operations paid off. In November 1992, Sea Ray's Cork, Ireland, plant was registered by the Irish Standards Authority under the ISO 9002 standard for quality systems.[42] The registration was the first in the world for a fiberglass pleasure-boat manufacturing facility.[43]

While the ISO recognition was a boon for Sea Ray's reputation, the domestic recreational boating statistics between 1990 and 1992 told a grim tale of decline in the industry. Unit shipments of outboards, inboards, and stern drives had dropped by more than 50 percent, from around 550,000 to approximately 265,000.[44] Sea Ray's prudent cost-cutting measures and efficient operation, however, allowed the company to record 1992 pre-tax profits of approximately $6 million, considerably smaller than usual but remarkable given the situ-

---

The 650 Cockpit Motor Yacht, which debuted in 1993, would temporarily halt the desire of Sea Ray designers to continue building larger yachts. The 75,000-pound behemoth had a 1,000-gallon fuel capacity and was offered with an optional 250 gallons of additional capacity.

Left and right: Sea Ray's 185 Spitfire and 190 Sportster, both introduced in 1993, were two of the three small, but powerful, ski boats debuting that year as serious contenders in the tournament ski-boat market.

ation.[45] Barrington recalled the extraordinary fiscal stability of Sea Ray during these years:

> *On a positive note, during that three-year period from 1990 through 1992, we never lost money. We always had some positive earnings, and that included all the provisions we had, the accruals we had to make for closing facilities and laying off people. So our guys did a bang-up job of managing [the situation]. It's almost unheard of to cut the size of a company in half during that period of time and not lose money in any year.[46]*

Nevertheless, such a dramatic drop naturally diminished Sea Ray's production activity and profits, with the declining revenue stream inevitably affecting manufacturers that supplied Sea Ray and boat dealers that carried the Sea Ray line. "Twenty-five percent of our dealers went out of business during that time period," recalled Stone.[47]

Sea Ray's corporate sales department personnel struggled to secure at least 30 new dealers in a year to replace all the ones that were folding during the depths of the "Great Boating Depression." The pressure was immense to maintain a sufficient dealer network. The vice presidents within the dealer sales and dealer development divisions at this time—Parmentier, John Simonsen, Doug Mohney, and Scott Noble—along with their sales managers, were the most directly involved in these Herculean efforts.

Sea Ray management devised numerous methods to help its dealer sales team achieve its goals. A special Quota Incentive Program was developed based on market conditions and retail activity during the previous year. A Market Share Bonus Program encouraged dealers to focus their attention on Sea Ray boats. A special Yacht Financing Program helped dealers that carried Sea Ray's largest yachts. Sea Ray also increased its financial underwriting of dealer floor-plan costs as well as its flexibility with boat deliveries to dealers. Once new dealers were signed up, the company's increased dealer development and training efforts during this time were important in keeping them viable.[48]

Sea Ray's efforts in maintaining a solid dealer network during these trying times were successful, although upheavals did occur. As always, it was ultimately the personal dedication and strong work ethic of Sea Ray employees that allowed the Knoxville firm to survive. "We saw our way through every one of those deals and the impact on production schedules [as well as] the impact of our obligations on what to do with the inventory," said Stone.[49]

Sea Ray was not the only manufacturer affected. Every domestic boat manufacturer's sales fell drastically during this period, and recreational boat dealerships of all kinds were failing. Indeed, Sea Ray was faring far better than most marine manufacturers.

The National Marine Manufacturers Association (NMMA) and Houseboat Industry Association (HIA) blamed the federal luxury tax that had been initiated in 1990 for the drastic drop in boat sales. The two marine organizations later estimated that between 1990 and 1992, the tax, in combination with a recession, had caused an astounding 80 percent decline in the sale of boats subject to the tax and a loss of approximately 25,000 jobs.[50]

By the beginning of 1993, the sales figures for calendar-year 1992 showed a slight increase in unit shipments of runabouts and stern-drive boats. The increase was minimal, and it would take considerably more to bring the industry back to healthy levels. Nonetheless, in 1993, the numbers had been steadily and drastically dropping for three years, so any increase was welcome.

Meanwhile, Sea Ray continued to advance its inexpensive, smaller boat models. Jim Steffens and Bob VanNorman, both working out of corporate headquarters in Knoxville since the Oxford plant closed, teamed with Michalak to develop a new jet-powered model. To build the new jet boat, Sea Ray decided in 1993 to reopen one of its buildings at Cherokee Cove, the manufacturing site it had closed in 1989. After operating out of Cherokee Cove for just a few months, however, MasterCraft Boat Company, a small East Tennessee boat company specializing in tournament ski boats, expressed interest in purchasing the facility. Sea Ray agreed to sell the site, and subsequently reopened one of the buildings at the closed Riverview plant as a replacement, retooling it for the new jet boat.[51] Steffens was named vice president and general manager of the reopened Riverview plant.

By the summer of 1993, with one domestic plant sold and another reopened, Sea Ray reevaluated its situation in Europe. Company executives decided Sea Ray's attempt to generate increased

sales overseas through the Frankfurt, Germany, office had proved cost-ineffective. While the facility had helped increase European sales, the increase was insufficient to justify the cost of running the facility during a depleted domestic market. Sea Ray closed the Frankfurt office that July.

Thankfully, the summer of 1993 brought good news. Congress passed the Omnibus Budget Reconciliation Act (OBRA) of 1993, and on August 10, first-year President Bill Clinton signed the revised tax legislation into law, retroactive to January. The new law repealed the luxury tax on boats that had been included in the 1990 OBRA. Sea Ray's top-line models were now, in effect, less expensive.

### Sea Rayder, Signature, and Select

Pleased with the Cork plant's ISO 9002 success, Sea Ray expanded its most rigorous TQM program to all of its domestic plants in the fall of 1993. Meanwhile, the slight increase in sales and repeal of the luxury tax gave Sea Ray executives reason to believe the recreational boat market would recover. In August 1993, the company offered an exciting new lineup of 60 boats, ranging from 13 to 65 feet for the 1994 model-year. Three refinements were offered in the popular Sundancer series—the 300,

By 1993, Sea Ray's dealer merchandising materials had grown to include an appealing array of items such as flags, banners, T-shirts, and caps, which clearly targeted a younger audience for the company's new jet boats in 1994.

A group of Sea Ray veterans celebrated company founder C. N. Ray's 70th birthday in 1994 at Lake Tahoe. Pictured from left to right: C. N. Ray, Steve Helwig, Mike Meyer, Arch Mehaffey, Jerry Michalak, and Murray Shektman.

290, and 270—as each offered exceptional value in mid-sized sport cruisers. The 300 received a power upgrade with twin 230-horsepower MerCruiser stern drives.

Several sport boats also received makeovers. The 180, 200, and 220 Bow Riders featured new deck treatments, upgraded power, and deep-V hulls for higher deadrise. The 1994 220 Overnighter had a longer, wider hull and a more powerful engine. It was also offered in a luxurious Select model, the new designation that replaced the Limited designation previously used for specially appointed boats.

In another change in designation, all of Sea Ray's sport boats, with the exception of the new Sea Rayder (a 13-foot boat that blasted a water jet from a nozzle in the stern) and the 230 Sundancer, were now considered part of the Signature series (in marketing materials, this series name was always rendered in italicized, faux-signature font).[52]

Perhaps the most significant news for 1994 was the reemergence of the jet boat. Sea Ray had not produced a jet boat since the 1970 vintage Pachangas, so its introduction of the Sea Rayder was a major step. The bold-colored jet boat, which could reach 40 miles per hour, was powered by a 90-horsepower Mercury Sport-Jet. A color-coordinated trailer also accompanied the boat. Initially, Mercury offered its Sport-Jet engine only to Sea Ray and Bayliner.

**Sundancer Style and Rayder Raves**

Well received in the marketplace, the Sea Rayder proved a popular addition to Sea Ray's lineup, combining "terrific control and tracking with

Introduced in 1994, the jet-powered Sea Rayder was just 13 feet long and could top 40 miles per hour.

an ability to slide and spin on command" and debuting to "rave reviews."[53] The affordable jet boats were relatively simple to manufacture, easily trailerable, and required little room on the showroom floor. Sea Ray was soon building 100 per week in only one building at the Riverview plant.[54]

Sea Ray built upon the Sea Rayder's success with two new 1995 jet-boat models, offered in August 1994. The Sea Rayder F-16, powered by Mercury's Sport-Jet 120, added three feet in length to the basic Sea Rayder and increased the boat's horsepower by 25 percent. The limited-edition Sea Rayder Select was offered in a rich, gold color and added special amenities not found on the more basic Sea Rayders.

Sea Ray's 1995 models did not depend solely upon the Sea Rayder for refinement. A 630 Sundancer was added to the lineup, along with redesigned 370, 330, and 250 Sundancers.

The 630 Sundancer was a current 630 Super Sun Sport hull and deck with twin inboard diesel engines at the transom connected to Arneson Surface Drives. This placed the engines farther back in the engine room, allowing for more interior cabin space, the addition of a mid-stateroom, and raising of the helm—the trademark of a Sea Ray Sundancer. Sea Ray had never built a boat with Arneson Surface Drives previously and has not done so since.

The 370 and 330 Sundancers offered refinements such as more comfortable amenities in the helm and extra storage space in the galley. The 250, a new trailerable Sundancer, joined the 230 and 270 as examples of easily transportable models. Its size was noted to "strike a perfect balance between accommodations and trailerability," according to *Trailer Boats* magazine.[55] At about $40,000, the 250 came with plenty of amenities and a 250-horsepower MerCruiser stern drive.

In 1993, the American Bureau of Shipping recognized Sea Ray for its excellence in manufacturing. The well-respected organization judged Sea Ray's production facilities on quality and safety standards.

Sea Ray also offered Select versions of its 200 Overnighter and Bow Rider, and refinements of the 195 and 175 Bow Rider for 1995.

As the midpoint of the decade approached, Sea Ray executives reflected on the past few years with pride. Despite the "Great Boating Depression" of the early 1990s, Sea Ray had managed to accrue a profit every year, while continuing to expand its line of boats. The company had earned recognition in *Fortune*® magazine, which rated Sea Ray boats as one of the 10 best American-made products; the Cork, Ireland, plant had received the prestigious ISO 9002 certification; a new plant at Sykes Creek on Merritt Island was opened and awarded the American Bureau of Shipping's Certificate of Quality Assurance;[56] and Tennessee Governor Ned McWherter had awarded Sea Ray with the Tennessee Quality Achievement Award in 1993 and 1994.[57] Fortunately, by 1994, the recreational-boat market numbers had reversed their decline and climbed back to mid-1980s levels, providing some relief after several years of downturn.

Beyond the highlights of the past few years, the near future looked promising for Sea Ray. The market seemed poised for a continuous, gradual recovery; PACE and other efficiency and quality programs were producing results, and additional refinements to the company's quality directives were being developed. In addition, Brunswick was beginning the process of establishing an organizational distinction that would broaden Sea Ray's mission, while the company's international operations were on the verge of significant change.

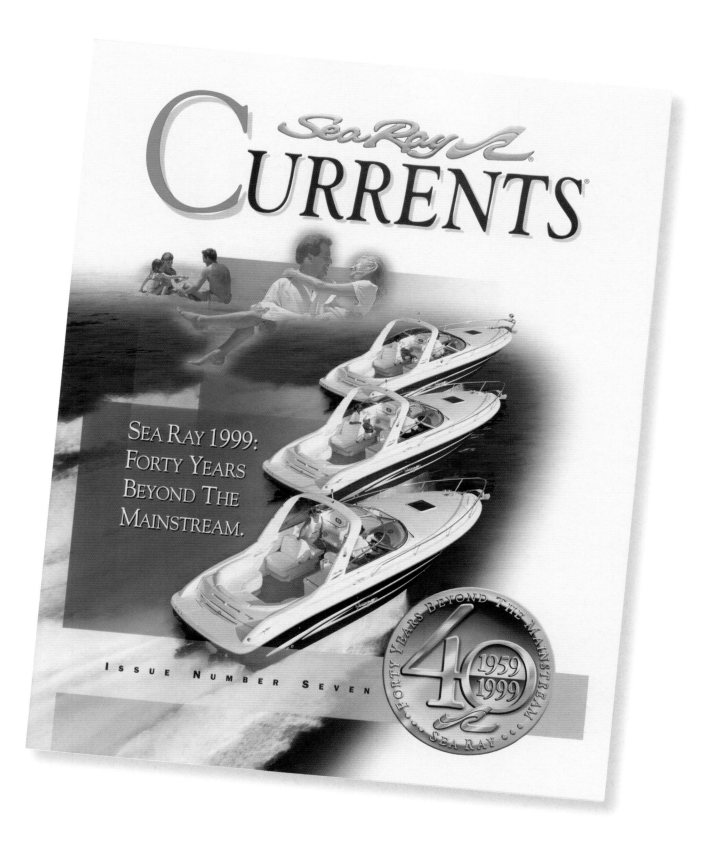

Sea Ray's 1999 marketing materials commemorated the company's 40 years of boatbuilding.

## CHAPTER EIGHT

# SHIPSHAPE AND SEAWORTHY

## 1995–1999

*Bill [Barrington] surrounded himself with the best people he could. He was a really good numbers guy, [but] he knew that he didn't know everything about everything. He hand-picked one of the best staffs in the entire industry, and he gave everybody the autonomy to execute their ideas. He liked to hear new things. He liked to hear how we could grow the company. That's [when] we took the company to another level.*

—Rob Parmentier, executive vice president[1]

WITH THE NATIONAL RECES-sion easing and the luxury tax no longer hampering the industry, boating shipments had increased slightly for 1993 and even more significantly for 1994. By 1995, boat shipments were more than 15 percent higher than they had been for the previous six years.[2]

During that time, Sea Ray's numbers rose at an even faster rate than the industry average. The company had prospered for many reasons, but much of Sea Ray's continuing success was a result of one of its greatest strengths—its handling of the dealer network. Sea Ray had taken great care in rebuilding the network after the loss of many of its dealers during the disastrous market drop in the early part of the decade.[3] It was, as Sea Ray CEO Bill Barrington characterized it, "a real mess."[4] As he recalled:

*It was very difficult. We had to go in and pick up all the boats. In a lot of cases, we didn't have the responsibility to pick up the boats that were left [when a dealership folded], but I always elected to do that. At the same time, you're out interviewing other players that are in the market selling boats.[5]*

Choosing to uphold the attributes of its dealer network, Sea Ray replaced each failed dealership with just one new dealer to maintain a limited

number of Sea Ray dealers within relatively large territories. This policy was one of the defining features of the Sea Ray dealership network that contributed to the strength and success of the company's dealerships. Barrington also wanted to maintain the high quality of dealers that characterized the Sea Ray dealership network. "It wasn't hard to get a dealer to stand up and say they wanted the Sea Ray franchise, but you had to make sure you had the right guy," Barrington said.[6]

Although rebuilding the dealer network to full strength was a major Sea Ray objective in the early to mid-1990s, the company also focused on maintaining good working relationships with the dealers who had survived one of the industry's most difficult periods. Like founder C. N. Ray, Barrington believed in spending a lot of quality time with the dealers.[7] He often accompanied Rob Parmentier, then vice president/general manager for Eastern region sales and product manager for Laguna Sport Yachts and Yachts, on customer service trips. Parmentier remembered the close business relationships that he and Barrington cultivated with Sea Ray dealers:

---

Bill Barrington served as Sea Ray president from June 1989 until February 2001, longer than anyone else except C. N. Ray.

*Every week, we would visit two or three dealers. Even when we didn't have to, we would. Globally, on our plane. We would [stay] with them. We wouldn't stay in a hotel. We'd stay at their house. We'd play golf with them. We'd go to their customer-appreciation events. We'd go to their [kids'] First Communions. We'd go to their weddings. We'd go to their funerals. [And that is why there is that loyalty still today].*[8]

While the heart of Sea Ray remained rooted in its dealer network and the personal relationships it had established over the years, the company's continuing efforts at quality and efficiency management also played a central role in its growing fortunes. The implementation of a fully integrated material requirements planning (MRP) program, the PACE (People Achieving Customer Expectations) Process, and an increasingly formalized production-efficiency process were all crucial components of those efforts. One indication of the growing recognition of Sea Ray in the Total Quality Management (TQM) field was the March 1995 appointment of Mike Mitchell, the

company's director of quality, to the Malcolm Baldridge Board of Examiners.

Sea Ray's quality and efficiency efforts paid off even more several other times in 1995. In February, the company's main Merritt Island, Florida, production facility became the first fiberglass pleasure-boat manufacturing plant to receive International Standards Organization (ISO) 9002 registration in the United States.[9] Sea Ray's Phoenix, Arizona, plant received the same distinction in June.[10] The Palm Coast, Florida, and Knoxville and Tellico, Tennessee, facilities received ISO 9002 registration in November.[11]

Nevertheless, even quality checks of Sea Ray's caliber could not guarantee perfection. While more than 4,000 Sea Rayders had been built at Riverview in model-year 1994, and the inexpensive jet boats were extraordinarily popular in 1995, there were persistent problems with the starters. Even though immediate measures were taken to find a solution, they were unsuccessful at first.[12] "A substantial portion of [starters] failed in the market," recalled Barrington. "We replaced them, or Mercury would come in and replace them

**February 1995:** The 450 Sundancer debuts at the Detroit Boat Show.

**February 1995:** Merritt Island production facility becomes the first fiberglass boat manufacturing plant to receive ISO 9002 registration.

**June 1995:** Phoenix plant receives ISO 9002 certification.

**September 1995:** Ray Industries, Inc., purchases Baja Boats, Inc., for $22.5 million.

**November 1995:** Knoxville, Tellico, and Palm Coast plants receive ISO 9002 certification.

**Summer/Fall 1995:** Sea Ray introduces its 1996 lineup. New boats include the 420 Aft Cabin; 400 Sedan Bridge; 210 and 280 Bow Riders, Sea Ray's largest bow rider; 240 Sundeck, Sea Ray's first deck-style boat; 240 Sundancer; 215 Express Cruiser; 175 Closed Bow stern drive, Closed Bow outboard, and Closed Bow XL; Laguna 21 Dual Console; and Sea Rayder F-16.

**March 1996:** The Riverview plant receives ISO 9002 certification. Sea Ray becomes the world's first recreational fiberglass boat manufacturer with all of its production facilities operating under the ISO 9002 quality system.

with what they thought was the fix, and then they would fail again."[13]

Sea Ray's other boat models, however, continued to prove reliable. The 450 Sundancer, a second-half 1995 model-year yacht that debuted at the Detroit Boat Show in February, replaced Sea Ray's 44-foot Sundancer. It featured additional space and a cored hull, along with various equipment upgrades. Sea Ray used end-grain balsawood coring in the bottom and sides of some of its larger yachts to reduce weight and increase buoyancy. Cored hulls allowed boats to run faster and reduced fuel consumption, regardless of speed.

### Aft Cabins, Sundecks, and the Baja Acquisition

When Sea Ray introduced its 1996 lineup in August 1995, the company introduced a newly refined bridge-style boat. Powered by twin 310-horsepower V-8 inboard engines, the 400 Sedan Bridge was a model of performance, luxury, and versatility. Even the standard model featured many accessories and options. Two bridge plans, two floor plans, and four optional engines were available as selections. The "Monte Carlo Package" offered upgraded amenities such as stainless-steel sliding doors and windows as well as custom veneer wood treatments. The boat was a superlative, versatile addition to the Sea Ray lineup.

Sea Ray also debuted its largest bowrider model in 1996. The 280 Bow Rider featured a bow door with a walk-through windshield leading to a spacious and well-padded bow with ample storage space. The new boat also offered far more amenities than typical for a 28-footer. Sea Ray introduced a 210 Bow Rider the same year.

Meanwhile, Sea Ray made its first attempt at producing a deck-style boat. Although the boat lacked the graceful lines of most recreational powerboats, it had been around for years as a small-percentage niche product for family boaters limited to lake boating. Sea Ray had never pursued the ungainly style until its popularity began to grow in the mid-1990s. *Trailer Boats* magazine reported that Sea Ray "did a good job softening the lines." In regard to the boat's mechanical systems, the magazine reported that the 240 Sundeck "shines."[14]

Another 1996 Sport Cruiser, the 240 Sundancer, replaced the 230 Sundancer for the domestic mar-

**1996:** Jerry Michalak, Sea Ray's original boat designer, retires. He had created revolutionary boat designs during his 37 years with Sea Ray.

**August 1996:** Sea Ray initiates a new computerized dealer communication system called RayNet.

**July 1996:** Sea Ray introduces "Legacy," the marine industry's first certified pre-owned boat program.

**May 1996:** Ray Industries, Inc., purchases Boston Whaler from Meridian Sports for $26.6 million.

**Summer/Fall 1996:** Sea Ray introduces its 1997 model-year lineup. New boats include the 580 Super Sun Sport; 400 Sundancer; 370 Aft Cabin; 370 and 330 Express Cruiser; 280 Sun Sport; 280 Cuddy Cabin; 230 Overnighter; 230 and 210 Bow Rider; 190 Bow Rider and Closed Bow; 185 Bow Rider; and the Sea Rayder F-16 XR.

Sea Ray had never before manufactured a deck-style boat until introducing the 240 Sundeck for 1996. The Sundeck was essentially a hybrid that gave a V-hull to a pontoon-type deck.

ket, while the 230 was offered strictly in the international marketplace. Sea Ray initiated changes with its sport boats as well. The company rebranded its opening models as the "Five Series," with the 215 Express Cruiser, a smaller Boat, Motor, Trailer (BMT) cruiser with a two-person berth, as the most prominent model. Other Five Series entries included three new closed-bow variations: the 175 Closed Bow, 175

Closed Bow outboard, and 175 Closed Bow XL. The 175 Closed Bow outboards featured a Mercury engine with 90 horsepower, and an optional fish and ski package that increased the horsepower to 115 and offered swivel bucket seats, a live-bait well, and a trolling motor. The 175 Closed Bow stern-drive model featured MerCruiser Alpha I engines with 135 horsepower. The 175 Closed Bow XL model had an Alpha I with a horsepower of 160 and featured swivel bucket seats. All of the 175s were BMT models and were sold complete with trailers.

A new Laguna model was also produced in 1996. The Laguna 21 Dual Console, unlike other Lagunas, lacked a walk-around deck, creating extra space that was used for separate, full consoles on each side of the deck. Located farther forward than center consoles on other Laguna models, the dual console offered a larger aft cockpit and an open

**November 1997:** Sea Ray closes its Cork, Ireland, plant (above).

**Summer/Fall 1998:** Sea Ray introduces its model-year 1999 lineup, including the 280 Sun Sport Anniversary Edition, which commemorates Sea Ray's 40th anniversary, and the 270 Sundancer Special Edition. Other new boats include the 460, 380, and 260 Sundancer; 450 Express Bridge; 260 Overnighter; 190 Cuddy Cabin; and 180 Dual Console.

**Summer/Fall 1997:** Sea Ray introduces its 1998 model-year lineup. New boats include the 540, 310, 290, and 270 Sundancer; 480 and 210 Sedan Bridge; Select versions of the 260 and 230 Bow Rider and 230 Overnighter; and 180 Bow Rider and Bow Rider outboard.

**Late 1998:** The Sea Ray Boat Group consolidates its three companies into a new international division.

bow as well as a longer, wraparound windshield that offered more protection from wind and spray.

Other events occurring that year included Sea Ray's renaming the new version of its basic Sea Rayder, which featured 25 percent more horsepower, as the Sea Rayder F-16. Another change, which did not go unnoticed, was the removal of Weekender models from company brochures for 1996, when Sea Ray's innovative Sun Sports and Sundecks temporarily pushed the model out of the lineup.

At the Fort Lauderdale Boat Show® in October 1995, Sea Ray debuted its new 420 Aft Cabin for 1996. Aft-cabin hull configurations allowed for maximum privacy, with staterooms at opposite ends of the boat separated by a salon. Twin 340-horsepower MerCruiser engines powered the boat. Orders for the new model proliferated during and after the show. Commenting on this great response, a writer for *Motor Boating & Sailing* magazine noted that what really "... won raves from the crowd was the way in which Sea Ray has enhanced the design by offering about as much comfort and convenience as is conceivable in a 42-foot cruiser."[15]

As 1996 models began to hit showroom floors, Ray Industries, Inc., acquired a new boat manufacturer, Ohio-based Baja Boats, Inc., on September 29, 1995.[16] Baja Boats had been operating under Chapter 11 bankruptcy since February 1994, which complicated the transaction. Sea Ray had to reach an agreement with Genmar Industries, Inc., which had purchased the boat manufacturer's bank note from National City Bank of Cleveland.[17] Sea Ray and Genmar reached a series of agreements that included several different transactions, with the final price reaching approximately $22.5 million. Bill Barrington, Sea Ray president at the time, recalled:

*Irwin Jacobs [chairman of Genmar] had jumped in and purchased, for pennies on the dollar, the debt that was outstanding. So, in effect, he owned the company. We took Baja off his hands. We had a number of successful years with it. It was a whole new business.[18]*

The Baja acquisition provided Sea Ray with an entry into the high-performance boat market segment, which it had not pursued since retiring

**Early 1999:** Sea Ray licenses boatbuilders in New Zealand and Brazil to manufacture Sea Ray boats for the international market using Sea Ray molds and materials.

**April 1999:** Sea Ray becomes the first company to receive a prestigious Horizon Award from the American Boat and Yacht Council.

**August 1999:** Sea Ray introduces its model-year 1999 lineup. New boats include the 510, 410, and 240 Sundancer; 290 Amberjack; 245 Weekender; 240 and 190 Sundeck; and a reintroduced 190 Closed Bow.

**March 1999:** Sea Ray becomes the exclusive North American representative for Torino, Italy–based Azimut cruisers and yachts.

the Pachanga series in 1992. Although Baja had only a small percentage of the overall recreational boat market, it was the world's largest manufacturer of high-performance boats. The deal also allowed Sea Ray to keep the Baja brand name.

### ISO 9002 Certifications and the Boston Whaler Acquisition

Sea Ray reached a major milestone in early 1996, when its quality management efforts culminated in industry recognition of all areas of the company. In February, Sea Ray's Sykes Creek plant in Florida achieved ISO 9002 certification, and the Riverview plant in Knoxville was certified in March. With the Riverview certification, Sea Ray became the world's first recreational fiberglass-boat manufacturer to operate all of its production facilities under the ISO 9002 quality system. All registered plants were placed on a semiannual surveillance audit schedule to ensure maintenance of ISO 9002 standards. By this time, Sea Ray's PACE Process had resulted in an increase in the company's Customer Service Index for the past three model-years and a reduction in warranty failures per unit for the past three fiscal years.

Another important event occurred in the spring of 1996, when Ray Industries, Inc., expanded further through its acquisition of Boston Whaler from Meridian Sports for $26.6 million. Completed on May 31, the acquisition brought Sea Ray a well-known brand of fishing and commercial boats with a superb reputation.[19] Boston Whaler's previous parent corporations had failed to give it priority status within their operations, so the company had become stagnant, particularly in new-product development. It was first acquired by athletic shoemaker Reebok, and then by New York financier Ronald Perelman, who purchased the marine manufacturer in June 1993 as one of several company acquisitions made in the 1990s.[20] Perelman had become overextended during this period, and by 1995, he started selling off his marine-manufacturing assets. Barrington recalled how the Boston Whaler acquisition developed:

*We heard that [Perelman] was going to sell Boston Whaler. Boston Whaler [was] probably, if not the best brand in the recreational marine industry, certainly right up there with anybody. When we looked at the numbers, it was a company that had*

*just been abused. At best, they were a break-even company. Here's this great brand name that no one could figure out what to do with. So we went in. Of course, Brunswick helped.*[21]

Boston Whaler's manufacturing operations and dealership network were small, compared to Sea Ray, but of high quality. It was relatively easy to incorporate Sea Ray's quality management directives and dealership incentives into the new Sea Ray operation. Ed Boncek, director of dealer-development at the time, remembered how smoothly Boston Whaler's dealer network fit into the Sea Ray Master Dealer scheme:

*Whaler's brand tenets and Sea Ray's brand tenets were very similar. With a program like [Sea Ray's Master Dealer Program], you really have to be a dominant brand in the business. A lot of Boston Whaler dealers were the dominant brand. The Whaler network, although very small, was made up of some very fine dealers that were open-minded and receptive. So the program transferred well to Boston Whaler.*[22]

Boncek had joined Sea Ray from Brunswick in 1992 to help establish a more formal dealer development program. In 1996, he had helped Sea Ray's manufacturing facilities achieve ISO 9002 certification and continued his focus on dealer development when Boston Whaler was acquired.

Perhaps even more crucial to Boston Whaler's future success, however, was Sea Ray's monetary investment in the newly acquired brand's product development projects. Barrington made sure to reinvigorate the company's creative capacity so the brand would sell successfully. He recalled:

*Within about two years, we doubled the sales. We took it from a break-even to a solid 10- to 12-percent pre-tax earnings company. It just took off like crazy. I believe that's still one of the best acquisitions Brunswick ever made, dollar for dollar.*[23]

In July 1996, Sea Ray initiated a standards-based dealer-certification program developed with Sandy Corporation, a Detroit, Michigan–based corporate training and communications firm with extensive experience in the automobile industry. As the

I N 1996, SEA RAY WAS THE FIRST MARINE manufacturer to offer a comprehensive owner-based benefits and privileges package. The new initiative, called the "Sea Ray Preferred Customer Club," began with the 1997 model-year and offered various product discounts and program enhancements, as well as a special newsletter. Initially, the program offered membership benefits only to buyers who purchased brand-new boats, but in 2000, the program was renamed the "Sea Ray Owners Club" and became available free of charge to all Sea Ray owners, whether their boat was purchased new or used.[1]

The Sea Ray Owners Club is the second-largest manufacturer's owners club, with almost 200,000 members. Membership is "inclusive" and the benefits are designed to enhance the key lifestyle elements of boating and develop important one-to-one communication with each member. New buyers of a Sea Ray are enrolled automatically upon warranty registration, while used Sea Ray owners can enroll for free via the Sea Ray Web site, by fax, or by mail. Membership includes a complimentary subscription to *Sea Ray Living* magazine, an award-winning, quarterly owners' publication.[2]

Over the years, thousands of members have received their share of more than $3 million in cash rebates through the club's loyalty earnings program. With every qualified purchase made at an authorized Sea Ray dealer, members earn 10 percent toward the purchase of their next new Sea Ray—up to $2,000—depending on the new Sea Ray purchased.[3]

Members also enjoy exclusive on-water and on-road towing coverage courtesy of the National Boat Owners Association (NBOA) for 12 months from the date of registration. Custom towing packages include 24-hour nationwide emergency assistance and $1,000 additional on-water and $150 on-road towing coverage. In addition, Club members are offered extended service contract protection through Brunswick Product Protection Corporation. Sea Ray also offers special members-only insurance rates through North America's top insurance providers.[4]

Colorful memorabilia, including limited-edition Sea Ray Owners Club hats and Sea Ray decals are available to members free of charge, while the complete line of Sea Ray apparel and accessories are sold at an exclusive rate of 15 percent off.

With regard to boat shows, members enjoy the convenience of e-tickets and 15 percent savings on all National Marine Manufacturers Association (NMMA) tickets purchased online through *www.searay.com*. A Sea Ray travel concierge is also available to offer pricing on airfare, upgrades, vacation packages, hotels, car rentals, and much more.[5]

Last but not least, Sea Ray Owners Club members may purchase custom-built, handmade scale replicas of their Sea Rays. Members enjoy 10 percent savings on all model purchases.

To learn more about Sea Ray Owners Club member benefits, interested parties may contact Member Services at 1-888-SEA-RAY-0 (1-888-732-7290) or by e-mail at memberservices@searay.com.

first of its kind in the boating industry, the Master Dealer program was designed to help Sea Ray dealers achieve their highest potential in service, sales, facility management, and parts management, and contained substantial instruction in the financial aspects of running a Sea Ray dealership.

The Master Dealer program evolved from Sea Ray's continual quality management efforts, including the company's PACE Process and the initiatives Sea Ray designed specifically for ISO 9002 certification, as well as the Dealer Performance Groups® program led by Performance Incorporated. The principal architects of these earlier Sea Ray programs included Sea Ray President Bill Barrington; Chief Financial Officer Rick Stone; back-to-back Vice Presidents of customer and consumer service Jim Carpinelli and Mike Mitchell; and Director of Quality Ed Boncek. However, it was Rob Parmentier, Sea Ray's senior vice president of domestic sales and marketing at the time, who established the new Master Dealer program with Sandy Corporation, bringing together the dealer-oriented quality measures into a comprehensive certification program.

Boncek, now the director of dealer certification, summarized the value of the Master Dealer program:

*I think the success really comes from repeated exposure and engagement with the dealer body and the dealer principals, and trying to expand their perspective on the key practices that make a dealer successful, while also helping them adopt better practices and procedures in their own business.*[24]

Also in July 1996, Sea Ray introduced the marine industry's first certified pre-owned boat program. The new program, known as "Legacy," was established by Parmentier, along with Kathy Link from Deep Haven, Minnesota–based Marine Innovations Warranty Corporation (now owned by Brunswick), and offered a one-year limited warranty on many Sea Ray models. Boats covered by the program were prequalified after passing a 60-point inspection conducted by the Sea Ray dealership.[25]

One month after the debut of the Legacy program, Sea Ray initiated a new computerized dealer communication system called RayNet, which allowed dealers to transmit boat orders, parts orders, and warranty claims directly to Sea Ray's corporate computer system. RayNet was tested at a number of Sea Ray dealerships before being implemented stage by stage at all domestic dealerships.[26]

## Boat of the Year

As new Sea Ray initiatives were being rolled out, Parmentier described Sea Ray's "aggressive retooling efforts" in the company's press kits, noting that Sea Ray was "developing and releasing more new product than most of [its] competitors [had] in their entire lineups."[27]

Sea Ray's 1997 lineup certainly supported his assertions. With 15 new models and numerous refinements, the 1997 model-year was shaping up as one of the best ever. Sea Ray introduced four new yachts for 1997: the 580 Super Sun Sport, the 400 Sundancer, the 370 Express Cruiser, and the 370 Aft Cabin. Each standard product came with a full Raytheon electronics package that included VHF marine radio, GPS, and Raydata, a multifunction digital display for navigational information, as well as a sophisticated C-phone marine telecommunication system with cell phone interface.

The largest new Sea Ray offering for 1997 was actually a downsized boat, a smaller version of its popular 630 Super Sun Sport. The 58-foot 580 Super Sun Sport offered much of the same extraordinary luxury and comfort as its predecessor but in a smaller package at a lower price.

That year Sea Ray also presented the 400 Sundancer. The new Sundancer had the same basic hull as the 1996 model-year's very successful 400 Sedan Bridge, but was provided in a Sundancer style.

The 370 Express Cruiser of 1997 featured an all-new hull with more "Carolina Flare" at the bow. It was designed as a dual-purpose boat equally good for fishing or cruising. The boat, 37 feet long and more than 14 feet wide at the beam, offered great stability and versatility. Twin 340-horsepower MerCruiser inboards gave the boat plenty of speed. By the end of 1996, *Boating* magazine named the 370 Express Cruiser "Boat of the Year."[28] A 330 Express Cruiser was also produced for 1997 to complement the series offerings.

The 420 Aft Cabin had been a phenomenal success in 1996, so it was no surprise when Sea Ray introduced another Aft Cabin model, the 370, in 1997. The 370 version offered value similar to that of its larger predecessor, but in a smaller package. *Motor Boating & Sailing* referred to both aft cabin creations as marking "… an evolutionary step in the history of aft-cabin cruisers" that was "… undoubtedly the shape of things to come in 'split-plan' style boats." The magazine also noted Sea Ray's "seamless integration of the aft cabin in the overall shape of the boat," and "the way in which the sheerline absorbs the high stern [making] traditional aft-cabin styling obsolete." The magazine heaped further praise of this model, adding, "Sea Ray has made sure that the 370's performance and seaworthiness match its go-for-it profile."[29]

Sea Ray also introduced two versions of a newly sized sport cruiser for the domestic market in 1997, with each boat at 28 feet. The 280 Sun Sport maintained the popular rounded styling featured in the larger versions of the model but at a more modest price. The 280 Cuddy Cabin was essentially the

same boat but with an additional aft lounge seat and a padded engine cover that also served as a seat. The interiors were identical. Meanwhile, at the Cork facility in Ireland, production began on a 200 Sun Sport designed strictly for the European market.[30]

For 1997, Sea Ray introduced five new or improved Signature sport boat models. The 230 Overnighter and 210 and 230 Bow Riders were refined, and the Bow Rider and Closed Bow versions of the 190 also received improvements. Each had new graphics, new interior fabrics, a trailer, and a depth-finder as standard equipment. The 190 Closed Bow was produced only at the Cork facility for the market in Europe, where the model had proven most successful.[31]

Below and inset: Sea Ray's 1997 Sea Rayder F-16XR featured the fastest jet engine ever produced. As one of Sea Ray's BMT models, a trailer accompanied the colorfully accented jet boat.

# EVOLUTION OF THE SUNDANCER

THE SUNDANCER IS THE QUINTESSEN-tial Sea Ray boat design. Of all the boats Sea Ray designers have created, the Sundancer proved the best example of new design parameters and became most readily associated with the Sea Ray brand. While Jerry Michalak was the primary designer of almost every Sea Ray boat during the company's first few decades, the first Sundancer was a design conceived and initiated in the mid-1970s primarily by Arch Mehaffey, who served as Sea Ray founder C. N. Ray's "right-hand man" and executive vice president at the time. Nevertheless, Michalak was the one to actually bring the design into fiberglass reality for the 1975 model-year.

The challenge that designers faced with the SRV 240 Sundancer was how to incorporate two sleeping areas into the limited space of a 24-foot boat. Mehaffey and Michalak's solution was to raise the bridge deck enough to situate a small mid-cabin underneath, keeping the boat's graceful lines intact. Surprisingly, Sea Ray's competition was uncharacteristically slow in adopting these new design features. As the Sundancer continued to sell well, however, the competition caught up and closely followed the refinements and redesigns Sea Ray created over the years.

One feature that designers changed on the first Sundancer was its forward-tilted wraparound windshield. The 1976 model fea-

In addition to the Five Series BMT models, Sea Ray added the 185 Bow Rider, which came with the same features as the 175 versions introduced the previous year.

Finally, Sea Ray offered a new and faster version of the Sea Rayder F-16—this one with the XR designation. The F-16 XR featured Mercury's Sport Jet 175 XR motor and new color choices.

After testing Sea Ray's newly refined 230 Overnighter for 1997, *Trailer Boats* writer Jim Barron wrote:

*Outstanding design means many things to many people. It's often difficult to describe, but most people know it when they see it. Some people judge a boat by its looks, and others by its*
*speed, utility, and handling qualities. Sea Ray is one of the few companies that manages to put it all together in a variety of packages.*[32]

### The Sea Ray Boat Group

As Sea Ray's 1997 models graced showroom floors, the company's marketing department released "The Dream Builders," a consumer video, in November 1996. Filmed at the product development & engineering (PD&E) facility on Merritt Island, it provided an overview of the dedication and expertise of Sea Ray's design and engineering employees.

In January and February 1997, Sea Ray trumpeted *Boating* magazine's selection of the new 370 Express Cruiser as "Boat of the Year" in

tured the type of back-slant windshield now common to most boats.

In 1979, designers refined the Sundancer even further, raising the foredeck to add more headroom space belowdecks on the SRV 260. Aesthetic quality was sacrificed for the sake of utility, however, as the boxy lines did not improve the boat's visual appeal.

The relatively square shape of the 1979 Sundancer foredeck was smoothed down into a gradual slope with the 1981 SRV 310 Vanguard model, establishing a stylistic breakthrough that was applied to many future boat models.

Increasing the size of the Sundancers, however, presented new engineering and design challenges. Early Sundancers had used stern-drive engines that were unable to propel larger-size boats, while inboard engines usually took up considerably more precious cabin space. Michalak managed to use inboards without sacrificing valu-

able mid- and fore-cabin volume by situating the engines aft and using V-drive transmissions. He also downsized the fuel tank.[1]

As Captain Chris Kelly, a boat tester, marine journalist, and cofounder of BoatTEST.com, wrote in a 1999 *Power & Motoryacht* magazine overview of the Sundancer's style changes: "[By] 1985 the metamorphosis into a sporty cruiser was complete, and the modern Sundancer was born."[2]

Sea Ray has made consistent, substantial improvements to its Sundancer design since that fundamental metamorphosis was "complete." Sea Ray's 2008 Sundancers range from the 240 Sport Cruiser version, a continuation of the model's original size, to the magnificent 61-and-a-half-foot 60 Motor Yacht, all with the appealing mid-cabin design and reverse sheer that Sea Ray perfected with the Sundancer line.

advertisements that appeared in four leading boat magazines. To attract consumers, for a limited time Sea Ray offered a free Raytheon electronics package with the purchase of any sport yacht.[33]

Raytheon had long been the manufacturer of choice for electronic systems, and Sea Ray had used their products for years. The state-of-the-art marine electronics package for 1997 included the R41XX multiscreen radar system, which offered a fish-finder, navigation, and a collision-avoidance function; the Raychart 600XX charting system; and the Raypilot 650 Autopilot, for accurate steering in inclement weather.

In the early part of the year, Sea Ray began advertising itself as the only boat manufacturer to have achieved ISO 9002 registration at

all of its facilities. Full-page ads appeared in boating publications.[34]

Meanwhile, Brunswick formed the Sea Ray Boat Group early in 1997. Baja and Boston Whaler were included along with Sea Ray in the newly structured unit. Barrington became president of the Sea Ray Boat Group, but his duties with Sea Ray Boats, Inc., continued as before. He also oversaw Baja and Boston Whaler operations.

Meanwhile, Sea Ray's "aggressive retooling" allowed for the introduction of considerable new product for the upcoming 1998 model-year. The most noticeable difference in August 1997, however, as Sea Ray announced its new lineup, was the absence of the boatbuilder's largest yacht, the 65-foot 650 Cockpit Motor Yacht. For 1998, Sea

Ray's 63-foot Sundancer and Super Sun Sport models remained as the company's largest yachts.

The 540 Sundancer was a new yacht, nearly 55 feet long and with almost 16 feet of beam, that offered extraordinary stability and comfort. Sea Ray's newest yacht did not replace the 500 but offered a layout with more room and even more luxurious accommodations. The standard model was powered with twin 553-horsepower diesel engines, but it also came with engines of up to 776-horsepower. Sea Ray's Sundancer series was so popular and the 540 so anticipated that five were sold before it hit showroom floors, based solely on model drawings.[35] Further evidence of the 540's luxuriousness was evident in a review in *Robb Report*, a magazine that billed itself as "the leading authority on the luxury lifestyle."[36]

Below and inset: The 540 Sundancer of 1998 was hailed by *Robb Report* as a "... luxury cruiser capable of small-craft performance." Twin 553-horsepower diesel engines provided the boat with plenty of power.

While the 630 was the largest Sundancer for 1998, Sea Ray further expanded its already resplendent Sundancer series with enhancements of its 310, 290, and 270 models. Sundancers continued to be Sea Ray's most definitive style—the one most readily associated with the company.

Meanwhile, the 480 Sedan Bridge added a new dimension to Sea Ray's sport yachts. The three-cabin flybridge yacht included innovative, layered use of interior space, which made it more comfortable than other 48-foot vessels.

Sea Ray also presented a new deck-style boat for 1998, the 210 Sun Deck. This new boat's smaller size and price fit a particular market niche. An ingenious bowrider/deck-boat hybrid, it was more successful than its larger predecessor, incorporating real style in a deck-style boat. Sea Ray designers managed to dispense with the typical clunky, squared-off deck-boat shape, rounding the bow gracefully without losing forward-deck or storage space. Sea Ray also furnished it with a full, walk-through windshield—an innovative feature for a deck boat.

In other new sport boats for 1998, Sea Ray offered specially appointed Signature Select versions of its 260 and 230 Bow Riders and 230 Overnighter. A newly refined 180 Bow Rider in stern drive and outboard versions was also presented.

By the 1998 model-year, Sea Ray's boats ranged from 16 to 63 feet. The suggested retail prices for standard models in the sport boat category ranged from as little as $16,500 for a basic 180 Bow Rider to $57,500 for a 260 Bow Rider Select. Sport cruisers were offered from $56,500 for the 250 Sundancer to $189,000 for the 330 Express Cruiser; sport yachts were priced from $276,500 for a 370 Sundancer to $620,000 for a 480 Sedan Bridge; and yachts ran from a little more than $713,000 for a 500 Sundancer to upward of $1.6 million for the top-of-the-line 630 Super Sun Sport.[37]

In the fall of 1997, as Sea Ray's manufacturing facilities bustled with activity in preparation for distributing the new 1998 model-year boats to dealers around the nation, the company's activity in another nation slowed to a halt. Sea Ray closed its Cork, Ireland, international production facility in November 1997. In operation for 11 years, the plant had once been an asset but ultimately failed to meet expectations. With so much ocean-freighter shipping traffic between the United States and Europe, it was often cheaper to ship product directly from the United States to a European destination than from Ireland.

"Virtually everything we built [at Cork] had to get on a ship and go to the mainland and then be trucked somewhere," explained Roger Giles, vice president of international sales in 1997 and a former Cork plant manager. "There isn't that much traffic between Cork, Ireland, and the body of Europe."[38]

Furthermore, the Cork facility had never manufactured more than a half-dozen of Sea Ray's lineup, which included more than 50 boat models.

### Happy 40th Anniversary

In the fall of 1998, Sea Ray introduced its 40th anniversary model-year boats. In celebration, the company produced the 280 Sun Sport Anniversary Edition for 1999, which was available for only one year. This sport cruiser came in new gel-coat colors and featured amenities such as an Italian mahogany–accented steering wheel and a console with burl wood accents. The boat was powered with twin 240-horsepower stern-drive engines and was offered at a special price of about $93,000. *Motor Boating & Sailing* magazine called the limited-edition 280 Sun Sport "an outrageously classy 28-footer," and named it the "Sportboat of the Month" for March 1999.[39]

In another limited-edition boat, Sea Ray offered the 270 Sundancer Special Edition, a 27-foot version of Sea Ray's popular mid-cabin cruiser at a reduced price.

Other 1999 Sundancers also received significant redesigns. The 460, 380, and 260 Sundancers were popular boats, with sleeping accommodations for six people and cockpits arranged for entertaining, with design improvements enhancing all three models. The relatively boxy transom (the crosswise

Below and inset: The 1999 Sundancer redesign allowed for even more graceful lines than its predecessors. The 460 Sundancer decks also featured ample padded space for sunbathing.

# EVOLUTION OF THE MASTER DEALER

FROM THE BEGINNING, SEA RAY UNDERstood the importance of establishing and nurturing a strong dealership network and believed it was wise to assist dealers with occasional sales and service workshops. In October 1992, Sea Ray Director of Dealer Development Ed Boncek oversaw the introduction of Sea Ray dealers into the company's evolving quality-management systems.[1]

Sea Ray's increasing focus on its dealers was underscored when Doug Mohney, then vice president of sport boats, accepted the position of vice president of dealer development and training in 1993, a new executive-level position that oversaw the quality systems as they applied to dealers.

The mid-1990s saw the development of regularly scheduled workshops in a more structured program for Sea Ray dealers. During this time, then Sea Ray Chief Financial Officer Rick Stone initiated a relationship with Performance Incorporated, a Chantilly, Virginia–based firm that specialized in helping retailers develop optimal operating procedures with special emphasis on financial management.[2] Performance Incorporated collaborated with Sea Ray to develop a Dealer Performance Groups® program ideally suited for boat retailers in general, and Sea Ray dealers in particular.

With typically no more than 10 dealers in a Dealer Performance Group®, activities were manageable and allowed for the in-depth analysis required by the program. Mike Burke, Sea Ray vice president of sales since 1998, praised the Master Dealer program:

*It's a group of dealers that get together with a moderator. Dealers have to be roughly the same size—not in markets that are right next to each other—so there's not any pressure to withhold*

*information. They do an exploration of their profitability. They break it down by department, by function, by overhead, by product. It's a best-practice forum where all of the dealers participate in understanding everybody's financials; where the weaknesses [and] strengths are, who is doing better than the other guy. It's the opportunity for dealers to understand their cost structure to a level they've never known before so that they can have a positive impact on it. It's been an extraordinarily successful program.[3]*

In 1996, Sea Ray Senior Vice President of Domestic Sales and Marketing Rob Parmentier initiated a standards-based dealer certification program developed with Sandy Corporation. The voluntary Master Dealer program was the first of its kind in the boating industry, incorporating the Dealer Performance Groups® and other dealer operations designed to help Sea Ray dealers achieve their highest potential in service, sales, facility management, and parts management, with particular attention to overall financial management.

There are three levels within the Master Dealer program—gold, master, and ambassador—with each level requiring progressively demanding standards. Ambassador Dealer is the highest level of achievement, requiring sheer excellence in every facet of operation.

Perhaps the most remarkable aspect of the Master Dealer program is its great success despite the fact that Sea Ray does not underwrite dealer expenses for their participation. According to Burke, the reason for the program's success is simple:

*It helps the dealer[s] make more money. ... It's an investment on their part and they com-*

*mit to it. The returns have been tremendous. ... It helps [Sea Ray] maintain a strong relationship with [its] dealers and it helps them do a better job of meeting the expectations of their employees and customers.*[4]

In 2006, Sea Ray's highly prized Master Dealer program celebrated its 10-year anniversary. The company also invested more than $5 million in the program during the 2007 model-year.[5] The initiative has served as a major focus of operations in Sea Ray's Master Dealer department, which Ed Boncek manages.

Nancy Luster, senior dealer operations advisor, is another Sea Ray veteran committed to the continued success of the Master Dealer program. Luster, who has worked for Sea Ray since 1979, became the Knoxville, Tennessee, plant's first female plant manager in 1988. Nine years later, she was promoted to vice president of customer service, warranty, and parts, before accepting her current position four years after that. She has spent the past six years working full-time on the Master Dealer initiative, encouraging non-participating dealerships to sign up for the program:

*Our job is to help the dealers get certified. We look at CSI [Customer Satisfaction Index]. We look at market share. We spend time in human resources, operations, facilities, service, sales, and parts. We go in and have access to the entire dealership from succession planning [to] long-term business plans—we really look at their entire operation.*[6]

Sea Ray's parent company is also well aware of the great value of the Master Dealer program. Dustan "Dusty" McCoy, Brunswick chairman and CEO, recognizes the importance of the initiative to Sea Ray and the concept of dealer certification to Brunswick as a whole:

*We, because of our experience with Sea Ray, understand that dealer certification, through a process that is oriented toward a particular brand's needs, produces much more successful dealer–OEM relationships, permits the dealer to be more profitable and permits the dealer to be more successful in his or her market. We learned that from Sea Ray—and because of that learning, we've been so very focused on bringing it to all of our brands-certification processes.*[7]

Boncek has now added these broader Brunswick dealer certification efforts to his continuing Sea Ray dealer development duties. Boncek notes the ongoing development of the program and the increasing importance of the Internet for dealer operations:

*Master Dealer is [continually evolving]. I think the challenge we see for dealers today and the things we are struggling to help them with ... the Internet and Web-based marketing, Web site presence, Internet-lead management. It's an education process with dealers. We're putting a lot of energy and effort into it. In the last 12 to 18 months, we've seen some improvement in our Internet lead [sales] close rate nationally and hope to continue to see that improve.*[8]

Today's Master Dealers must meet more than 140 operational guidelines, as determined by annual on-site evaluations conducted by an independent consultant, covering virtually every aspect of their operation. Master Dealer status is earned on a store-by-store basis, so dealers with multiple facilities must earn certification for each location separately. Furthermore, dealers must continue to achieve high scores on the Customer Satisfaction Index questionnaires sent to Sea Ray owners and service customers to maintain Master Dealer status. As of 2007, about 90 percent of Sea Ray dealers had participated in the Master Dealer certification program.[9] There are approximately 41 Ambassador Dealers, 54 Master Dealers, and 28 Gold Dealers at more than 150 participating locations worldwide.[10]

section of the stern) that broke up the otherwise graceful curves of previous Sundancers was replaced in the 1999 models with transoms that flowed well with the rest of the boat. Other aesthetic improvements made by Sea Ray's PD&E team included a quieter exhaust system that pulled exhaust down through a fitting in the bottom of the hull in the new Sundancers.[40] Also, additional luxuries and amenities were offered with each step up in size. The top-of-the-line model of this 1999 trio, the 460, offered far more room, a much larger instrument panel, a full complement of electronics at the helm, electrically powered controls throughout the boat, and amenities such as a large foredeck sun pad and a washer and dryer.

Sea Ray also replaced its 550 Sedan Bridge with the 560 version for 1999. The added length allowed for an even more spacious interior.

Keeping with its recent successful attempts at designing hybrid boat models that combined the best of two styles, Sea Ray introduced the 450 Express Bridge for 1999. The 450 Express Bridge was a cross between an express cruiser and a flybridge cruiser, and featured an L-shaped helm layout with seating for 10 and a swivel helm seat. A pair of 292-horsepower diesel engines propelled the sport yacht.

Two new 26-foot Sea Ray sport boats were developed for 1999—the 260 Sundancer and the

Left and below: Sea Ray commemorated its 40th-anniversary model-year of 1999 by offering several special boat models, including the 280 Sun Sport Anniversary Edition. All anniversary models featured a 40th-anniversary logo and a serialized placard on the glove box.

Overnighter—and each was upgraded with electronics and galley features. Meanwhile, Sea Ray produced a Select version of the 230 Bow Rider that included an upgraded engine—the 310-horsepower Bravo III MerCruiser stern drive—as well as upgraded deck appointments.

At the smaller end of the spectrum was Sea Ray's new 190 Cuddy Cabin, which offered a remarkably large cabin for a 19-foot boat, without sacrificing cockpit space. The 190 Cuddy Cabin was available in three cockpit layouts. Also offered was the new 180 Dual Console, which had only one seating arrangement but included a passenger console with a remarkable amount of easily accessible storage space for such a small boat.

### Charting International Waters

A few months after the debut of the 1999 boats, Sea Ray named Constantinos Constantinou, vice president of international operations, to the position of group senior vice president of international sales and marketing. Added to Constantinou's continuing international sales, marketing, and distribution efforts was oversight of the new consolidation of all three Sea Ray Boat Group companies (Sea Ray, Boston Whaler, and Baja Marine) into a new international division. By this time, Sea Ray's worldwide distribution network covered 80 countries.[41]

Constantinou's original association with Sea Ray was as a dealer in Cyprus. Barrington had promoted him to vice president of international operations in 1995, and the multilingual Constantinou would play a prominent role in globalizing Sea Ray's sales and distribution.[42]

Sea Ray continued to increase its international profile during the late 1990s. In 1999, the company approved a licensing agreement with Rae Line Boats in New Zealand that allowed the company to use Sea Ray molds and materials to build its boats. A similar arrangement was made soon thereafter with a manufacturing facility in Brazil.[43]

In some cases, the international connection played out in the United States. In March 1999, Sea Ray became the exclusive North American representative for Torino, Italy–based Azimut cruisers and yachts. Under the agreement, a limited number of North American Sea Ray dealers began handling the Azimut line, providing a distinct strategic advantage for Sea Ray. At the time, company executives had decided Sea Ray's line should be no larger than 65 feet, while Azimut made high-quality yachts up to 100 feet long. Offering the Azimut line brought in buyers of large yachts who may have never had a reason to frequent Sea Ray dealerships otherwise. It also accommodated Sea Ray customers who were considering upsizing from the company's largest offerings, making it unnecessary for them to go outside the Sea Ray dealership.[44]

### Quality Management and ISO Expertise

In 1999, as Sea Ray charted new opportunities in the international marketplace, the company's reputation as an expert in the field of TQM (Total Quality Management) programs and ISO 9000 implementation continued to grow. In March, Dave Marlow, Sea Ray's director of product integrity and customer service, was named to two prestigious posts in the marine industry: chairman of the board for the American Boat and Yacht Council (ABYC), the industry source on standards and recommended practices for recreational boating,[45] and member of the National Boating Safety Advisory Council, which advises the U.S. Department of Transportation and the U.S. Coast Guard on federal regulations regarding major boating safety matters.[46]

One month later, Sea Ray became the first company to receive a prestigious ABYC Horizon Award, which honors contributions to the future success of boating.[47] The press release announcing the award included a quote from Tom Hale, ABYC vice president and technical director:

*This award reflects Sea Ray's long-term contribution to the technology base needed by not only boatbuilders, but also regulators, insurance adjustors, and boat owners. Sea Ray is unique in that it has a representative on each of ABYC's 20 committees. Over the past 10 years, Sea Ray has donated employees' time and travel expenses to represent the marine industry at every committee meeting, which average 35 per year.*[48]

The company was regularly participating in quality-benchmarking exercises with corporations such as Saturn, Bell Helicopter, and Piper Aircraft.[49] When the Sea Ray Group acquired Baja Boats and Boston Whaler in 1995 and 1996, respectively, Sea Ray Boats was established as the model for the new sister companies' operations, including sales, marketing, accounting, inventory, MRP, purchasing, and production systems. Boston Whaler and Baja Boats were restructured to mirror Sea Ray's methodologies in these areas; the same process would eventually occur at US Marine, another Brunswick company.[50]

By 1999, through the company's PACE process, Sea Ray employees were making suggestions about how to improve quality at 10 times the national average for such programs. The company's TQM efforts had resulted in a 75 percent reduction in Cost of Quality, the projected costs associated with not achieving various quality benchmarks. Meanwhile, Sea Ray's Customer Satisfaction Index had increased for five years straight to reach the highest level ever.[51]

Up to this point Sea Ray had achieved remarkable quality improvement, primarily by following efficiency standards the company had developed naturally over 40 years of manufacturing and by working to meet specified ISO 9002 certification guidelines. It wasn't until the late 1990s that strictly formalized quality-management systems were implemented at Sea Ray facilities. Ken Harrell, general manager at the Knoxville production facility since 1999, credited Robert VanNorman for pioneering the company's first such system during his stint as the Tellico plant general manager starting in 1998. VanNorman initiated the "Five S" (sort, set in order, shine, standardize, sustain) program at the lakeside facility.[52] Harrell subsequently began to implement a system that combined elements of the Lean manufacturing and Six Sigma production-oriented process-improvement programs in 2000.[53]

The Lean and Six Sigma programs Harrell was instrumental in initiating at Sea Ray were complementary—Lean is concerned primarily with production speed and efficiency, while Six Sigma focuses on precision and accuracy to allow for data-driven decision-making. Harrell was responsible for outlining the appropriate procedures, designing the training, and incorporating both programs into existing manufacturing facilities—a daunting task. As he recalled, "on the front end, [it was] very difficult."[54]

Harrell's introduction to Sea Ray had been unusual. Hired early in 1989 based on his experience in computerized MRP, he had the misfortune to begin his Sea Ray career just as the company was initiating layoffs and plant closings. As a consequence, he worked in four different manufacturing facilities in less than a year before finally settling at the Pickel Island plant, where he had served as an operations manager. He is currently vice president and general manager of the Knoxville plant.[55]

### New Millennium Innovation and Retrospective

In 1999, Sea Ray prepared to present its new lineup for the inaugural year of the new millennium. In July, the company approached officials in Brevard County, Florida, to propose the addition of a 200,000-square-foot manufacturing complex to its Merritt Island facilities. Plans called for Sea Ray to add some 400 employees to the 1,200 the company already employed on the island.[56] The proposal-approval process became stalled as county officials considered the environmental impact of the additional manufacturing on the island.

Meanwhile, as the new 2000 model-year boats were introduced, Sea Ray showed both forward-looking innovation and an appreciation for classic styles. One retrospective offering was the Amberjack, a style not seen in a half-dozen years. As one of Sea Ray's original fishing boat designs, it had been absent from brochure pages since 1994. The 29-foot 290 Amberjack was redesigned as a comfortable family sport cruiser, with an optional package rigged for serious fishing.

The other classic Sea Ray model that reappeared was the Weekender, not seen as a new boat for five years. The new 245 Weekender was offered at a moderate price and size but still offered exceptional comfort and convenience.

As usual, Sea Ray offered renovations and refinements to its dependably popular Sundancer series. For 2000, 510 and 410 models of the Sundancer were created, and the 240 model was refined. The 510 Sundancer replaced the 500, with the new model slightly longer at the centerline and wider at the beam. It also had a 50-gallon increase in fuel capacity, as well as an increase in horsepower for its standard twin-inboard engines. As always, various amenities and luxuries were also added. A similar transformation occurred with the 410, which replaced the 400.

The 240, the smallest of the Sundancer series, received new refinements and a more powerful 220-horsepower stern-drive engine.

Boat testers and reviewers loved the new Sundancers. Describing the 510, *Boating* magazine wrote: "Ruggedly built, this sport yacht possesses crisp handling, an exquisite finish, and fine detail. It has more gadgets than 007's Aston Martin, and you can handle it alone."[57] The magazine called the 410 "... a near-perfect case study of how to combine luxury and function in a boat."[58] Meanwhile, the 240 was hailed as a boat that "... puts stylish cruising well within the financial reach of just about everyone."[59]

In the sport boat category, Sea Ray made several changes for 2000. The acclaim garnered by the 1998 debut of the restyled 210 Sundeck encouraged Sea Ray to bring to the 240 Sundeck of 2000 a closer approximation of the 210's innovative hybrid styling. The new 240 Sundeck still sported the high gunwales of a deck boat, exceptional storage capacity, and a spacious cockpit that could accommodate up to 10 people. The new version also included the 210's curved bow and windshield, as well as more appealing lines. It quickly became the recreational boating industry's market-share leader for boats in this class. A smaller Sundeck was also produced for 2000, a 19-foot outboard model called the 190 Sundeck Outboard.

Left and right: The 210 Sundeck's hybrid design combined the best of a runabout with the utility of a deck boat. Like many Sea Ray models, the Sundecks offered a Sunbrella-brand canvas convertible top and optional deck covers.

In other changes in the sport boat category, Sea Ray reintroduced its 190 Closed Bow to the domestic marketplace for 2000. The lineup now included four versions of 19-foot sport boats—the Bow Rider, the Closed Bow, the Cuddy Cabin, and the Sundeck.

In addition to these significant changes, Sea Ray also upgraded a number of its models. The cockpits of the 280 Sun Sport, 280 Bow Rider, and 185 Bow Rider received equipment upgrades. The cockpit dashboards of the 420 and 380 Aft Cabin and the 400 Sedan Bridge were refined. An enclosed hardtop was added to the 480 Sedan Bridge, and its salon was upgraded. A salon upgrade was also implemented on the 380 Aft Cabin.

With the impending start of the new millennium, Sea Ray was once again poised on the brink of major change. This time, however, change would ultimately shake employee morale and stifle new product development, when the nation suffered an unnatural disaster that would mark a pivotal point in American history.

The broad range and variety of Sea Ray's line has always been one of the company's most important assets.

## CHAPTER NINE

# CHANGING COURSE

## 2000–2005

*[Sea Ray President Cynthia Trudell] had a lot of good ideas. ... Basically, changed the way we thought as Sea Ray. Some of her management methods were different than we had ever experienced.*

— Jim Steffens,
senior manufacturing advisor[1]

THE BEGINNING OF THE NEW millennium looked promising for Sea Ray Boats, Inc., and the recently established Sea Ray Group. Sales of most types of recreational boats were rising, and Sea Ray manufacturing facilities were taking advantage of new technologies in an effort to increase productivity and profitability.

In 2000, the duties of several Sea Ray executives were broadened to encompass the entire Sea Ray Group, and their respective titles were changed accordingly: Senior Vice President and Chief Financial Officer Rick Stone became Sea Ray Group senior vice president and chief financial officer, and the same Group distinction was added to the titles of Gary Stoecker (manufacturing), LuAnn Jarnagin (human resources), Constantinos Constantinou (international sales and marketing), Doug Kitts (general counsel), Bruce Thompson (new product development), and Scott Noble (consolidated distribution).[2] Bill Barrington continued as Sea Ray Group president.

Sea Ray Boats also established a significant presence at Baja Marine Corporation's production facility in Bucyrus, Ohio, and began listing the facility on the "Manufacturing Plants" page of its Annual Report.[3] Jim Carpinelli, who had previously served as a Sea Ray plant manager in Fort Mill, South Carolina, and later as a vice president of customer/consumer service, worked out of the Bucyrus plant as Sea Ray's

regional vice president/general manager in Tennessee and Arizona.[4]

Meanwhile, Sea Ray continued to upgrade its production facilities and methods. In 2000, the Palm Coast, Florida, plant installed 14 new computerized workstations in assembly areas for improved on-the-floor documentation accessibility, a significant advantage in streamlining workflow, and in maintaining ISO 9002 (international quality standards maintained by the International Standards Organization) certification. Sea Ray plans called for implementation of similar technology at all of its manufacturing facilities.[5]

At the time, the Palm Coast facility was building several of Sea Ray's largest sport yachts at the rate of approximately 450 a year, with a third of them shipped to Europe. This plant had grown to include more than 175,000 square feet in three buildings and employed 725 people.[6]

Sea Ray designers decided to introduce a new flagship for the company's lineup for model-year 2001—the luxurious 680 Sun Sport, which appeared in the summer of 2000. The 680 Sun Sport was more

Computerized information and communication systems on the production floor of Sea Ray plants help ensure efficient, high-quality manufacturing.

The 680 Sun Sport debuted in 2000 as the sleek and sophisticated flagship of the Sea Ray fleet. The beautiful behemoth could hold 1,000 gallons of fuel and 200 gallons of water.

than 70 feet long, including the swim platform, and its expansive cockpit featured an ample aft lounge that converted to a sun pad. The main deck salon sported custom teak flooring, leather bench seats, and a wet bar with a refrigerator concealed in an attractive storage cabinet. The helm offered more leather seating, a retractable sunroof, electric side windows, and full helm instrumentation. Below deck were three extraordinarily comfortable and well-appointed staterooms, a full-service galley, and an air-conditioned salon equipped with a deck skylight and retractable sunshade.

**July 2000:** Sea Ray's New Zealand licensee, Rae Line, debuts its first Sea Ray boats at the Sydney International Boat Show in Australia.

**October 31, 2000:** Sea Ray Boat Group merges with the newly formed Brunswick Boat Group.

**Summer/Fall 2001:** Sea Ray introduces its 2002 lineup. New boats include the 550, 360, and 300 Sundancers; two limited-edition Sundancers, the 410 and 380 Monaco Editions; 480 Motor Yacht; 270 Sundeck; and 220, 200, and 176 Bow Riders.

**Summer/Fall 2000:** Sea Ray introduces its 2001 lineup, including the 680 Sun Sport, Sea Ray's largest yacht and the line's newest flagship; 540 Cockpit Motor Yacht; 340 Amberjack; 290 Sun Sport; 290, 230, and 185 Bow Riders; 280 Sundancer; and 225 Weekender.

**February 2001:** Former Saturn Corporation President Cynthia Trudell is named Sea Ray Group president. Bill Barrington becomes president of Brunswick's US Marine Division.

Above left and right: The 680 Sun Sport entertainment center offered a 42-inch Sony plasma-screen TV and VCR/DVD/CD player, while the staterooms included queen-sized beds with innerspring mattresses and cedar-lined lockers. The helm featured state-of-the-art electronic instrumentation.

The 680 Sun Sport was designed for great performance as well as comfort. It featured Raytheon electronics, VHF radio, and a telephone/intercom system that also included a cell phone antenna. For power, the 680 Sun Sport had massive twin inboards that generated a remarkable 1,358 horsepower.

Bruce Thompson, group senior vice president of New Product Development, cites one of the most awe-inspiring moments of his career as the day

**Spring 2002:** Brunswick Boat Group moves its headquarters to downtown Knoxville, Tennessee.

**Summer/Fall 2002:** Sea Ray introduces its model-year 2003 lineup. New boats include the 420 and 340 Sundancers; 200 Sundeck; and 182 and 176 SRX Bow Riders. Sea Ray also enters into a Contract Manufacturing Agreement with Slepsk in Augustow, Poland, to build Sea Rays for the European market.

**Early 2003:** More new models are introduced, including the 500 Sundancer, 390 Motor Yacht, and 185 BRX Outboard, Sea Ray's first outboard model in several years. Sea Ray also wins its first J. D. Power and Associates award for "Highest in Customer Satisfaction with Express Cruisers."

**February 2002:** Sea Ray introduces its Navigator System, an exclusive, computerized navigational device developed jointly with Maptech, at the Miami International Boat Show.

**Spring 2003:** Sea Ray completes the development of Robotic In-Mold Fiber Reinforcement (RIMFIRE), which uses a robot to coat the inside of a mold with pressurized fiberglass before the mold is closed for subsequent manufacturing procedures.

they popped the prototype hull of the 680 Sun Sport. It was the biggest fiberglass part the department had ever made. According to Thompson, "Our goal is to deliver to the customer what they want even before they know they need it. We design products that the customers are compelled to buy—and grow with our brand."[7]

The company's original plans called for the 680 Sun Sport and the next-largest boat in Sea Ray's 2001 lineup, the 580 Sun Sport (the 630 Sundancer had been dropped), to be manufactured at a new Merritt Island, Florida, facility called the Cape Canaveral plant. Its name was derived from its location near the famed Florida city and NASA site. Due to resistance from Brevard County officials and the U.S. Environmental Protection Agency (EPA), however, construction of the new plant was delayed indefinitely. So, manufacturing of Sea Ray's two largest models was moved to the Sykes Creek facility on Merritt Island.

Sea Ray also reintroduced a cockpit motor yacht for 2001. The motor-yacht design allowed boat owners maximum indoor comfort by extending the upper cabin further forward. The new 540

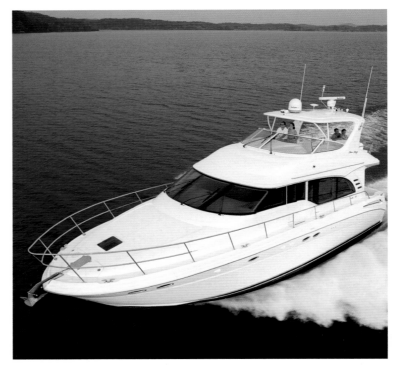

The 540 Cockpit Motor Yacht was one of six Sea Ray yacht models built at the Sykes Creek plant for 2001.

**Summer/Fall 2003:** Sea Ray introduces its model-year 2004 lineup. New boats include the 420 Sedan Bridge, 215 Weekender, 200 Sport, and the redesigned 185 Outboard Sport.

**Summer/Fall 2004:** Sea Ray introduces its model-year 2005 lineup. New boats include the 500 Sedan Bridge; 460 and 260 Sundancers; 290 Sun Sport and an upgraded version called the 290 Select EX; and the 245 Weekender.

**Early 2004:** Sea Ray introduces the 550 Sedan Bridge and 390 Sundancer.

**September 2004:** Brunswick Boat Group announces a $22 million expansion and modernization of Sea Ray's Knoxville, Riverview, and Tellico plants.

Cockpit Motor Yacht was a fine example of the style, with an enormous salon, a large galley, three state-rooms, and a pilothouse with an L-shaped sofa on the portside, complete with a state-of-the-art entertainment center. The 540 Cockpit Motor Yacht was propelled by twin 640-horsepower diesels.

Sea Ray manufactured several new or upgraded sport cruisers for 2001. The Amberjack, a model reintroduced to the lineup the previous year, was produced for 2001 in a larger size. The 340 Amberjack had a more spacious cabin, additional amenities, Raytheon electronics, and more powerful inboard engines rather than the smaller version's stern drives.

Other new sport cruisers included the 290 Sun Sport and the 280 Sundancer. The 290 Sun Sport offered a wider beam than the 280 Sun Sport and additional amenities. The 280 Sundancer added length to the 270 Sundancer and had more horsepower than the 290 Sundancer, which was dropped the following year.

Sea Ray's Bow Riders also received substantial attention for 2001. The 290 Bow Rider replaced the 280 Bow Rider, another boat model dropped the following year, as the largest and most luxurious Bow

In 2001, Sea Ray's 290 Bow Rider was one of the largest bowriders on the market. The optional Sport Package included a fiberglass sport spoiler with overhead lighting.

Rider. The new version offered a wider beam and a larger cockpit and "head" (bathroom) than the 280. Other developments in the Bow Rider line included refinements of the 230 Bow Rider for 2001 and a new size for the model, which debuted as the 185 Bow Rider. The 185 was a half-foot longer than the

**Early 2005**: Sea Ray introduces the 48 Sundancer, 270 Amberjack, and 270 Select EX. The new Sundancer reflects the company's new two-digit designations for all new boats in its sport yacht and yacht categories.

**Summer/Fall 2005**: Sea Ray introduces its model-year 2006 lineup. New boats include 38, 290, and 240 Sundancers and the 195 Sport.

**October 2004**: Brunswick Boat Group formally announces a broad initiative to change the way its marine manufacturing operations conduct business.

**Early 2005**: Sea Ray wins the J. D. Power and Associates award for "Highest in Customer Satisfaction with Express Cruisers" for the third straight year, as well as the National Marine Manufacturers Association Marine Industry Customer Satisfaction Index Award for the Sport Boat category.

# SEA RAY INTERNATIONAL

SEA RAY'S OVERSEAS MANUFACTURING operations had commenced in 1986 with the establishment of the plant in Cork, Ireland, as well as a commissioning and delivery hub at Hellevoetsluis, Netherlands. The Cork plant remained in operation for 11 years until Sea Ray closed the manufacturing facility in 1997.

The year after Cork was shut down, Sea Ray entered into its first licensing agreement, established with Rae Line, a boatbuilder in New Zealand. Rae Line founder Peter Rae and other important personnel visited Sea Ray's Knoxville, Tennessee–area plants for training. Under the arrangement, Sea Ray provided 180 Bow Rider and 180 Outboard molds and other necessary parts to Rae Line for assembly at its Kaiapoi, New Zealand, facility. The first boat Rae Line built was finished in August 1999 and was shipped back to Sea Ray for inspection. The newly licensed boats were produced for the international marketplace in New Zealand and introduced with the Sea Ray brand name to great acclaim at the 2000 Sydney International Boat Show, where 35 Sea Ray boats were sold. Later that year, Rae Line added Sea Ray's 190 Cuddy Cabin and 215 Express Cruiser to its production schedule. In March 2006, Sea Ray ended the licensee agreement with Rae Line, although Sea Ray continues to provide certain materials and components to the New Zealand company. Rae Line now brands its boats with its own name.[1]

In 2002, Sea Ray initiated another international production arrangement, this one with the Slepsk boat manufacturing plant in Augustow, Poland, which had been building boats for Brunswick since 1990. After Sea Ray trained some workers from the Slepsk plant, which was owned and founded by Jozef Wiszniewski, the company shipped 176 Bow Rider hulls to the Augustow plant, where the first round of Sea Ray boats were manufactured.[2] Subsequently, a number of Sea Ray veterans visited Augustow to ensure that operations were running smoothly, including Constantinos Constantinou, senior vice president of international sales and marketing; Roger Giles, vice president of international corporate operations; Jim Steffens, vice president of international manufacturing; and Mike Mitchell, vice president of quality.

By 2005, Slepsk produced 220 and 240 Sun Sports, the former winning "European Boat of the Year" in its class for 2005. A 255 Sundancer was added to the production schedule for 2008. The plant currently builds about 300 boats a year for Sea Ray.[3]

Sea Ray established another international manufacturing connection early in 2007, when Brunswick handed Sea Ray ownership of a facility in Zhuhai, China, where Sea Ray initially produced a 17-foot Bow Rider. Robert VanNorman, vice president of manufacturing, remembered the establishment of the China operation:

> We did the 175 Bow Rider, what we called the 175 Sport. We knew there was not an immediate market in China for that boat, so we'd have to export. Well, boats are difficult to export because they don't really fit well in containers, and when you have to ship them by themselves, it's fairly expensive. We figured a way, through working with some container people, to be able to put four [175 Sports] in a container. So we started exporting to Australia, and for probably the first six months, it was all going to Australia. Then the group took a look at [getting] to Europe from there, and it was cost-effective to ship them to Europe.[4]

Sea Ray introduced a second boat, a 185 Outboard model, in the late summer of 2007 for the 2008 model-year. The Zhuhai facility employed about 75 people at the time and built about 25 boats a month.[5] "They are very proud to be Sea Ray employees," said VanNorman. "In fact, we've had one turnover in two years, which is very

unusual for China. They have stayed [on] and really [feel] like they're part of the Sea Ray family."[6]

Sea Ray's international business has grown dramatically. Approximately 2,000 boats are sold annually in the international marketplace outside North America, accounting for nearly 17 percent of the company's overall sales in 2007.[7] All Sea Ray boats are properly equipped to meet the specialized requirements of any market worldwide.

**Key Players and Locations**

As of 2008, several key individuals coordinate Sea Ray's international manufacturing operations from the company's world headquarters in Knoxville, Tennessee. These include VanNorman; Shane Stanfill, director of international manufacturing; Rob Parmentier, executive vice president; and Kelly Henry, international sales manager.[8]

There are four geographically based sales and operational divisions: Sea Ray Australia, New Zealand, and the Pacific, based in Dandenong, a suburb of Melbourne, Australia (John Pfeifer, pres-

ident of both Brunswick Marine EMEA and Brunswick Global Structure); Sea Ray Europe, Africa, and the Middle East, based in Amsterdam, Netherlands (Marcel Rijnbeek, managing director of European Operations); Sea Ray Asia and Far East, based in Singapore (Edwin Lim, general manager; Masanori Tokuno, general manager/Japan); and Sea Ray Latin America and Caribbean (regional office), based at Sea Ray's Sykes Creek facility on Merritt Island, Florida (Roberto Cox, manager).[9]

There are approximately 90 international dealers around the world, in places as diverse as Argentina, Bulgaria, Egypt, Finland, and South Africa. Australia, France, and Germany boast the most Sea Ray dealers of all nations outside of the United States.[10]

Sea Ray's new manufacturing plant in Zhuhai, China, is located north of Macau and west of Hong Kong. The facility is a testament to Sea Ray's recognition of the extraordinary potential of the Asian marketplace.

180 model, and its 190-horsepower stern drive added substantially to the boat's power. It also offered three seating plans.

Following the successful reintroduction of the Weekender the previous year, Sea Ray debuted the 225 Weekender in 2001. The new version offered features similar to its larger predecessor but at an even more manageable size and price point. Meanwhile, the 245 Weekender received upgrades in seating, fabrics, and other features. Sea Ray also upgraded its 420 Aft Cabin, 400 Sedan Bridge, and 260 Overnighter for 2001.

A few months after the introduction of the 2001 lineup, on October 31, 2000, Sea Ray's parent company, the Brunswick Corporation, announced the formation of the Brunswick Boat Group. The move merged the Sea Ray Group and the US Marine Division, along with other Brunswick marine manufacturers, with the newly formed group, headquartered in Lake Forest, Illinois, in the suburbs of Chicago. Brunswick Vice President and General Counsel Dustan E. "Dusty" McCoy was named Brunswick Boat Group president.[8] Sea Ray Group's Stone became vice president and chief financial officer of the newly formed Brunswick group, and was given the additional responsibility of serving as managing director of Brunswick's Sealine International, a luxury boat manufacturer based in Kidderminster, United Kingdom, in July 2005.[9] Dan Freeland, Sea Ray vice president of transportation and distribution, was named Brunswick Boat Group vice president of logistics, while Kitts, general counsel for Sea Ray Group, took the same position with the Brunswick Boat Group.[10]

One of the boat companies the Brunswick Boat Group merged into its new corporate structure, Boston Whaler, had improved its position considerably due to its two-year affiliation with the Sea Ray Group. The company had doubled its sales and improved its status consistently from a break-even company to one of the most profitable boat companies in the marine industry.[11]

Like many other boat manufacturers, sales for calendar-year 2000 were disappointing for Sea Ray. Registrations of mechanically propelled fiberglass recreational boats had dropped almost 100,000 units since 1999.[12] Meanwhile, the number of stern-drive boats sold industry-wide had fallen by about 2,000 units in the same period. The only powerboat

Cynthia Trudell served as Sea Ray president from March 2001 until February 2006.

sector performing well at that time was the outboard sector, a product category in which Sea Ray had minimal investment.[13] Although this slump was far from the "Great Boating Depression" of the early 1990s, the numbers were troubling.

Compared to other boatbuilders, Brunswick's US Marine Division manufacturers had suffered the most from the market downturn, a fact that most likely contributed to Brunswick's decision to move Sea Ray Group President Bill Barrington to its top position at the US Marine Division in February 2001. Barrington's tenure at Sea Ray had been remarkably productive, especially considering the poor market conditions that had emerged soon after he became president in 1989. During the industry-wide decline of the early 1990s, Sea Ray sales had fallen to approximately $265 million, but by the time Barrington left, the company's sales had risen to $900 million, with the company ledger showing 29 consecutive quarters of increased sales and earnings.[14] Barrington's time with Arlington, Washington–based US Marine would last only about a year and a half, however, before he left to pursue another opportunity.

### Trudell Takes the Helm

Cynthia Trudell, the first woman to head a major U.S. automaker, replaced Barrington at Sea Ray. Trudell had been in the automotive industry for more than two decades in a variety of positions, becoming president of Saturn Corporation, a General Motors subsidiary with facilities in Tennessee, in 1999. Trudell was named the new Sea Ray Group president on March 29, 2001.[15]

Additional changes took place as Trudell succeeded Barrington. Rob Parmentier became senior vice president of operations, Terry McNew was promoted to vice president of manufacturing, and Jeff Skuda moved from vice president of manufacturing to vice president of technology. Parmentier, who had been with the company for almost 20 years, had experience on both the production floor and in sales and management, gaining the broad scope of knowledge and experience necessary for upper-level management in the operations department. McNew had started out at Sea Ray's product development & engineering (PD&E) facility and steadily progressed in key manufacturing roles at the company. Skuda had also been with the company in production-related roles and management capacities for many years, serving as the vice president and general manager of the Knoxville plant before being promoted to department management positions.

On April 25, Brunswick announced plans for additional job cuts and cost-saving measures.[16] Brunswick had already laid off more than 1,300 US Marine Division employees that year, and yet another fiscal-quarter's poor showing had pushed management to take further action. The announcement also noted the suspension of construction at Sea Ray's nearly completed Cape Canaveral manufacturing facility in Florida, which had still not received approval from EPA and officials in Brevard County, Florida.[17]

Also in 2001, Sea Ray officially introduced its Multiple Insert Tooling (MIT) Technology, the company's proprietary state-of-the-art, closed-mold

automated manufacturing system.[18] Sea Ray had started implementing the resin transfer molding (RTM) method of closed-mold production several years earlier, using the technology on an experimental basis for small parts, such as doors and lids, on select boat models. By 2001, there were RTM "work cells" (workstations) of some variety at every Sea Ray manufacturing plant. The integration of the technology for forming hulls was hailed internally as the culmination of the company's automated production development process.[19]

At Sea Ray, RTM essentially consisted of automated low-pressure injection of resin into closed,

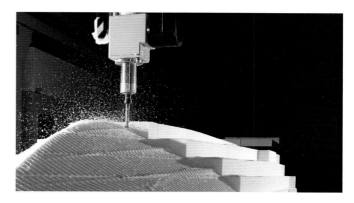

Right (top to bottom): By the turn of the 21st century, Sea Ray used sophisticated resin transfer molding (RTM) techniques and state-of-the-art robotics for several key facets in its manufacturing operations.

# MARINEMAX: SEA RAY'S NO. 1 DEALER NETWORK

AS THE NATION'S LARGEST MARINE retailer in the nation, Clearwater, Florida–based MarineMax provides Sea Ray with its largest dealer network, controlling about 40 percent of the total Sea Ray market.[1] The marine retailer is a consolidation of more than 20 individual companies, with 90 retail stores that collectively generated $1.26 billion in sales in fiscal-year 2007.[2] Almost all MarineMax retail centers are primarily Sea Ray dealerships. Although the marine conglomerate handles lines other than Sea Ray, they are generally not directly competing lines.

MarineMax has had a prominent business connection to Sea Ray from its earliest days. The company was formed in January 1998, when six Sea Ray dealerships with 28 locations in Florida, Georgia, Texas, Arizona, and California consolidated operations in Clearwater, Florida. Even at the organization's inception, with combined revenues of approximately $170 million for the previous fiscal year, the six founding MarineMax dealers accounted for about 20 percent of Sea Ray's total domestic sales.[3] MarineMax raised additional funds by selling public shares in June 1998 through an initial public offering (IPO), and the organization has been acquiring boat dealerships ever since.

While MarineMax was not established until 1998, Sea Ray had associated with its principals since the 1970s, when MarineMax Chairman, President, and CEO Bill McGill, one of the original driving forces behind the company, became a Florida Sea Ray dealer. McGill recalled a conversation with C. N. Ray during those early years:

*This is probably the late 1970s or maybe early 1980s, and we were the No. 2 dealer in the world, and I said to C. N. Ray, "C. N., being No. 2 is great, but I really want to be No. 1. So we're going to go and be your No. 1." He kind of put his arm around me and said, "Bill, you're No. 1 if you're doing what's right for your customer and for your team members. That's the name of the game. Always do what's right for your customer, and treat them the way you want to be treated, and like they're part of your family, and you will be No. 1." I'll never forget when he did that because the man truly lived it.[4]*

McGill apparently took Ray's credo to heart, as did another MarineMax founder, Richard Bassett. Bassett's family had been selling Sea Rays in its Bassett Boat Company dealerships, primarily in the New England states, since the

high-quality composite moldings with fiberglass reinforcement. The technology improved part quality and consistency while lowering labor costs and, because it allowed for resin injection into a closed part rather than a part open to the environment, it reduced air emissions of potentially harmful chemicals by 90 percent.[20]

MIT technology was used to build the 2002 model-year 185 and 182 Bow Rider hulls on the first and only closed-mold hull work cell at the Riverview plant in Tennessee. Plans called for the

completion of a second work cell by the end of 2001 and the expansion of the process for manufacturing the balance of 17- to 21-foot sport boats within the next three years.[21]

Various small parts for a number of boat models were also being manufactured at four separate RTM work cells at Knoxville, Tellico, and Phoenix. A fifth cell was to be completed at Riverview by the end of the year. This type of small-part manufacturing was deemed cost-prohibitive for Sea Ray's yacht and sport yacht prolate 1960s and had become quite close to Sea Ray founder C. N. Ray. Bassett led the expansion of his family's company to Florida in 1979, and in 1994, he established his own dealer network in the state under the name Bassett Boat Company of Florida before establishing MarineMax. Bassett served as director and senior vice president of MarineMax until retiring from the company in 2002.[5] He remembered C. N. Ray's profound influence on him, professionally and personally:

*We cared so much about the manufacturer, and the manufacturer, through C. N., truly cared about his dealers. We were a family ... we all cared jointly about our customer. We were a Sea Ray [dealer] owner, and by God, I'm telling you we all had a philosophy. Just fix the boat. Worry about paying for it later. Just take care of that customer. That whole quality and culture just carried on throughout our whole professional careers together. C. N. would listen to his dealers and listen to his customers, and we would listen to C. N., and we were just a great family. We grew leaps and bounds together.[6]*

While many factors have contributed to MarineMax's success, much of its prosperity has resulted from the company's dedication to customer education and service. For example, MarineMax initiated "Women on Water" and "Kids in Boating" classes so that every member of a family could make the most of their boating experiences. MarineMax also hosted "Docktail" parties at local marinas, which encouraged local area boat

owners to meet and socialize. In addition, the company ensured that all customers received the necessary mechanical services. According to McGill:

*[Show] them how to have fun, teach them how to use their boat, get the whole family involved, and service them second to none with mobile service trucks and [also] go to their homes and to their marina and take care of them there. It all goes back to the same philosophies that C. N. Ray had. Whatever you give to the customer, you get back.[7]*

duction facilities in Florida because of their smaller production volumes.[22]

Sea Ray also continued to utilize robots for part-trimming and hole-cutting at Knoxville and Riverview. Tellico, meanwhile, had a robotic gelcoat sprayer work cell.

### Significant Change

Model-year 2002 shaped up as one of Sea Ray's finest. Sea Ray designers added length and beam

refinements to the 510 Sundancer to produce the 550 Sundancer, the largest Sundancer in production at the time. The 550 was nearly 58 feet, including the standard swim platform, and had a beam of almost 16 feet. The spacious cabin featured wood finishes in cherry or clear maple. The salon was large as well, offering amenities such as an entertainment center with a plasma-screen TV and VCR, among other features. The 550 Sundancer also had two large and luxurious staterooms. The deck, meanwhile, had a standard enclosed hardtop and an air-conditioned cockpit. Twin 640-horsepower diesel inboard engines provided the power.

Also created for 2002 were the 360 and 300 Sundancers. Both filled appealing size niches in the market. The 360 had an enormous cockpit for a boat its size, and a comfortable salon with plenty of storage space. The 300 Sundancer probably garnered more acclaim than her larger sister ship, however, as sale numbers and Sea Ray customer feedback indicated, the 30-foot size and price range was a favorite. Sea Ray had spared nothing in designing the 30-foot sport cruiser, which was "large enough to entertain a crowd, while remaining agile enough not to require inboard propulsion."[23] The 300 Sundancer was loaded with amenities, with numerous options allowing for a high degree of customization. Its open, single-level mid-cabin design came in two interior floor plans, each offering plenty of floor space. Ingeniously designed storage space—another feature inspired by customer feedback—provided twice the volume of competitive models. The new Sundancer was propelled by twin MerCruiser stern drives, each with 260 horsepower.

Sea Ray produced two limited-edition Sundancers for 2002, the 410 and 380 Sundancer Monaco Editions. Each boat offered custom fabrics and other luxurious custom appointments, including Hampton Cherry (antiqued) wood finishes. A custom engraved plaque with the owner's name was also added after purchase.

The 480 Motor Yacht was another standout for the new model-year. It featured a raised foredeck that sloped high and gracefully over the cabin to the cockpit, giving the boat an exceptionally stylish silhouette. Large cabin windows that ran nearly the length of the cabin itself offered extraordinary views. The boat's three staterooms were large and accommodating, and luxury abounded. A hardtop roof and curved, trisected windshield sheltered the air-conditioned cockpit.

---

Ingeniously designed storage providing twice the space of competitive models was just one of the many features that made Sea Ray's new 300 Sundancer an extremely popular boat.

Another compelling innovation in the 2002 Sea Ray lineup was the 270 Sundeck. Sea Ray's hybrid deck-style boats had been selling well, and the 270 offered a truly unique addition—sleeping quarters. In their never-ending quest to design boats that maximized space efficiency, Sea Ray engineers had formed a lighted storage area large enough to double as sleeping quarters. The 270 Sundecks exhibited extraordinary space-saving design in other ways as well, affording maximum utility in the relatively small package of a 27-foot boat.

In the realm of bowriders, several Sea Ray 2002 models received extensions and upgrades similar to those of the 182 Bow Rider introduced earlier in the year. The 220 and 200 Bow Riders had more power than the 210 and 190 Bow Riders they were replacing (although the older models remained available during the transition year), and they offered more deck and storage space. Meanwhile, the new 176 Bow Rider became the smallest boat in Sea Ray's lineup, even though it had almost as many standard amenities as its larger sister models.

In August 2001, the new boat models had barely been taken off the production line when Sea Ray announced the elimination of 74 positions in the Knoxville area, 140 at two Florida plants, and 15 in Phoenix. The continuing market slump that had adversely affected other Brunswick Boat Group manufacturers had begun to take a significant toll on Sea Ray as well.[24]

Soon thereafter, however, a profound impact of an entirely different scale would affect the entire nation, when Islamic terrorists attacked the United States on September 11, 2001. Life and business would change forever.

### Strategic Adjustments

While the nation grappled with the repercussions of the September 11 attacks, the general population attempted to return to some semblance of normalcy. Despite the still-shaky tenor of the times, Sea Ray managed to set record sales at the Fort Lauderdale International Boat Show®

in late October 2001, an event that had grown into one of the premier boat shows in the nation.[25]

In addition, on October 25, Brunswick announced the closing of Sea Ray's Phoenix plant, which had approximately 370 employees.[26] By the end of 2001, National Marine Manufacturing Association (NMMA) figures indicated wholesale dollar receipts for boats were down 15 percent industry-wide, and unit shipments were down 16 percent.[27]

A few months later, at the Miami International Boat Show, Sea Ray introduced the Navigator System, an impressive computerized navigational device developed jointly with Maptech, an Amesbury,

---

With the 2002 debut of the 270 Sundeck, Sea Ray designers' talent in optimizing use of limited space resulted in the creation of a small berth in the starboard helm, a rare feature for deck-style boats.

Introduced in 2002, Sea Ray's Navigator System provided helmsmen advanced two- and three-dimensional color screens that operated through convenient touch-screen technology.

PASS to replace RayNet as Sea Ray dealers' primary tool for placing boat and parts orders, processing warranties, and performing myriad other administrative and customer-service tasks.

As the year progressed, Sea Ray established a relationship with a boat manufacturer in Poland that was already building boats for another Brunswick boat line. While Sea Ray continued to license two other international manufacturers to use Sea Ray hulls to build and market their own boats, the Slepsk boatbuilding plant in Augustow, Poland, would operate as a Sea Ray contractor, building select models of Sea Ray boats directly for the company.

Meanwhile, Sea Ray's 2002 model-year unit sales and dollar sales were down significantly. By the end of the model-year, unit sales had dropped nearly 40 percent and revenues more than 30 percent from the previous year.[29]

**More Change Ahead**

Sea Ray began producing fewer new boats and introducing them more intermittently throughout the 2003 model-year. Sea Ray offered only seven new boats, the first full year's production overseen by Trudell, and several of them were essentially refinements rather than true redesigns. In contrast, there had been 10 new boats for model-year 2002, several created as the largest of their respective series, and all debuted near the beginning of the model-year.

One redesigned boat for 2003 was Sea Ray's largest sport cruiser, the 340 Sundancer. The new version was more than a foot longer than its predecessor and had four degrees more deadrise (the angle between the bottom of a boat and its widest beam). Both features contributed to a sleek, racy new profile for the 37-and-a-half-foot boat. It also featured a unique cockpit-seating layout with dual bucket seats, portside bucket seat, and U-shaped aft seating. The standard model included SmartCraft™

Massachusetts–based software development firm. The system utilized the most advanced software of its kind to provide Sea Ray boaters a variety of navigational aids, including a GPS (global positioning system), depth sensor, and remote power source, as well as the Maptech Digital ChartKit, which delivered official National Oceanic and Atmospheric Administration (NOAA) charts, photos, information on tides and currents, and more to the boat's Navigator screen. The Navigator System was available on Sea Ray boats 36 feet and longer. Robust boat sales at the Miami show were partly attributed to this new and popular feature.[28]

Another technological development in 2002 concerned Sea Ray's dealer communication system: The company established a new, more sophisticated Web-based system named COM-

Diagnostics, a sophisticated new instrumentation package, and a choice of stern-drive or inboard engines. Once again, Sea Ray designers had improved their most popular series.

Sea Ray added the 200 Sundeck to the popular series lineup for 2003, which already included 19-, 22-, 24-, and 27-foot versions. The 200 Sundeck replaced the 190 and 210 models, becoming the smallest deck-style boat Sea Ray offered, with a 260-horsepower motor, thus filling the niche in size and power between the two previous versions. Sea Ray also created two new versions of its 182 and 176 Bow Riders for 2003, offering both in SRX editions with special graphics and additional amenities. Each was offered as a package that included a trailer.

All of the boats produced for 2003 at the Knoxville production facility had been formed in part by a pair of new Automation Model 6400 Foundry series robots made by Zurich-based ABB Robotics. The massive orange robots trimmed excess boatbuilding material and drilled holes in boat decks, taking only 16 minutes to do automatically what it had previously taken four people more than an hour and a half to do.[30]

By late 2002, when Sea Ray presented its earliest new entries for 2003, the 75 Brunswick Boat Group employees, including then Sea Ray Chief Financial Officer Stone, had moved to a new headquarters office in downtown Knoxville. Brunswick Boat Group operations had been moved from Brunswick Corporation's Chicago-area headquarters to Knoxville earlier in the year.[31]

By the end of 2002, it was clear that the terrorist attacks of September 11, 2001, had not precipitated as drastic a decline in business for Sea Ray as originally feared. As noted by Trudell in a profile appearing in the local Knoxville newspaper, "the drop was not as dramatic as the company anticipated."[32]

The introduction of new boats continued into the new year. In January 2003, the 500 Sundancer displaced the 510 model. The 500 Sundancer was virtually the same size as the 510 but had additional curves and a distinctive bow profile. The helm offered a more ergonomically designed arrangement and an upgraded instrument panel, while practical luxuries filled the space below deck. Both the 500 Sundancer and

the newly upgraded 420 Sundancer, which was also introduced that year, featured SmartCraft™ Diagnostics as a standard feature.

About the same time, the 390 Motor Yacht debuted to complement the previous Motor Yacht version, the 480. Also equipped with the SmartCraft™ Diagnostics package, the 390 Motor Yacht was yet another innovative hybrid created by Sea Ray designers. As opposed to most motor yacht helms, which were positioned on a flybridge above the roofed aft deck, denying the pilot much opportunity for socializing, the helm of Sea Ray's 390 Motor Yacht was on the same level as the aft deck, under a hardtop roof.

During this time, Sea Ray also reintroduced an outboard model for 2003. It had been several years since Sea Ray had offered an outboard, but a variety of technological and market-driven developments had encouraged the move. The new 185 BRX offered a choice of three outboard engines: The standard motor was a 125-horsepower Mercury, the next step up was the fuel-injected 115-horsepower, and the new state-of-the-art fuel-injected V-6 135-horsepower OptiMax outboard represented the top of the line. The new outboard boat offered several advantages over the stern-drive version. While most earlier outboard motors were less fuel-efficient than stern drives, Mercury's OptiMax outboards achieved better mileage than the 190-horsepower MerCruiser engines that came standard with the stern-drive version of the 185 Bow Rider. In addition, although the stern-drive version featured more horsepower, the OptiMax propelled the outboard version faster.[33] The 185 SRX Outboard Bow Rider replaced the 182 Bow Rider (both the basic and the SRX versions), complementing the current stern-drive 185 Bow Rider.

Other factors that affected Sea Ray's new outboard boat model production were weather and location. Saltwater corrosion and winter storage, especially in northern climates, were particularly troublesome with stern-drive models of the day, but far less so for outboards. In addition, because outboard engines were outside of the boat, they allowed for significantly more stern seating space as well as more room in the cockpit. The technology of Sea Ray's new outboard models did, however, command a high price—a few thousand dollars more than that of the stern-drive version.[34]

### Ready, Aim, RIMFIRE!

Another company achievement in early 2003 was the completion of Sea Ray's development of another advanced production tool to complement its RTM methodology—a new, sophisticated fiber-application technology dubbed RIMFIRE (Robotic In-Mold Fiber Reinforcement). The RIMFIRE system used a robot to coat the inside of a mold with pressurized fiberglass before the mold was closed for subsequent manufacturing procedures. In just 14 minutes, RIMFIRE completed a task that had pre-viously required about a half-hour of labor from three people.[35]

While Sea Ray continued to upgrade its production technology, the Brunswick Boat Group began preparing to integrate various new areas of the recreational-boating business, such as parts

Sea Ray's award-winning RIMFIRE, completed early in 2003, allowed automated and precise application of fiberglass to an open boat mold.

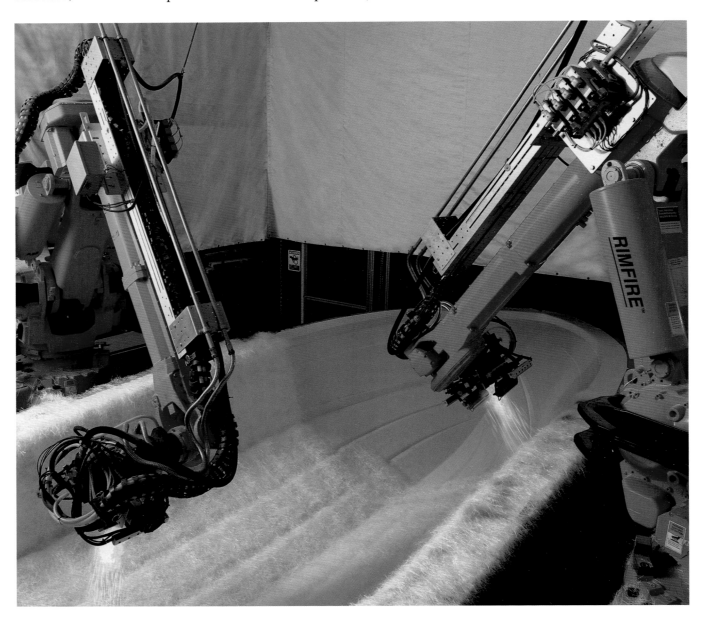

distribution, into in-house operations in an effort to provide dealers and individual boat owners with faster service. In June 2003, Brunswick acquired Land 'N' Sea, the world's largest marine parts distribution business, for $52 million.[36] Later that year, it purchased Attwood Corporation, another marine products business, for $47.9 million.[37]

These acquisitions, combined with the implementation of state-of-the-art production technology by Brunswick Boat Group manufacturers, including Sea Ray, signaled a broad effort to make significant changes in the way Brunswick Boat Group companies conducted business. It was late in 2004, however, before these efforts were announced in the media as a new initiative.

Meanwhile, Sea Ray introduced seven new boats for 2004. Sea Ray focused primarily on its sport boats for the earliest 2004 model-year entries, establishing new product groupings within the category. The sport boat category now included 15 boats 25 feet or less in the Sport, Select, Sundeck, Weekender, and Sundancer series. Three new sport boats were produced for 2004, two in the Sport series and one Weekender. The new 200 Sport became the longest in the series, while the redesigned 185 Outboard replaced the 185 SRX Outboard. The basic 185 Bow Rider, meanwhile, was designated the 185 Sport. The other new sport boat, the 225 Weekender, was an updated version of the 215 Weekender—two feet longer, with an extended swim platform, and priced accordingly, but otherwise essentially unchanged.

The largest of the new Sea Rays offered in the summer 2003 opening of the new 2004 model-year was a downsized version of its 480 Sedan Bridge. The 420 Sedan Bridge was a smaller version, but still provided luxurious accommodations and excellent speed (36 miles per hour), thanks to its aerodynamic styling and a pair of 420-horsepower Cummins MerCruiser diesel inboard engines.

As the second-half 2004 line was introduced in January 2004, Sea Ray continued to surprise its customers. A newly designed 550 Sedan Bridge featured a broad 16-foot beam and a new standard hardtop roof. The flybridge offered an overhead console with "head-up" engine monitoring gauges (gauges that a pilot could view without having to look down), a significant improvement in terms of both comfort and safety. In addition, the boat's salon

featured luxurious appointments and exceptionally large windows for maximum viewing.

The 390 Sundancer, also introduced in January, was a lengthened and refined version of the 380 Sundancer. The new version had an expansive cockpit featuring an array of high-quality electronics. A stylish sport spoiler served as a platform for electronic equipment, while also providing overhead lighting. With an optional enclosed hardtop roof, the 390 Sundancer had a forward master stateroom and a salon with a conversation pit that converted into a bedroom.

That same month, Sea Ray's RIMFIRE system received the 2003 Innovation in Manufacturing Process Award for Excellence & Innovation from the American Composites Manufacturers Association (ACMA).[38]

In April, Brunswick took another step in augmenting the services its boat manufacturers could provide to dealers and, by extension, to retail customers, when it purchased the assets of Marine Innovations Warranty Corporation, a Minnetonka, Minnesota–based warranty firm. This purchase expanded the warranty services Sea Ray dealers were able to offer their customers.[39]

**Moving Targets**

Sea Ray used its new technology wisely when it produced its line for 2005. The company complemented the newly designed 550 Sedan Bridge produced the previous year with the smaller yet equally luxurious 500 Sedan Bridge for 2005. The 500 Sedan Bridge came with a hardtop roof and fully enclosed air-conditioned bridge, as well as wood flooring, custom-decorated staterooms, and two full "head" compartments.

Sea Ray did not neglect the Sundancers for 2005. The 460 Sundancer featured SmartCraft™ Diagnostics and a Raymarine® electronics package. The Sea Ray Navigator II, the second generation of the impressive computerized navigational system, was optional. Meanwhile, the 260 Sundancer was significantly redesigned. The newly shaped hull offered two degrees more deadrise, which, along with the model's four lifting strakes, created a boat that was relatively quick to plane and could cut well through choppy waters. The new boat also featured new colors and design features.

In the sport boat category, Sea Ray offered two 29-foot versions for 2005, a "Sun Sport" closed bow and the new 290 Select EX Bow Rider. Both versions featured upgraded electronics, a stainless-steel windshield, and a fiberglass spoiler as one of several options. The 290s also featured steering wheels from Troy, Michigan–based Delphi Corporation, equipped with Vessel Control Systems integrated among the boats' other electronics. The system allowed those at the boat's helm the ability to control radio functions and various diagnostic instruments. The system was also available as an option on other Select and Sundeck models.[40]

In further developments, Sea Ray used its Bucyrus, Ohio, plant, which normally produced Baja boats, to build a new sport boat, the new 245 Weekender.[41]

Less than two months after the 2005 model boats were delivered around the nation, Brunswick Boat Group announced plans for a $22 million expansion and modernization of Sea Ray's Knoxville and Tellico facilities. The plans called for doubling the Tellico plant's capacity and adding 75 people to its 510 employees. The Knoxville plants would add 125 to the 1,175 employed at Riverview and the main plant on Pickel Island. Part of the modernization would involve the expansion of the company's new RIMFIRE process.[42] By this time, Sea Ray had added its 20-foot Bow Riders and 22-foot Sundecks to the 180s and 185s already receiving the RIM-FIRE treatment.

Sea Ray secured $4.4 million in local and state incentives to assist the company in its ambitious plans, including a $1.7 million tax abatement, a $1 million technology capital grant, and approximately $1.7 million in workforce development applications. Brunswick Boat Group President McCoy indicated a two- to three-year timetable for the expansion.[43]

Just a month after Sea Ray's modernization plans were announced, the Brunswick Boat Group formally announced a broad-based and ambitious initiative aimed to radically change the way the company conducted its boat-manufacturing business. The plan primarily entailed the expansion of robotic state-of-the-art manufacturing methods, development of same-day or next-day boat part delivery, enhanced repair service, a better-structured used-boat business sector that would offer full warranties on used products, and better financing options for dealers, all within a three- to five-year period.[44] In an October 2004 *Knoxville News-Sentinel* article, McCoy described the goals of the new initiative:

> *We're going to provide a product that is designed, specified, and fully integrated by us that has an end-to-end warranty and for which any dealer or consumer can get any part for that product on [a] same- or next-day basis. We are determined that we're going to change the way this product is made, the way it's put to the marketplace, the warranty standards around the product, [and] the quality standards around the product.*[45]

Furthermore, Brunswick had established Brunswick Financial Services, also housed in its downtown Knoxville offices, another fully in-house program that allowed dealers greater ease in borrowing money to purchase boats.

As Brunswick and Sea Ray worked to integrate the various facets of the new corporate vision for boat manufacturing and service, Sea Ray introduced the 48 Sundancer Sport Yacht at the winter boat shows early in 2005. The boat reflected the change in nomenclature that Sea Ray had initiated for all of its new sport yachts and yachts, in which a two-digit rather than three-digit number was used to refer to models in the two boat categories. The resulting number specified the boat's approximate length. Due to print production time constraints, however, this change was not reflected in the earliest 2005 model-year boat brochures.

Although the 48 Sundancer was four inches shorter than the model it was replacing (the 460), several new features made it 5,600 pounds heavier. The new model had a fully integrated hardtop roof with two large sunroof hatches and a curved-glass windshield. Salon-side windows and a skylight at the forward end of the cabin provided additional light. The 48 Sundancer's helm featured SmartCraft™ Diagnostics. Despite a 212-horsepower

---

Debuting in 2005, the 550 Sedan Bridge was powered by twin 765-horsepower V-8 inboards and outfitted with an unusually large fuel capacity for a boat its size.

increase furnished by its larger diesel inboards, the new boat's top speed remained about the same, as a result of the additional amenities.[46]

The 270 Amberjack, a sport cruiser, was also introduced in the second half of 2005. Its hull was based on the 260 Sundancer, which had been brought out several months earlier, but featured additional open cockpit space to facilitate fishing. The 270 Amberjack came standard with a 300-horsepower MerCruiser stern-drive engine. Once again, the standard version of the Amberjack was an appealing cruiser suitable for casual fishing, whereas the optional fishing package was best suited for more devoted anglers.

Another boat of similar size also debuted at this time. The 270 Select EX offered a smaller version of the well-appointed 290 Select EX that had come out earlier in the model-year. One boat magazine reviewer suggested it could be the "best bow rider ever."[47]

## More Boats Introduced

The summer of 2005 brought with it the new 2006 model-year lineup, which showed considerable differences from the previous model-year. All yachts, including sport yachts, reflected the new two-digit designation. The 68 Sun Sport remained as the flagship, but the equivalent of the earlier 600 Sun Sport was unavailable. The 550 Sedan

The reverse sheer of Sea Ray's 48 Sundancer was more gradual than the 460 Sundancer it replaced, but still retained the stylish hull feature long associated with Sea Ray.

Bridge was replaced with a longer and refined 58 version, while the 52 Sundancer took over for the 500 Sundancer.

Only one motor yacht remained, the 40 Motor Yacht, while the number of Sedan Bridge sport yachts doubled. Sundancer sport yachts also remained constant in number, with the new designations reflecting refinements and one redesign. Sport boats and sport cruisers received less substantial alteration, although five boats in these two categories received slight resizing or refinements.

New boats appearing in July included a 240 Sundancer that replaced the earlier version. The new 240 Sundancer, still the smallest version of Sea Ray's most heralded series, offered more seating configuration options for the cockpit and ingenious use of removable furniture components, once again achieving maximum space and comfort in a small package.

Before the end of the year, Sea Ray introduced three additional boats. The new 38 Sundancer, which featured a seamlessly constructed fiberglass arch with a molded-in hardtop roof and an aft canvas top, was available at a length between that of the previous 360 and 390 Sundancers. The new Sundancer could accommodate six people, with its interior featuring stylishly appointed seating and cherry wood finishes on its cabinetry. SmartCraft™ Diagnostics was a standard feature, while Raymarine® and Sea Ray Navigator II instrumentation was optional.

The 290 Sundancer was another 2006 model boat introduced in late 2005. At approximately 31 feet, it filled another niche in the burgeoning Sundancer series. With its integral swim platform, the 290 Sundancer sport cruiser had many of the same features of the new 38 Sundancer but at a smaller size and more modest price.

Also debuting late in the year was the 195 Sport. This new entry-level sport boat was a larger and redesigned version of the 185 Sport. It provided bucket seats, more comfortable aft seating, an extended swim platform, and a sun pad. The optional Wakeboard Package included a tubular aluminum water-sports tower with wakeboard racks, an integrated bimini top, and exceptionally colorful hull graphics.[48]

With Sea Ray facilities continually producing new boats and keeping dealership floors busy, business seemed to run extraordinarily well for the boatbuilder. After all, in recent years, Sea Ray had introduced innovative new production technologies, one of which had won an award from a major manufacturing organization. The company was also undergoing modernization of its Knoxville-area plants, all while augmenting its secondary service functions through Brunswick's expansion into marine parts and service-oriented areas. Furthermore, Sea Ray had won the prestigious J. D. Power and Associates award for best "Customer Satisfaction for Express Cruiser" three times in a row, as well as the coveted NMMA Marine Industry Customer Satisfaction Index Award in several categories.[49] Sales meanwhile had risen about 10 percent from the previous year in units sold, reflecting higher-than-ever revenues of more than $1 billion.[50]

Clearly, Sea Ray's business was successful. Unfortunately, the previous several years had introduced some challenges for the company, particularly within the PD&E area. Because of the demands placed on product development, approximately half of the 175 product-development employees at Sea Ray had either quit or been fired.[51]

In the fall of 2005, Sea Ray conducted a survey among its employees. Since the company had issued a 200 percent employee bonus the year before, positive numbers were expected on the survey. Instead, the scores indicated dissatisfaction among Sea Ray workers. These results were part of the equation that led fairly quickly to significant change for Sea Ray in the coming years.[52]

*Sea Ray Living* is an elegant lifestyle magazine designed to enhance the lives of Sea Ray boat owners. Seasonal coverage of Sea Ray events, destinations, and cruises coexists with the latest in style, culture, entertaining, and travel, both domestically and abroad. *(Printed with permission from* Sea Ray Living *magazine and Dino Publishing.)*

## CHAPTER TEN

# A HALF CENTURY OF BUILDING BOATS

## 2006 AND BEYOND

*I think the biggest thing we have to do as a company is stay tuned into what's going on in the market for our dealers. ... Our responsibility is to build a good boat ... with a lot of innovative features.*

—Rick Stone, Sea Ray Group president, 2007[1]

IN JANUARY 2006, SEA RAY INtroduced several new boats, including one particularly magnificent example of the company's most definitive series: the 60 Sundancer. At more than 61 feet, the new model was the largest of the series with several new features, including a sloped window line and hardtop with distinctively fresh styling, and reduced reverse sheer.

Twin MAN V-10 1100 CR V-drive diesel engines generating more than 1,000 horsepower gave the 60 an abundance of power, along with excellent fuel efficiency and reduced air emissions. These water-cooled, long-lasting, four-stroke engines allow for lower oil and fuel consumption than two-stroke engines. They also have a high torque rise, which allows for fast acceleration. The 60 also featured standard bow and stern thrusters that allowed for easy docking of the large yacht.[2]

As Sea Ray's newest flagship, the 60 also included luxurious interior features such as cherry wood paneling and cabinetry, a teak sunroom floor and cockpit chairs, a wooden galley floor, and wooden window blinds. The yacht's climate-controlled cockpit sunroom with two large sunroofs was equipped with a 27-inch flatscreen pop-up LCD high-definition TV with a DVD player and a Bose Lifestyle® 48 sound system. The master stateroom featured a queen bed and Ultraleather HP™ sofa, cedar-lined hanging locker, washer and dryer, fully appointed

head (bathroom) with shower, and deluxe entertainment center with a flatscreen TV. The forward and guest staterooms also included deluxe entertainment systems and comfortable accommodations.

Sea Ray designers ensured a pleasant experience for anyone piloting the 60 Sundancer. An adjustable leather helm chair offered comfortable access to a full complement of navigation aids, including Raymarine® Autopilot, Raymarine® E120 GPS/Chartplotter/Radar, and Sea Ray Navigator III. Other luxury options abounded, including a grill and wine chiller and a premium Northstar electronics package.

One boating magazine reviewer called the 60 Sundancer a "worthy new flagship for the Sundancer brand."[3] Another declared that the yacht captured "the essence of a successful three-decade run."[4]

While the 60 Sundancer attracted the most attention among the boats in Sea Ray's 2006 lineup, another model proved successful in a different size niche: the newly designed 31-foot version of the series,

---

Rick Stone was named Sea Ray Group president in February 2006. He brought to the position more than 20 years of financial management experience with Sea Ray and Brunswick Boat Group. *(Photo by Jerry Amos Photography.)*

known as the 290. The 290 Sundancer featured design refinements and a large, translucent deck hatch plus four portlights that provided an abundance of light. Sea Ray's extraordinary use of space was also evident throughout this sport cruiser model, which had a large (four-person) dinette that converted into a bed and a forward V-berth—a sleeping space shaped like a triangle due to the shape of the forward hull—that doubled as a family room and a bedroom.

Sea Ray's new flagship, the magnificent 60 Sundancer, debuted in January 2007. Its helm (inset) featured Raymarine® electronics, including Raypilot and VHF radio, as well as Sea Ray Navigator III.

In January 2006, Sea Ray also introduced a new Sedan Bridge sport yacht: the 36. The 36 Sedan

**Summer/Fall 2006:** Sea Ray introduces the majority of its 2007 lineup. New boats include the 310 Sundancer, 260 Sundeck, and 210 Select.

**January 2006:** New models are introduced, including the 60 Sundancer, the largest and most luxurious Sundancer ever built; an upgraded 280 Sundancer; 36 Sedan Bridge; and 250 Select EX.

**April 2006:** Terry McNew is named senior vice president of product development and engineering (PD&E); Gary Zimmer is named vice president of quality and manufacturing technology.

**February 2006:** Rick Stone is named Sea Ray Group president, and Rob Parmentier is promoted to executive vice president.

**July 2006:** The inaugural AquaPalooza takes place.

**April 2006:** Sea Ray launches a completely redesigned Web site at *www.searay.com*.

Bridge offered an enticingly sporty silhouette, including a wide fiberglass spoiler, an aft-facing arch with a Sunbrella® canvas bridge cover, and eye-catching striping at the waterline that ran almost the entire length of the boat. The helm was equipped with Northstar electronics, and twin 370-horsepower MerCruiser inboard engines offered plenty of power.

The new Sedan Bridge featured an air-conditioned salon and an impressive entertainment center. A sliding glass door led to the lower cockpit area. The boat also included two luxurious staterooms, a galley with hardwood flooring, and an upright refrigerator and freezer.

Also introduced in January was a new offering in Sea Ray's premium luxury sport boat Select EX series. The cockpit of the new 250 Select EX featured rare luxuries for such a small boat, including

The 60 Sundancer's salon included an Ultraleather HP™ curved sofa, while its master stateroom featured a queen-size bed with an innerspring mattress that also had a massage function and an electrically adjustable backrest and footrest.

**January 2007:** Sea Ray officially introduces the 55 Sundancer.

**Summer/Fall 2007:** Sea Ray introduces the majority of its 2008 lineup. New boats include the 47 Sedan Bridge; the 330 Sundancer, which joins the 55 Sundancer as a new boat in Sea Ray's most popular series; 290 Amberjack; 290 Sundeck; a refined 205 Sport and a redesigned 175 Sport; and two brand-new models, the 230 and 210 Select Fission.

**2007:** Sea Ray begins introducing select boats with three valuable new marine technologies: Cummins MerCruiser Diesel's Zeus propulsion; Mercury's SeaCore stern-drive engine-corrosion control; and the Mercury Axius joystick docking system.

**Summer 2007:** Sea Ray opens its Cape Canaveral facility in Florida and begins equipping it as a state-of-the-art wood-component manufacturing facility. Dubbed "Project Cypress," the new operation marks the beginning of Sea Ray's commitment to producing its own hardwood cabinetry and other wooden components and increasing the use of real wood in its lineup.

**2009:** Sea Ray celebrates its 50th anniversary.

**Early 2008:** Sea Ray introduces the 270 Sundancer, 350 Sundancer, 200 Select EX, and 210 Sundeck.

# SEA RAY MISSION STATEMENT

SEA RAY BOATS, EMPHASIZING OUR 48-year history, tradition, and heritage, will continue to lead the marine industry in the manufacture and sale of an extensive line of superior-quality fiberglass boats.

Our products will combine innovative styling, design and advanced engineering concepts with distinct and prestigious brand images. We will promote our growth, market share, and profitability by distributing our products through a worldwide network of marine dealerships to which we will provide appropriate training, support, and development.

Our mission will be accomplished by continuing to attract and develop highly motivated and skilled employees.[1] In support of our mission, the following statements commit us to:

- *Produce high-quality, cost-efficient boats using superior people, quality materials, and state-of-the-art manufacturing equipment and facilities.*

- *Provide our employees with a quality work environment and reward them for superior performance.*

- *Ensure that Sea Ray customers realize superior satisfaction with our products, suppliers, services, dealers, and employees.*

- *Promote a partnership attitude with our suppliers in an effort to improve our products and services.*

- *Designate dealers and sales locations that have the potential to achieve desired market penetration and dealer profitability while better serving the retail customer.*

- *Employ market development strategies in concert with our dealers with the goal of expanding and improving existing and potential dealerships.*

- *Continue our international strategy of addressing foreign competition and opportunities by emphasizing specially designed, engineered, and manufactured products for international markets.*[2]

fiberglass-backed bucket seats, a padded L-shaped bench, and a wet bar with a stainless-steel sink and faucet. A 300-horsepower 350 Magnum MPI Bravo I MCM stern-drive engine powered the boat, which also had a water-sports tower option for wakeboarding enthusiasts.

### Solid as Stone

A month after the introduction of new 2006 model boats, Sea Ray underwent a major change in management, with the departure of Sea Ray Group President Cynthia Trudell on February 27. Brunswick Boat Group Chief Financial Officer Rick Stone immediately took over the position.[5]

The move brought Stone back into the Sea Ray fold, albeit in a new capacity. He had worked as a Sea Ray financial executive for 16 years prior to his 2001 position at Brunswick Boat Group, which allowed him to maintain a peripheral working relationship with Sea Ray. Stone's comments to the *Knoxville News-Sentinel* indicated his determination to maintain the strategies that had made Sea Ray successful:

*We're going to continue to grow and to keep ourselves aligned with the goals of Brunswick, keep our market share position, keep our quest for quality products on the forefront, make sure our dealers get taken care of, make sure our employees get taken care of, be a good community participant.*[6]

Stone's long experience with Sea Ray, financial acumen, and leadership abilities made him the ideal person to take the helm of the company. Having built a solid relationship with the Sea Ray dealer network, Stone's previous management duties had already addressed dealer credit and financing needs. His seminal and continuous involvement with the Performance Group initiative, which formed the backbone for Sea Ray's much-lauded Master Dealer program, provided an additional venue for interaction with dealers, thus increasing Stone's understanding of dealers' perspectives (both personal and professional).

Offering the Sea Ray Group presidency to Stone in 2006 was an easy choice for Brunswick CEO Dusty McCoy. He and Stone worked together for nearly five years at the Brunswick Boat Group until McCoy was named Chairman and CEO for the parent company. McCoy recalled:

> Rick [Stone] is highly intelligent, a great leader, and understands people. He is the most unselfish leader I've ever had the opportunity to be with. Rick wants everyone in his organization to be successful, and Rick cares about everyone in his organization. I asked Rick to lead Sea Ray because I felt his knowledge of the brand, his love for the brand, his relationship [to] the organization, which is a key part of the Sea Ray success, would permit the organization to rally behind Rick.[7]

Soon after becoming president of Sea Ray, Stone made several important changes to his executive management team. Terry McNew was rehired in April 2006 as senior vice president of product development and engineering (PD&E). McNew had worked in PD&E for Sea Ray for many years, moving up to become vice president of manufacturing in 2001 before leaving the company in 2004 to serve as president and CEO of Orlando, Florida–based Correct Craft Boats. McNew

would work out of Sea Ray's PD&E facility in Merritt Island, Florida.[8]

Another personnel change Stone initiated was the promotion of Rob Parmentier from senior vice president of sales, marketing, and customer service to Sea Ray executive vice president and president of Baja Marine. While Parmentier was named president of Baja Marine in 2002, he would relinquish the Baja position in 2007 to provide needed focus and guidance in the Sea Ray International business division. With more than 25 years of experience in virtually every facet of boatbuilding, Parmentier, nicknamed "Mr. Electric," exudes an infectious, positive energy as well as a strong work ethic. McCoy lauded his contribution to the company:

> [Rob Parmentier has a] love for the brand, a desire [to help] every one of … his personal dealers and personal customers. … And Rob knows neither night nor day nor weekend nor holiday. It's all the same to him. [His attitude is,] "What do I have to do to make my dealers and the people who buy our product enjoy themselves and be successful?"[9]

Sea Ray dealers all over the globe also appreciate Rob Parmentier's energy and work ethic. Ian Williamson, founder and 30-year managing director

Few embody the spirit of Sea Ray like 25-year veteran and Executive Vice President Rob Parmentier. His energy and enthusiasm have served him well in many areas of Sea Ray's operations, including production, customer service, marketing, sales, and management.

of the New Zealand–based Sports Marine dealership, has enjoyed handling Sea Ray boats and pays special tribute to Parmentier:

> *Regardless of procedure, Rob always does the right thing. Rob's support and ability to get things done immediately make problems disappear. [Also], his determination when facing competitors has to be acknowledged. Rob can be trusted, and a Sea Ray dealer can take certain business risks that he might not normally take when dealing with Rob.*[10]

It is safe to say that Williamson's comments could well represent the judgment of the entire Sea Ray dealership network.

Stone was well aware of the impressive depth of talent and experience within the Sea Ray organization and advertised it heavily. "[I] said, 'You know what, we're going to take the chains off and let them start making decisions and get on with what they need to do.'"[11]

While Stone was making strategic promotions in April 2006, Sea Ray also launched an entirely redesigned Web site at *www.searay.com*. The new site streamlined information searches, making it easier to preview new products, download product archives, and access a vast array of technical information about Sea Ray products as well as general content about the Sea Ray lifestyle. Sea Ray Group President Stone described the style and features of the company's new Web site:

> *It's all about the customer. The new site offers captivating images and intuitive site navigation that make it easier to find what you are looking for. Everything is just one click away—from our comprehensive product lineup to [other menu] items such as gear, fashion, local events, charts, maps, a towing guide, and service help.*[12]

### The Transitional Model-Year

With the arrival of summer in 2006, Sea Ray introduced its 2007 lineup. There were only four new boats for 2007, a model-year that had been planned while Trudell was still president. Three of the new boats debuted in late summer/early fall of 2006, while the official introduction of the 55 Sundancer was deferred until January 2007. An all-new Sundancer, the 310, was unveiled in August 2006. Designers of the 310 Sundancer traded the side walkways of the 300 Sundancer for a walk-through windshield, giving the boat nearly an extra foot in helm and cockpit width. The helm featured SmartCraft™ instrumentation and plenty of space for adding optional electronics. Aft on the boat was a standard fiberglass spoiler with an integrated arch-top and aft canvas sunshade. Also aft was a new foldout transom seat overlooking the large swim platform mounted on the rear of the boat.

Sea Ray's new Sundancer included a stateroom that also served as a conversation area and a private V-berth. The galley featured a stainless-steel sink, refrigerator, and two-burner stove, among other amenities. The 310 also came with other types of luxury appointments typical of Sea Ray boats.[13]

In addition to the new Sundancers, Sea Ray offered a new deck-style sport boat for 2007. The 260 Sundeck was longer and had more amenities than the 240 Sundeck (which remained in the lineup). As a family-oriented day boat, the 260 Sundeck offered plentiful seating throughout and exceptional storage space, ingeniously fitted on the deck, under seats, and under the floor, as well as in other areas of the boat.

The helm of the 260 Sundeck was carefully laid out to accommodate piloting in both seated and standing positions. Powered by a 300-horsepower MerCruiser 350 Magnum MPI with a Bravo III counter-rotating propeller stern drive, the 260 also featured a SmartCraft™ monitoring package and could reach 48 miles per hour with a light load, a remarkable speed for a deck boat of its size.[14]

In October, Sea Ray introduced the 210 Select. The 210 had a 260-horsepower engine and SmartCraft™ instrumentation, easily controlled through the standard electronic Vessel Control System steering wheel. Entertainment equipment included a Clarion® stereo with a CD player and an MP3 port as well as a Sirius satellite receiver with six months of complimentary service of Sirius Satellite Radio®.

In December 2007, select Sea Ray dealers and owners received an early introduction to the new 55 Sundancer at the Sea Ray Yacht Expo at Sea Ray's Merritt Island facilities. The 55 Sundancer was 60 feet long, including the standard swim platform, and nearly 16 feet at the beam, filling a

size and price niche just less than its larger sister boat, the 60 Sundancer, introduced about a year earlier. The layout of the 55 was essentially the same as that of the 60, featuring similarly luxurious amenities and sophisticated electronics. One new feature was a fully adjustable queen bed with an electronic massage system. The new yacht was powered by a T-MAN 800 or 900 CR V-drive diesel inboard engine.[15]

The Sea Ray 55 Sundancer was one of several boats featured in 2008 advertisements that used Sea Ray's latest tagline: "Where Land Ends, Life Begins."

**Marketing Magic**

Historically, Sea Ray has had a relatively small national advertising presence. The company has frequently been featured, however, in premiere recreational boating magazines, and has offered carefully conceived, localized cooperative advertising opportunities to its dealers. Sea Ray's marketing department also produces stellar promotional events and marketing materials, providing ample consumer information in product brochures and catalogs as well as videos and CDs featuring breathtaking photography and graphic art. Sea Ray also offers many high-quality promotional items, including clothing, bedding, posters, sunglasses, and jewelry, most of which are decorated with the well-known Sea Ray logo.

Sea Ray's marketing operations have undergone some changes in the past decade. Longtime Sea Ray sales and marketing veteran Mike Burke was promoted from marketing manager to vice president of sales and marketing in 1997.[16]

That same year, Robert Noyes became vice president of marketing. Noyes had come to Sea Ray in 1987, following six years in sales and marketing at Boston Whaler, prior to its acquisition by Brunswick Corporation. His first position with Sea Ray was vice president of Central region sales and Sport Cruiser product manager.[17]

In 1998, the multitasking Rob Parmentier was promoted from senior vice president of domestic sales and marketing to senior vice president and general manager. The next year, Sea Ray's marketing department added staff devoted specifically to planning special events for Sea Ray and

# Sea Ray Superlatives

- World's largest manufacturer of superior quality pleasure boats

- Offers more variety than any other boat manufacturer, with 40-plus models ranging from 17 to 62 feet

- J. D. Power and Associates award for "Highest in Customer Satisfaction with Express Cruisers" four years in a row (2003–2006)

- Eight National Marine Manufacturers Association Customer Satisfaction Index awards for 2006, with top honors in every category in which it was eligible

- Three consecutive years winning National Marine Manufacturers Association Customer Satisfaction Index awards

- Two consecutive years leading the industry in National Marine Manufacturers Association Customer Satisfaction Index awards

- Five Star Diamond Award from the American Academy of Hospitality Sciences, the international organization's most prestigious award

- Customer satisfaction rating among the highest in the world

- Exceeds standards set by the U.S. Coast Guard, the National Marine Manufacturers Association, the American Boat and Yacht Council, and the International Organization of Standards (ISO)

- First boat manufacturer to receive ISO 9002 certification

- Sea Ray Master Dealer program is the first standards-based continuous-improvement program in the marine industry

- Sea Ray Owners Club is the largest boat owners association in the United States

- Resale values among the highest in the world

- Most searched-for boat brand on the Web

- Hosts AquaPalooza, the largest boating party in the world[1]

its dealers. These expanded capabilities allowed Sea Ray to offer more active and professional assistance for dealers that were planning and coordinating boat shows, demonstration days, open houses, and other kinds of special promotions.[18]

In another kind of marketing venture two years later, in 2000, Sea Ray established a full-color, quarterly lifestyle magazine for Sea Ray Owners Club members called *Sea Ray Living*. The magazine offered boaters informative and entertaining articles on a wide variety of boats, people, and issues associated with Sea Ray. *Sea Ray Living* has strived to enhance the lifestyles of Sea Ray family members. It has grown into one of largest circulated magazines in the boating industry. World-class photography and feature writing tell the stories of owners enjoying the exclusive Sea Ray lifestyle across the world.

*Sea Ray Living* has won the gold award in the International Marine category of the International Mercury Excellence awards, three silver Mercury Excellence awards, three Gold Millennium awards, two Crystal Awards of Excellence from the Communicator Awards competition, and other print-media recognition.[19]

In 2006, the Sea Ray marketing department established an extraordinary nationwide on-water summer event celebrating the Sea Ray lifestyle. They called the event "AquaPalooza," a fun-sounding name that played off the annual Lollapalooza music festival that first became popular during the 1990s. The inaugural AquaPalooza kicked off in July 2006 with fireworks, giveaways, and musical performances on a floating stage on Fort Loudon Lake near Sea Ray's Knoxville headquarters. More than 80 Sea Ray dealerships around the nation organized their own regional versions of the event. All boating enthusiasts were welcome to attend AquaPalooza.[20]

AquaPalooza's second year was even better than its first, drawing significant media attention and more than 10,000 boats and 30,000 boating enthusiasts to 120 events worldwide. Similar to Harley Davidson's Bike Week, engines revved and the fun was fired on all cylinders. In terms of number of participating boats and people, event attendance increased by more than 40 percent from the inaugural year. Prince William Marine Sales of Woodbridge, Virginia, sponsored the 2007 signature event on the Potomac River near Washington, D.C., where an estimated 1,300

boats gathered. Sea Ray's third annual marine extravaganza in 2008 created even greater buzz, drawing a record 50,000 guests to 150 lakes, rivers, bays, and harbors all across the world. Hosted by MarineMax Lake Ozark, MarineMax Osage Beach, and MarineMax Laurie, the festivities featured food, drinks, music, games, giveaways, and much more.[21]

"We're creating quite a stir in the industry with AquaPalooza," said Stone, president of Sea Ray. "It's really incredible that so many people show up in so many places at the same time. The event is Sea Ray–inspired, but really it's all-inclusive, and everyone is welcome. It's a testament to the boating lifestyle. And no other boat company can replicate AquaPalooza because we already invite everyone. It will always be wide open, but always associated with Sea Ray."[22]

By 2007, Sea Ray's marketing department management still included Mike Burke and Rob Noyes, each in their respective positions, as well as Joe Cacopardo, director of marketing; Chris Helton, marketing manager; a few 25-year Sea Ray veterans, including Mike Hungerford, Greg Garland, and Gary McCloud; Sharon Blazer; and Nicole Bales.

Sea Ray dealers benefit from the company's marketing and advertising efforts, and many recognize the quality of the work that the company's marketing team produces. "Their marketing is just incredible," said Rodney Bensz, co-owner of Michigan City–based B&E Marine, a Sea Ray dealership. "Rob [Noyes, Sea Ray vice president of marketing] always does an excellent job. Their brochures, their videos—everything is No. 1."[23]

Rod Malone, owner and president of Sail & Ski Center, a Sea Ray dealership based in Austin, Texas, has a similar opinion of Sea Ray's marketing department, including its event management staff. Malone has had the opportunity to participate in numerous Sea Ray dealer events. "Their marketing department is top-notch," said Malone. "They know how to put on a program. They know how to select venues, and they know how to organize the trips so that they're fun and convenient."[24]

### Manufacturing Excellence

The new year of 2007 began with a shakeup at Brunswick Corporation when Peter Hamilton retired in January as Brunswick Boat Group president after just a year in the position. Soon thereafter, Brunswick CEO Dusty McCoy eliminated the position, resulting in Sea Ray President Stone reporting directly to McCoy, as he had prior to 2006, as a Brunswick Boat Group chief financial officer during McCoy's presidency.[25]

Also in 2007, Brunswick Corporation's Marine Division established a new initiative—Manufacturing

AquaPalooza, also known as the "World's Largest Boating Party," takes place at the end of July each year. The multi-location, action-packed extravaganza celebrates life on the water, as boaters and non-boaters alike enjoy games, giveaways, food, drinks, and music. *(Photo courtesy of www.johnbildahlphotography.com, printed with permission from Dino Publishing.)*

Skilled Sea Ray workers ensure Sea Ray boats receive the attention to detail possible only with hands-on craftsmanship.

Excellence—that divided its boat manufacturers into three groups: an aluminum group, a sport boat group, and a cruiser and yacht group. Boatbuilders in these three groups subsequently started a formalized process for sharing best practices.[26]

More so than ever before, Sea Ray remains dedicated to production-oriented teamwork, both within the Brunswick organization and among the various Sea Ray facilities. Amidst this spirit of teamwork, Sea Ray supervisors and managers aim to ensure joint efforts within the company do not squelch employee initiative. "You don't want to lose your entrepreneurial spirit," said Ken Harrell, vice president/facility manager at the main Knoxville plant. "It's a fine line because sometimes people are just waiting for the next best idea versus healthy competition on who's going to come up with something. We've been able to balance that over the last 20 years."[27]

Through the years, Sea Ray has introduced many practices into its manufacturing operations and production administration designed to ensure

Sea Ray's boat molds are carefully sanded and coated with high-polish molding gel, ensuring a smooth finish on hull and deck parts.

the highest level of quality. In 2006, for instance, quality management was elevated from an administrative role to a vice president position that reported directly to the president rather than the engineering department (as per standard quality management reporting patterns). Gary Zimmer, whose 30 years of marine engineering experience had prompted Sea Ray to recruit him, initially served as vice president of PD&E for two years before becoming the first vice president of quality and manufacturing technology in 2006.[28]

Bob VanNorman, vice president of manufacturing operations, offered an overview of Sea Ray's current manufacturing approach:

*We concentrate a lot on our process control. We certainly have taken a lead from the Toyota production system and understand that if we don't have good operating procedures, you're going to have a lot of variation. So we have made a big press for standardized work. A lot of standard operating procedures have been written. We have cooperated with a lot of local universities to get some good industrial engineering talent—the University of Tennessee, Tennessee Tech, the University of Central Florida. We've added a supplier of quality function that reports to the vice president of quality. ... We've gotten a quality we need out of our suppliers. So, those are some of the things we have done to continually ensure that our quality is really up to standards.*[29]

All wiring on Sea Ray boats is hand-assembled and color-coded with Underwriters Laboratories, Inc.–approved high-quality connectors that are weather-resistant and provide better crimp, thus minimizing the possibility of electrical shorts.

Along with the overall production standardization, Sea Ray simultaneously returned to a higher level of handcraftsmanship in its manufacturing environment, an element that had always characterized Sea Ray production, but that decreased somewhat during the high-tech initiatives of the 21st century. While the company still makes great use of robotics for precision cutting and similar functions, it has eliminated automated production applications that failed to achieve the level of craftsmanship of a highly skilled Sea Ray production worker.

These efforts to achieve manufacturing excellence have led to success in the marketplace as well as pride in the workforce. Dwight Cobble, vice president of Sport Cruisers and a 27-year Sea Ray veteran who worked on the production floor for many years before moving to customer service and then sales, explained the meaning of the "Sea Ray Way":

*We stand behind our product because we believe in our product. One thing I think separates us from the competition is we really do care about our customer. We want our customer to be happy. We want them to be satisfied. If they're not, we go that extra mile to make that happen. When you've got 65 percent repeat business, you have to be doing something right, and simply put, I think it's because we really do care. We will, without a doubt, right or wrong, stand behind our product.*[30]

Forrest Weyant, an engineering technician who has been with Sea Ray for 40 years, also stressed the importance of caring about the final product. "We're providing the weekend relaxation for [Sea Ray owners] and their family," said Weyant. "You want it

right. The whole company has always been based on that—to try to get the quality the best we possibly can and make sure everybody is happy."[31]

Another longtime employee, Bob Scott, production manager at the Riverview plant and a 35-year Sea Ray veteran, expressed a similar perspective: "The best thing about this company, as far as I'm concerned, is they're always looking out for what's best for not only the employees, but the users," Scott said. "When I see a Sea Ray boat going down the road on a trailer, I'm just as proud today as I was the day I was hired."[32]

Brunswick conducts employee opinion surveys every two years throughout its various companies to remain aware of employees' concerns and recommendations. Employees are afforded the opportunity to comment on many aspects of business, including management, supervision, safety, communications, quality, company competitiveness, and image in the marketplace. The overall results for 2007 surpassed the results of 2005 and significantly improved from the results of 2003. Ninety percent of the 2007 survey responses showed improvement from the previous survey. Clearly, Sea Ray employees, always the lifeblood of this remarkable American business success story, are fired up about the company and its products.[33] Gary Montavon, vice president of human resources at Sea Ray since 2006 and vice president of employee relations at Brunswick since 2002, recognizes and appreciates the dedication of Sea Ray employees:

*I've been at this [Human Resources] for more than 30 years now. I've worked with employee opinion surveys the entire time. What our Sea Ray employees told us in 2007, even in the toughest of times for our industry when production schedules are being reduced and we are sizing ourselves to the business we have, was amazing. They are standing tall. They are committed. Their heads are in the game. They validated that they are being openly communicated to, fairly treated, and truly respected for the skills and talents they bring to us every day. It's an honor to be able to work alongside this work-force and management team.*[34]

### The Future Begins

Sea Ray's 2008 model-year, the first full model-year under Stone and his executive staff's leadership, featured one of the most impressive lineups of new boats the company had ever produced. With a reinvigorated commitment to producing new product, Sea Ray debuted nine new boats across six series.

The 2008 model-year production schedule assigned crucial boatbuilding responsibilities to the company's domestic production facilities: The Knoxville plant manufactured Sundancers 35 feet and shorter (except the 240 and 260); Riverview produced a mix of boats shorter than 30 feet; Tellico developed every sport boat 24 feet and shorter (except the Weekenders and the 175 Sport); Merritt Island

manufactured Sundancers 38 to 44 feet long, plus the 36 Sedan Bridge; the Palm Coast plant produced several 40- to 52-foot models; and Sykes Creek produced almost all yachts more than 50 feet long.[35]

Along with the 55 Sundancer, which had been introduced earlier in the year, the 330 was introduced in August, replacing the 320 Sundancer for 2008. The 330 Sundancer featured larger stern-drive motors with digital throttle and shift operation and a walk-through windshield that provided easy access to the foredeck. Four huge hull windows, a large deck hatch, and two skylights added substantially to this sport cruiser model's interior light.

The 330 Sundancer also featured upgrades of luxury items offered in the 320. The master

---

Sundancers in the 30- to 35-foot range have always been exceptionally popular. The 330 Sundancer for 2008 was a resplendent addition to the series.

stateroom contained an island-style double bed with an electronically adjustable extension and a Sealy Posturpedic® backrest with an elastic foam mattress. The cabin featured a 26-inch flatscreen TV with a remote DVD player, and a premium Clarion® stereo system.[36] One boat tester described the new 330 Sundancer as a cruiser "filled with better mousetraps" that "stands tall" compared with its competition.[37]

The 47 Sedan Bridge also debuted in August 2007. A step up from the 44 model, the 47 was more than five feet longer (including a swim platform) and had a wider beam that provided additional space and stability. A larger fiberglass rooftop was also added, and a raised-bridge deck offered more seating and entertaining space in the form of a large U-shaped seating area forward of the helm, which also featured a drawer-style refrigerator and a wet bar with sink and countertop. Other entertainment features included a 26-inch pop-up TV with a remote DVD player and a premium Clarion® stereo system. The boat's wood-floored galley featured an upright refrig-

erator/freezer, a two-burner stove, a microwave oven, and a coffeemaker. In addition, the 47 Sedan Bridge's panoramic windows brought in plenty of sunlight.

Two luxurious staterooms were well situated in the 47 Sedan Bridge. The full-beam master stateroom featured an innerspring queen berth with an eight-paneled headboard. Other amenities included a 20-inch flatscreen TV with a DVD player, a settee, and a cedar-lined hanging locker. The guest cabin rivaled most master staterooms, with its own innerspring queen mattress and a flatscreen TV with DVD player.

The extra size and amenities of the new Sedan Bridge model made it 9,000 pounds heavier than the 44 model. However, twin 574-horsepower Cummins

---

Sea Ray's Amberjack is a stable and comfortable sport cruiser that offers an optional fishing package.

Debuting for 2008, the Select Fission was Sea Ray's newest series. Offered as 230 and 210 models, these sporty bowriders came with a Fission Wakeboard Package for water-sports enthusiasts.

MerCruiser V-drive engines more than compensated for the additional weight.

The 47 Sedan Bridge featured piloting electronics such as SmartCraft™ VesselView display and diagnostic instruments, VHF radio, and a Clarion® stereo. It also offered a full complement of options such as bow and stern thrusters, and Sea Ray Navigator III.[38]

Sea Ray's 290 Amberjack was similarly upgraded but maintained its identity as a great dual-purpose family cruiser with an optional fishing package. Upgrades included a larger engine and fuel tank as well as additional storage space. The boat's 21-degree deadrise (the angle between the bottom of a boat and its widest beam) made it sturdy enough for any rough weather conditions. A designer-decorated cabin with cherry-finish wood interior cabinetry, matching hardware, and two comfortable berths provided a soothing environment.[39]

Another 290 model—the 290 Sundeck—was also introduced for 2008. As Sea Ray's most family-friendly sport boat model, the Sundeck series offered maximum deck and storage space to accommodate as many people as possible within a limited space without sacrificing style. The new 290 was the largest Sundeck, with three additional feet in length and several more inches of beam, compared to the 270 Sundeck it replaced. A 320-horse-power MerCruiser 6.2 MPI Bravo III with a digital throttle and shift propelled the boat, with optional power up to 425 horsepower.[40]

In other sport boat developments, Sea Ray refined its 205 model and redesigned the 175—both small, popularly priced bowriders that came with painted trailers. The 175s were built in the United States for domestic dealers and in China for Asian and European dealers. The new 205 sport boat for 2008 offered three floor plans, with the standard one featuring two swivel bucket seats and a motor box flanked by jump seats. The 205, like all Sport Boat models, offered four vibrant, two-tone color options, custom graphics, and an optional water sports tower. A 220-horsepower MerCruiser 5.0L Alpha I engine provided the boat with power.[41]

The 175 Sport Boat was Sea Ray's smallest boat. At 17-and-a-half feet long, and just 7 feet at the beam, the 175 weighed a relatively light 2,100 pounds. A 136-horsepower Alpha I MCM stern-drive engine powered the model. Like the larger sport

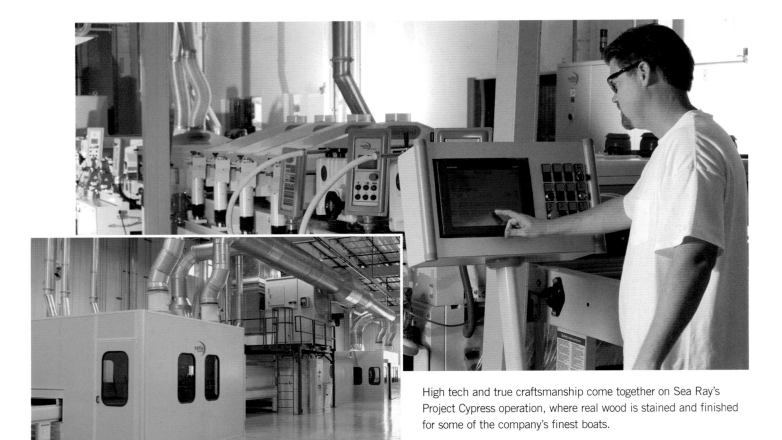

High tech and true craftsmanship come together on Sea Ray's Project Cypress operation, where real wood is stained and finished for some of the company's finest boats.

boats, the 175 offered a choice of floor plans plus several graphics options.[42]

While all of Sea Ray's new 2008 boats garnered attention, perhaps none excited younger recreational boating enthusiasts like the new 210 and 230 Select Fissions. These two runabouts were based on Sea Ray's premium 210 and 230 Select Bow Rider models but offered upgrades and additional amenities that transformed them into water-sport "dream boats." The 300-horsepower MerCruiser 350 Magnum Bravo III with digital throttle and shift transformed the boats into high-performance versions, while standard SmartCraft™ Smart Tow digital speed control provided quick and consistent acceleration. The Select Fissions sported two-tone gel coats on the hull and custom graphics, as well as a matching trailer.[43]

By the 2008 model-year, Sea Ray was building 19 sport boats, 10 sport cruisers, eight sport yachts, and five yachts, for a total of 42 boats. The lineup ranged in size from the 17-and-a-half-foot 175 Sport Bow Rider to the 61-and-a-half-foot 60 Sundancer.

Sea Ray boats ranged in price from about $20,000 to almost $2 million.

## Zeus, Axius, and SeaCore

With technological development a constant factor in Sea Ray's quest to improve its high-quality products, three developing propulsion-related technologies began to enhance Sea Ray's lineup by 2007.

The first technology, named Zeus, was created through a joint venture between Cummins MerCruiser Diesel, Sea Ray's primary engine manufacturer, and Columbus, Indiana–based Cummins, Inc., a major engine manufacturer that supplied Sea Ray with propulsion products. Under development for years, Zeus was first introduced by Sea Ray at the 2006 Fort Lauderdale International Boat Show® and formally introduced to dealers at Sea Ray's 2008 Dealer Meeting, which took place in mid-July at Sea Ray's Knoxville headquarters. By the time Sea Ray offered Zeus in 2008 products, the technology had been thoroughly tested and validated. Sea Ray sales associates from six continents and 34 countries had taken a Zeus-equipped 44 Sundancer on extensive sea trials. Further Zeus tests were conducted on 38 and 48 Sundancers. The response to the new propulsion system was enthusiastic.[44] Cummins MerCruiser's new technology delivered up to 15 percent better fuel economy, unsurpassed handling at high and low speeds, vessel systems integration unparalleled in the marine industry, and increased power density (up to 550 horsepower) that resulted in a 15 percent increase in top speed.[45]

Sea Ray integrated another new technological system into its boats called SeaCore, a new corrosion-control system for marine engines created by Mercury Marine. It used industrial hardcoat anodizing, a closed-cooling system, and a wide variety of stainless-steel components to achieve maximum corrosion protection all the way to the core of an engine (unlike other corrosion control systems that simply enclosed the drive components in a plastic shell). As SeaCore is particularly useful for stern-drive boats frequently used in saltwater, it should help alleviate the concerns of boat owners living in saltwater areas who have been reluctant to purchase a stern-drive boat.[46] Sea Ray featured SeaCore technology on many of its 2008 boats.

Axius, another new stern-drive development, provided even more technological innovation to Sea Ray boats. Using twin, independently operating MerCruiser Bravo III stern-drive engines to allow for joystick docking, Axius offered boaters remarkably easy and subtle maneuvering (laterally, at an angle, forward, backward, or even turning in a circle on its axis) through intuitive joystick control.[47] Sea Ray plans to feature Axius, which is particularly useful on larger boats, on select models. Brunswick CEO McCoy believes boats equipped with the new technology will be far more "user friendly" and will greatly enhance boaters' enjoyment of their craft:

*The release of the joystick docking systems, which are enabled by all of the fly-by-wire technology and the GPS technology that we have in Mercury, gives Mercury the opportunity to change boating for both stern-drive and the traditional diesel bigger boats in a way that's never happened before. I think as we watch those products coming to market, we'll see them change boating behavior, boating buying*

*habits, and we'll bring people into boating who have been intimidated by operating twin-engine boats at both the gas and diesel level.[48]*

### Project Cypress

Sea Ray opened its long-delayed Cape Canaveral facility in 2007 and spent $5.2 million to transform it into a state-of-the-art wood-component manufacturing facility for a special initiative called Project Cypress, in which workers process hardwood, stain it, and finish it with a high-gloss sealant for use on Sea Ray boats.[49] The grand 60 Sundancer was the first model to use wood finished through this process. The 58 Sedan Bridge and the rest of the yacht lineup were then integrated in 2008.[50]

An in-house supply of hardwood components will give Sea Ray a distinct competitive advantage as well as significant savings on wood applications for its top-line boats. For example, when Sea Ray built the 68 Super Sun Sport and furnished the huge yachts with wood cabinetry, a prepackaged kit purchased from an outside supplier cost about $240,000 for the cabinetry alone. On the other hand, wood components supplied by the in-house Project Cypress process would have cost less than half that amount.[51]

Preparing for Project Cypress and fully integrating the system into Sea Ray's overall manufacturing schedule is an exciting initiative for the company that will likely require two years to fully implement. Sea Ray plans to eventually supply real wood components for all of its yachts and sport yachts and any sport cruiser models more than 29 feet long. Company executives envision the Cypress plant running two 10-hour shifts per day, four days a week, with a capacity to produce up to 50,000 square feet of finished wood per week.[52]

### Dealer Dynamics

By 2007, Sea Ray had more than 300 dealers worldwide and more than 200 in the United States, representing more than 100 principal owners.[53] (Sea Ray allows its dealers to own multiple dealership locations as long as they do not intrude into the territory of another established dealership).[54]

"A lot of manufacturers can't offer you a single product line that goes from 17 feet to 60 feet," said

Mike Burke, vice president of sales and marketing. "That is a huge benefit for our dealer body because they don't have to deal with different programs and different personalities and different salespeople and different commitments."[55]

Sea Ray management is fully aware of the mutually beneficial nature of the relationship between the Sea Ray Group and Sea Ray dealers. The care with which Sea Ray management has chosen its dealers and the fact that the company has, historically, established large and exclusive territories for its dealers are two important factors in the success of the Sea Ray dealership network. According to Burke:

*It's not only that we pick the best [dealers]; it's that we nurture the best. We worked with them to expand their business. One of the founding precepts of Sea Ray's relationship with our dealers is [that] we always give them very large territories. We treat them as exclusive dealers within their territory. They have a lot of area in which they can make money today, but also grow their business tomorrow. We've always prided ourselves that our distribution is probably our number-one competitive advantage because of the size and the quality and the financial wherewithal of the dealers, plus the fact that they've also aligned themselves with our strategy. In fact, in a lot of cases, they point us in the right direction in terms of consumer satisfaction and how you retain a long-term owner.[56]*

The average Sea Ray dealer tenure is around 18 years—extraordinarily long for the recreational-boating industry—and 70 percent are exclusively Sea Ray.[57] Burke also explained how the Sea Ray organization works to keep its dealers productive and successful:

*One of the key reasons we have the type of [dealer] tenure we have is that we go the extra mile with the dealer where a lot of other [original equipment manufacturers] will not. If a dealer is a small-market dealer and they're struggling to make their numbers work or we believe they are underperforming, our immediate reaction is not to put a bullet in them and go somewhere else. We work with them. We help them develop programs to help them grow their level of experience and expertise in the marketplace, and effectiveness in the marketplace, and we help them to be successful. We do it through a long-standing list of dealer programs that we offer, including Performance Incorporated, which helps them understand their financials and where they're making money.[58]*

Sea Ray has long demonstrated such reasonable flexibility in financing and business arrangements with its dealers. Lars and Göran Sundberg, presidents of Málaga, Spain–based Marina Marbella, have been in the marine business since 1965 and Sea Ray dealers since 1983. They have experienced the kind of agreeable—and personal—working relationship with Sea Ray that all its dealers can expect:

*Our relationship with Sea Ray, and especially with C. N. Ray, was always based on mutual trust beyond normal standards. For example, we were granted an open credit line without limitation for stocking boats from Sea Ray from 1983 until 1996. [It took] 12 years of continued growth to become the largest international dealer, and, needless to say, we never missed a payment or backed out of an order commitment—a fantastic relationship that we are*

Sea Ray has more than 300 dealers worldwide, with more than 200 in the United States, two-thirds of which are exclusive. The average tenure of Sea Ray dealers is 18 years.

*still enjoying today even without C. N. at the helm.
[We work with] great people and have a long-standing personal relationship with them.*[59]

Marina Marbella has Sea Ray dealerships in Spain, the United Kingdom, Sweden, Portugal, Gibraltar, and Morocco. It has been the largest international Sea Ray dealership since 1997, with 20 stores and 200 employees.

Sea Ray dealers also reap the benefits of Sea Ray's formidable marketing assets. High-quality brochures and other marketing materials are always available, and Sea Ray's marketing staff provides first-rate event planning. The company's marketing department also offers carefully collected data to help dealers understand the marketing dynamics at work in their respective regions. "It's absolutely critical to their success," explained Burke. "It helps them determine how to spend their money, how to measure the return, and then how to evolve so that they are spending their marketing dollars as effectively as possible."[60]

Due to Sea Ray's long-standing policy of protecting the integrity of existing dealer territories, Sea Ray executives feel the company currently has a full complement of dealers. However, there is still ample opportunity for growth within existing dealership territories through the addition of more store locations.[61]

Appreciation for its dealership network permeates the Sea Ray organization. Sea Ray Group President Stone is fully aware of the importance of the dealer network in Sea Ray's success, partially due to his participation in a dealer performance group in addition to his duties as president:

*I think it's important that we think about our dealers and [how] everything comes from that. Our goal is to make sure our dealers make a great living selling the boats that we offer and have a large enough territory to do that ... because in essence that ensures our long-term success. [That philosophy] has been successful for almost 50 years.*[62]

### A Future Propelled by the Past

By the 2008 model-year, Sea Ray employed about 4,000 in its seven domestic manufacturing facilities, producing more than 40 different boat models.[63] For each of the past two years, Sea Ray

sold around 14,000 boats worldwide, with sales approaching $1 billion.[64]

Calendar-year 2008 opened with several new Sea Ray boats. Two sport boats, one Select EX and one Sundeck, debuted in January. The 300 Select EX, a premium runabout powered by a MerCruiser 496 Magnum Bravo III gas stern drive generating 375 horsepower, features a digital throttle and shift. The 30-footer has a 21-degree deadrise and power-assisted steering. The boat offers not only thrilling acceleration but also precise handling.

The 300 Select EX's helm is loaded with functional and aesthetic finery, including a sleek dash with Chartplotter standard. The wood-accented wheel sports Vessel Control System thumb pads that offer convenient control of SmartCraft™ diagnostics and of the Clarion® stereo system, which includes a CD player, MP3 port, amplifier, and six speakers.

A roomy cockpit has adjustable bucket helm seats and back-to-back sliding loungers, along with a U-shaped cockpit lounge and two aft-facing seats. At the bow, there is a wraparound lounge and built-in cooler, all of which help create a comfortable boating experience.[65]

Sea Ray's 210 Sundeck is also new. The entry-level runabout has surprising features typically found only on larger models, including a wraparound windshield and a fiberglass bow block-off door, as well as an aft-facing bench in the rear. A 260-horsepower MerCruiser MPI Bravo III MCM gas stern drive gives the 210 Sundeck its punch on the water. A matching trailer makes for convenient land transport.[66]

Another new Sundancer, the 350 model, was presented in February at the 2008 Miami International Boat Show. At 37-and-a-half feet in length and with 21 degrees of deadrise, it is at the top of Sea Ray's sport cruiser lineup. Twin MerCruiser 496 Magnum MPI Bravo III stern drives provide 375 horsepower with digital throttle and shift.

The 350 Sundancer cockpit features a big L-shaped settee facing a solid-teak table, a pivoting double helm seat, and a single companion seat, as well as an entertainment center with stainless-steel wet bar, refrigerator, and optional barbecue grill. The cabin has an Ultraleather HP™ sofa, solid-wood dinette table, deep-pile carpet, and a 26-inch flatscreen TV with remote DVD player, all presented in excellent light provided by two over-sized hull windows and a pair of skylights. As

# DEALER FEEDBACK

PETE BEAUREGARD, SR., BEGAN SELLING Sea Ray boats in 1964. In 1971, he dropped the Chris-Craft line that had been his bread and butter, in favor of Sea Ray, and adopted a new name, Colony Marine.[1] Beauregard, Sr., remembered the tremendous impact of Sea Ray's Sundancer model on the recreational boating industry:

> Jerry [Michalak] brought out that Sundancer with the converted windshield, and my God, it revolutionized the industry! And then it just opened up the entire fleet. It was a gorgeous boat with so much practicality, and the market … it just took it by storm![2]

Algonac, Michigan–based Colony Marine is a Sea Ray Ambassador Dealer with three sales locations and three marina facilities—all with service centers located in Michigan. The dealership consistently rates in the top five of all Sea Ray dealers.[3]

Beauregard, Sr., remembered C. N. Ray fondly: "C. N. was the ultimate cheerleader. He was a class act."

Pete Beauregard, Jr., who eventually took over as president of Colony (although his father remains involved in the operation), described the Sea Ray culture:

> It's just amazing the heritage that is still there. [Jerry Michalak's] fingerprints are still on everything. Same thing when you talk [about] C. N. [Ray] and Arch [Mehaffey]. The Rick Stones and the Rob Parmentiers and Mike Burkes and the guys running the company today still have the passion as strong as it was the day Ray retired.[4]

․․․․․

Joe and Mary Wakeen own and operate Wakeen's Family Boating Center, Inc., a Sea Ray Ambassador Dealer based in Rock Island, Illinois,

with a facility in Davenport, Iowa, and a smaller store in East Dubuque, Illinois. Wakeen's Family Boating Center has the distinction of being the first dealership in the world recognized as a Sea Ray Ambassador Dealer.[5]

The Wakeen boating legacy began at Bud's Marina in La Crosse, Wisconsin, where Joe Wakeen worked as manager and, in 1968, began selling Sea Ray boats. In 1987, the Wakeen family bought the marina. Four years later, Joe Wakeen and his wife and business partner, Mary, moved the operation to Rock Island, rechristening it "Wakeen's Family Boating Center." Since then, the Wakeens' Rock Island operation has sold only Sea Ray boats.[6]

Joe Wakeen described his appreciation of Sea Ray leadership's recognition of the difficult conditions in the recreational boating market:

> It's nice to have someone who has been around a while and knows what the dealers are going through. [Rick Stone] is more in tune to the dealer's needs. So [Sea Ray] has a good leader right now who I think will make a big difference. He is really a super guy.[7]

․․․․․

Ronald Bensz founded B&E Marine with a partner in Michigan City, Indiana, in 1953, and the dealership began carrying Sea Ray boats in 1974. Bensz's sons, Barry and Rodney, eventually joined the company, becoming co-owners when their father retired. Barry Bensz remembered the close business relationship between B&E and Sea Ray:

> As Sea Ray grew, we grew with it. You could tell they always had high-quality dealers. The dealers all seemed to work well together. Sea Ray is far ahead of the rest of the industry. There isn't anybody else that's even close.[8]

Sea Ray's dealer network has been the backbone of its success, with more than 25 new stores opening in the past few years.

Younger sibling Rodney grew up equally impressed with the Sea Ray operation, particularly the company's focus on service. "There's no doubt that the product is superior in the marketplace, and when there's a problem, Sea Ray always does the right thing. And their customer and dealer support ... [out of] all the manufacturers we've had, is ... by far the best."[9]

Both Bensz brothers noted the Sea Ray Master Dealer program as an important factor in their success. "It keeps us accountable for our methods and processes and makes us more professional," Rodney said.[10]

B&E Marine employs about 45 people at its operation, which includes a full-service marina. With approximately $20 million in annual sales, the company scored the highest in the Midwest and ranked sixth out of 350 Sea Ray sales locations nationwide. It was also honored as one of Sea Ray's first Master Dealers and recognized for Excellence in Customer Service in Sea Ray's Customer Satisfaction Index (CSI).[11]

. . . . .

When Rod Malone, president and owner of Austin, Texas–based Sail & Ski Center, began offering Sea Ray boats in 1987, his dealership sold nearly 100 boats the first year.[12] "We thought we had died and gone to heaven," said Malone.[13]

Expanding quickly over the next few years, Sail & Ski established a new dealership in San Antonio and another in Lakeway, Texas, just outside of Austin. In 2007, the company acquired a 409-slip marina on Lake Travis, adjacent to the Lakeway store. Malone has always appreciated the training that Sea Ray has offered to its dealers:

*Sea Ray is the premiere company in supporting the dealerships in terms of training sales-people, training the dealership in good business practices, as well as good operational and sales practices. It's that understanding and investment in the dealer distribution that I think makes Sea Ray unique and is key to their success as well as our own.*[14]

In 2007, Sail & Ski Center was recognized as the winner of Sea Ray's highest CSI awards in both Sales and Customer Service—the first time one dealership won both top awards. Sail & Ski was also the first multiple-location Sea Ray dealer to achieve Master Dealer status.[15]

Malone believes Sea Ray's growth and success will continue. "I think there is a new excitement and energy as a result of Rick Stone's leadership and some of the things that are happening at the product development center at Merritt Island," said Malone. "I think there is a real sense of anticipation and a real renewed energy from everybody."[16]

always with Sea Ray boats, a number of attractive options exist to upgrade even boats like the 350 Sundancer that have exceptionally high–quality features in the standard model.[67]

The 270 Sundancer is also scheduled for a second-half model-year release. One brand-new feature will be a lever-release–operated helm seat that swivels 360 degrees.[68]

Sea Ray's present and future harks back to its storied past. There has been an energetic revival of the principles and practices engendered by Sea Ray founder C. N. Ray that proved successful for decades. Although Sea Ray strayed from some of those principles in the early part of the new millennium, the

company's new leadership and seasoned veterans brought the company back to its tried-and-true path. Stone's business approaches are reminiscent of those advocated by C. N. Ray. Bill McGill, chairman, president, and CEO of MarineMax, compares Stone to Ray:

*I have known Rick, as long as he has been with Sea Ray, from a business and personal relation-*

Sea Ray's half-century of experience building boats has created a distinctive "Sea Ray lifestyle" that will continue into the future as the company builds on the brand's quality and style.

The Sea Ray executive staff in 2008 included (back row, from left): Terry McNew, Bob VanNorman, Russ Nellis, and Gary Zimmer. Front row: Kristi Thomasson, Gary Montavon, Rob Parmentier, and Rick Stone. Golden Retriever Sadie is also pictured.

*ship. Rick is a man of utmost character who, like the original founder C. N. Ray, approaches business from the perspective that the dealer is the customer, and the success of Sea Ray is tied to the success of the dealer.*[69]

Over the past few years, Stone has made a renewed effort to further develop the kinds of personal relationships with Sea Ray dealers that C. N. Ray maintained during his establishment of the corporation and his long tenure as president.

In model-year 2007, Stone visited more than 20 dealerships, often with longtime Sea Ray veteran and Executive Vice President Rob Parmentier.[70] While Stone pays close attention to Sea Ray's domestic dealers, his hands-on approach has increasingly incorporated a worldwide perspective. In recent years, Stone and Parmentier have visited many countries, including Australia, China, Kuwait, Finland, the United Kingdom, Greece, Germany, Russia, Qatar, the United Arab Emirates, Saudi Arabia, Egypt, Singapore, and Italy.[71]

Stone has also revived rigorous new product development—another early element of Sea Ray's success, epitomized by Bill Barrington during his tenure as company president. In calendar-year 2007, Sea Ray's PD&E operation produced 15 new boats (versus just five boats in calendar-year 2006). According to Stone:

*Introducing innovative new product ... is a huge requirement in the industry. It's what the dealers need and what the customers are looking for. And we are now back on track with that, reinvigorating some of the Sea Ray spirit at our product development operation. To sum up our renewed new product emphasis, by the end of 2008, two-thirds of Sea Ray's product lineup will have been introduced in the previous 24 months, with another*

*[six] new models planned for 2009. In addition, at least 15 models will include 360° Total Control technology [Axius, Zeus, or Total Command] by year's end.*[72]

The products Sea Ray is now developing will have a great impact on the recreational-boating marketplace. Mike Burke, Sea Ray vice president of sales and marketing, puts it succinctly: "We have a number of boats that are [nearing] release, and they're going to rock the market."[73]

With a past as rich as the tradition and corporate culture established by company founder C. N. Ray, a present as dependable as its products, and a future as "rock" solid as Rick Stone's leadership, Sea Ray is guaranteed to experience at least another half-century of success.

Dusty McCoy summed up Sea Ray's extraordinary present position and future potential best:

*Sea Ray is the most unique organization I've had the opportunity to be associated with in my life. It is an organization that is "can do." They know no boundaries. There's nothing that will keep them from reaching any goal they've established.*[74]

# Notes to Sources

**Chapter One
Boating Brainstorm**

1. C. N. Ray, interview by Jeffrey L. Rodengen, digital recording, 13 December 2006, Write Stuff Enterprises, Inc.
2. Ibid.
3. Jim Sherman, "Sea Ray Great While it Lasted," *The Oxford Leader*, 9 January 1990.
4. Ray, interview; Arch Mehaffey, interview by Jeffrey L. Rodengen, digital recording, 14 December 2006, Write Stuff Enterprises, Inc.
5. Ibid.
6. Ray, interview.
7. Ray, interview; Mehaffey, interview.
8. Ray, interview.
9. Ibid.
10. "Carr-Craft Fiber Glass Boat Building Planned for Oxford Area," *Oxford Leader*, 2 December 1959.
11. Ray, interview; Mehaffey, interview.
12. Ibid.
13. Jerry Michalak, interview by Jeffrey L. Rodengen,

digital recording, 11 December 2006, Write Stuff Enterprises, Inc.
14. Ray, interview; Mehaffey, interview.
15. Ibid.
16. Mehaffey, interview.
17. Ray, interview.
18. Ibid.
19. Ibid.
20. Ibid.
21. Ibid.
22. Ibid.
23. Michalak, interview.
24. Ibid.
25. Ibid.
26. 1963 Sea Ray brochure.
27. 1964 Sea Ray brochure.
28. Ray, interview; Mehaffey, interview; Michalak, interview.
29. Ray, interview.
30. Michalak, interview; Ray, interview.
31. 1963 Sea Ray brochure.
32. Ray, interview.
33. Jim Sherman, "Sea Ray Great While it Lasted," *The Oxford Leader*, 9 January 1990.
34. Mehaffey, interview.
35. Ibid.
36. Ibid.

37. Ibid.

**Chapter One Sidebar
Finding Strength in Fiberglass**

1. Daniel Spurr, *Heart of Glass: Fiberglass Boats and the Men Who Made Them* (New York: McGraw-Hill, 2000), 13.
2. Owens-Corning, http://www.owenscorning.com/.
3. Spurr, *Heart of Glass*, 11–14.
4. American Chemistry Council, http://www.americanchemistry.com/.
5. Ibid.
6. Spurr, *Heart of Glass*, 22.
7. Ibid.
8. Ibid.
9. Spurr, *Heart of Glass*, 30–31.
10. Spurr, *Heart of Glass*, 32–34.
11. Spurr, *Heart of Glass*, 14.
12. Spurr, *Heart of Glass*, 95.

**Chapter One Sidebar
The Harley Earl Connection**

1. Harley Early, "The Da Vinci of Detroit," http://www.classiccar.com/.
2. Ibid.

## Chapter Two
## Sea Ray Style

1. Jerry Michalak, interview by Jeffrey L. Rodengen, digital recording, 11 December 2006, Write Stuff Enterprises, Inc.
2. C. N. Ray, interview by Jeffrey L. Rodengen, digital recording, 13 December 2006, Write Stuff Enterprises, Inc.
3. Michalak, interview.
4. Jim Steffens, interview by Jeffrey L. Rodengen, digital recording, 10 May 2007, Write Stuff Enterprises, Inc.
5. Michalak, interview.
6. Ibid.
7. Steffens, interview.
8. Michalak, interview; "Carr-Craft Fiber Glass Boat Building Planned for Oxford Area," *Oxford Leader*, 2 December 1959.
9. Ibid.
10. Steffens, interview.
11. Michalak, interview; Arch Mehaffey, interview by Jeffrey L. Rodengen, digital recording, 14 December 2006, Write Stuff Enterprises, Inc.
12. Mehaffey, interview.
13. Chicago Public Library correspondence.
14. 1966 Sea Ray brochure.
15. Ibid.
16. Ibid.
17. Ibid.
18. 1967 Sea Ray brochure.
19. Mehaffey, interview.
20. 1967 Sea Ray brochure.

## Chapter Two Sidebar
## The Stern Drive Package

1. Jeffrey Rodengen, *Iron Fist: The Lives of Carl Kiekhaefer*, (Fort Lauderdale: Write Stuff Syndicate, Inc., 1990), 364.
2. Rodengen, *Iron Fist*, 360–79.

## Chapter Three
## Full Speed Ahead

1. Jim Steffens, interview by Jeffrey L. Rodengen, digital recording, 10 May 2007, Write Stuff Enterprises, Inc.
2. Arch Mehaffey, interview by Jeffrey L. Rodengen, digital recording, 14 December 2006, Write Stuff Enterprises, Inc.
3. C. N. Ray, interview by Jeffrey L. Rodengen, digital recording, 13 December 2006, Write Stuff Enterprises, Inc.
4. Ibid.
5. Ray, interview; Mehaffey, interview.
6. Ray, interview.
7. Roger Giles, interview by Jeffrey L. Rodengen, digital recording, 10 May 2007, Write Stuff Enterprises, Inc.
8. 1968 Sea Ray brochure.
9. 1969 Sea Ray brochure.
10. Ibid.
11. Ray, interview.
12. Mehaffey, interview.
13. Jerry Michalak, interview by Jeffrey L. Rodengen, digital recording, 11 December 2006, Write Stuff Enterprises, Inc.
14. Ray, interview.
15. Ray, interview; Mehaffey, interview.
16. Michalak, interview.
17. National Marine Manufacturers Association (NMMA), Market Statistics Division, January 1999.

## Chapter Three Sidebar
## Phoenix Flights

1. C. N. Ray, interview by Jeffrey L. Rodengen, digital recording, 13 December 2006, Write Stuff Enterprises, Inc.
2. Howard V. "Mac" Mc Donald, interview by Jeffrey L. Rodengen, digital recording, 28 August 2007, Write Stuff Enterprises, Inc.
3. Ray, interview.
4. Mc Donald, interview.
5. Ibid.

## Chapter Four
## Sundancer Sensation

1. Jerry Michalak, interview by Jeffrey L. Rodengen, digital recording, 11 December 2006, Write Stuff Enterprises, Inc.
2. National Marine Manufacturers Association (NMMA), Market Statistics Division, January 1999.
3. Michalak, interview.
4. Ibid.
5. 1976 Sea Ray brochure.
6. Michalak, interview.
7. 1976 Sea Ray brochure.
8. Michalak, interview.
9. Ibid.
10. C. N. Ray, interview by Jeffrey L. Rodengen, digital recording, 13 December 2006, Write Stuff Enterprises, Inc.
11. Ibid.
12. Jim Steffens, interview by Jeffrey L. Rodengen, digital recording, 10 May 2007, Write Stuff Enterprises, Inc.
13. Ray, interview.
14. Ibid.

**Chapter Four Sidebar**
**Pickel Island**

1. C. N. Ray, interview by Jeffrey L. Rodengen, digital recording, 13 December 2006, Write Stuff Enterprises, Inc.; Arch Mehaffey, interview by Jeffrey L. Rodengen, digital recording, 14 December 2006, Write Stuff Enterprises, Inc.
2. 1880 United States Federal Census, District 12, Knox County, Tennessee; Ancestry.com and The Church of Jesus Christ of Latter-day Saints, Roll: T9_1265; Family History Film: 1255265, 309.3000; Enumeration District: 155, 1999; 1900 United States Federal Census, Civil District 17, Knox County, Tennessee; Ancestry.com and The Generations Network, Inc., Roll: T623, 1583; Enumeration District: 90, 2004.
3. Don K. Ferguson, "Commission OK's Buying Land," *Knoxville News-Sentinel*, 4 May 1966.

**Chapter Five**
**Southern Heading**

1. C. N. Ray, interview by Jeffrey L. Rodengen, digital recording, 10 April 2007, Write Stuff Enterprises, Inc.
2. National Marine Manufacturers Association (NMMA), Market Statistics Division, January 1999.
3. Rob Parmentier, interview by Jeffrey L. Rodengen, digital recording, 10 May 2007,

Write Stuff Enterprises, Inc.
4. Jerry Michalak, interview by Jeffrey L. Rodengen, digital recording, 11 December 2006, Write Stuff Enterprises, Inc.
5. Steve Helwig, interview by Jeffrey L. Rodengen, digital recording, 11 December 2006, Write Stuff Enterprises, Inc.
6. Helwig, interview.
7. Ibid.
8. Ibid.
9. 1980 Sea Ray brochure.
10. George Beuhler, *The Troller Yacht Book*, (New York: W.W. Norton & Co., 1999), 13–14.
11. NMMA, January 1999.
12. Ibid.
13. Parmentier, interview.
14. Bruce Thompson, interview with Mike Hungerford, Summer 2001.
15. NMMA, January 1999.
16. Arch Mehaffey, interview by Jeffrey L. Rodengen, digital recording, 14 December 2006, Write Stuff Enterprises, Inc.
17. "Brunswick Appoints William J. Barrington President of Sea Ray Division; Ray Extends Contract as Chairman," PR Newswire, 21 June 1989.
18. Rick Stone, interview by Jeffrey L. Rodengen, digital recording, 10 May 2007, Write Stuff Enterprises, Inc.
19. Ray, interview.

**Chapter Five Sidebar**
**The Meaning of "Yacht"**

1. The American Heritage Dictionary of the English

Language, Fourth Edition, 2000, http://www.bartleby.com/ 61/12/Y0001200.html/.
2. Ibid.

**Chapter Five Sidebar**
**The MerCruiser Connection**

1. Jeffrey L. Rodengen, *The Legend of Mercury* (Fort Lauderdale: Write Stuff Enterprises, Inc., 1998), 155.
2. Rob Parmentier, interview by Jeffrey L. Rodengen, digital recording, 10 May 2007, Write Stuff Enterprises, Inc.

**Chapter Six**
**Brunswick and Irish Stew**

1. C. N. Ray, interview by Jeffrey L. Rodengen, digital recording, 13 December 2006, Write Stuff Enterprises, Inc.
2. Reuters, "Aggressive Brunswick Making Waves for Outboard Marine," *Chicago Tribune*, 14 December 1986.
3. Rick Stone, interview by Jeffrey L. Rodengen, digital recording, 10 May 2007, Write Stuff Enterprises, Inc.; "Sea Ray Go for Ireland," *International Boat Industry*, April/May 1986.
4. National Marine Manufacturers Association (NMMA), Market Statistics Division, January 1999.
5. Sallie Gaines, "Brunswick Nets 2D Boat Firm-Sea Ray Maker Coming Aboard for $350 Million," *Chicago*

*Tribune*, 29 November 1986.

6. Howard Rudnitsky and Richard L. Stern, "Dollars Ahoy!" *Forbes*, 2 November 1987.

7. Stone, interview.

8. Robert VanNorman, interview by Jeffrey L. Rodengen, digital recording, 28 August 2007, Write Stuff Enterprises, Inc.

9. Murray Shektman, Sea Ray Dealer Info-gram #58, 17 January 1986.

10. 1985 Sea Ray brochure.

11. Mike Morrison, interview by Jeffrey L. Rodengen, digital recording, 4 October 2007, Write Stuff Enterprises, Inc.

12. "Sea Ray Boats' Business Bulges in Monroe," *Knoxville News-Sentinel*.

13. Richard Thiel, "Sea Ray Pachanga II Boat Test," *Boating*, March 1986.

14. Thiel, "Sea Ray Pachanga II."

15. Ibid.

16. Linda Hersch, "Ski Boats Pull in Profits," *Boating Industry*, May 1988.

17. 1987 Sea Ray Products & Programs manual.

18. Roger Giles, interview by Jeffrey L. Rodengen, digital recording, 10 May 2007, Write Stuff Enterprises, Inc.

19. Ibid.

20. "Sea Ray Go for Ireland."

21. Jim Steffens, interview by Jeffrey L. Rodengen, digital recording, 10 May 2007, Write Stuff Enterprises, Inc.

22. Denis Reading, "Minister Brings Good News on Jobs Front," (Cork) *Evening Echo*, 13 August 1986.

23. Giles, interview.

24. "Sea Ray Goes for No. 1," *International Boat Industry*, October/November 1986.

25. Ibid.

26. Ibid.

27. Sea Ray Boats Annual Sales, internal documentation.

28. Carl Weinschenk, "Brunswick Changes the Landscape; Brunswick Corp.," *Boating Industry*, January 1987.

29. Ibid.

30. PR Newswire, 25 July 1987.

31. Ray, interview.

32. Weinschenk, "Brunswick Changes the Landscape."

33. PR Newswire, 25 July 1987.

34. Ray, interview

35. Gaines, "Brunswick Nets 2D Boat Firm."

36. Brunswick Corporation 1986 Annual Report.

37. Ibid.

38. Rudnitsky and Stern, "Dollars Ahoy!"

39. Gaines, "Brunswick Nets 2D Boat Firm."

40. Weinschenk, "Brunswick Changes the Landscape."

41. Arch Mehaffey, interview by Jeffrey L. Rodengen, digital recording, 14 December 2006, Write Stuff Enterprises, Inc.

42. Ibid.

43. Rudnitsky and Stern, "Dollars Ahoy!"

44. Ray, interview.

45. Giles, interview.

46. Sea Ray Boats Annual Sales, internal documentation.

47. 1987 Sea Ray Sport Yachts brochure.

48. 1987 Sea Ray Products & Programs manual.

49. Bill Barrington, interview by Jeffrey L. Rodengen, digital recording, 31 August 2007, Write Stuff Enterprises, Inc.

50. Ibid.

51. Ray, interview.

52. Jack Lail, "Sea Ray Boat Expanding with Fourth Plant in ET," *The Knoxville News-Sentinel*, 25 August 1987.

53. Ramona Patterson, "Lancaster Rides the Waves of Sea Ray Boats' Success," *The Business Journal–Charlotte*, 23 January 1989.

54. Ibid.

55. Voris Williams, "Boat Plant to Bring 500 Jobs to Knox," *The Knoxville Journal*, 15 August 1987.

56. Lail, "Sea Ray Boat Expanding."

57. "Just Add Water," *1st Class*, 1986.

58. Lail, "Sea Ray Boat Expanding."

59. Ibid.

60. Stone, interview.

61. Sea Ray Boats Annual Sales, internal documentation.

62. NMMA, January 1999.

63. Ray, interview.

64. Ibid.

65. Carrie Hedberg, interview by Jeffrey L. Rodengen, digital recording, 13 September 2007, Write Stuff Enterprises, Inc.; 1987 Sea Ray Products & Programs manual.

66. Ray, interview.

67. "Brunswick Appoints William J. Barrington President of Sea Ray Division; Ray Extends Contract as Chairman," PR Newswire, 21 June 1989.

**Chapter Six Sidebar**
**Sea Ray Success for Brunswick**

1. Reuters, "Boat Engine Rivals Battle for Market Share," *The Globe and Mail* (Canada), 19 December 1986.
2. Robert Johnson, "Brunswick Corp. Agrees to Buy Bayliner Marine," *The Wall Street Journal*, 10 November 1986.
3. Brian Bremner, "Why Brunswick Boat Buys Could Hurt its Engine Sales," *Chicago Business*, 8 December 1986.
4. Ibid.

**Chapter Six Sidebar**
**Popping the Cork**

1. Roger Giles, interview by Jeffrey L. Rodengen, digital recording, 10 May 2007, Write Stuff Enterprises, Inc.
2. Ibid.
3. Jim Steffens, interview by Jeffrey L. Rodengen, digital recording, 10 May 2007, Write Stuff Enterprises, Inc.
4. Ibid.
5. Ibid.
6. Ibid.
7. Steffens, interview; Rick Stone, interview by Jeffrey L. Rodengen, digital recording, 10 May 2007, Write Stuff Enterprises, Inc.

8. Steffens, interview; Parliament of Ireland debate minutes, 30 September 1997, http://www.gov.ie/debates-97/30Sept97/adjourn.htm/.

**Chapter Seven**
**Batten Down the Hatches**

1. Bill Barrington, interview by Jeffrey L. Rodengen, digital recording, 31 August 2007, Write Stuff Enterprises, Inc.
2. 1989 Sea Ray brochures.
3. 1990 Sea Ray Products & Programs manual.
4. Jerry Michalak, interview by Jeffrey L. Rodengen, digital recording, 11 December 2006, Write Stuff Enterprises, Inc.
5. Ibid.
6. 1989 Sea Ray brochures.
7. Rob Parmentier, interview by Jeffrey L. Rodengen, digital recording, 10 May 2007, Write Stuff Enterprises, Inc.
8. "Sea Ray Boats Closing for a Week," *Knoxville News-Sentinel*, May 1989.
9. Ibid.
10. Lois Reagan Thomas, "Sea Ray to Lay Off 190 Employees in ET; Low Sales in April Blamed," *Knoxville News-Sentinel*, May 1989.
11. Internal Sea Ray memorandum with news release attached, Bill Barrington, 20 July 1989.
12. "Brunswick Appoints William J. Barrington President of Sea Ray Division; C. N. Ray Extends

Contract as Chairman," PR Newswire, 21 June 1989.
13. Barrington, interview.
14. Ibid.
15. Rick Stone, interview by Jeffrey L. Rodengen, digital recording, 10 May 2007, Write Stuff Enterprises, Inc.
16. Ramona Patterson, "Sea Ray Boats Loses Fight to Stay Afloat; to Close in Sept.," *The Business Journal-Charlotte*, 31 July 1989.
17. 1990 Sea Ray Sport Yachts brochure.
18. Michalak, interview.
19. Marlene Sokol, "Powerboat Industry Flooded with Product," *St. Petersburg Times*, 9 October 1989.
20. Robert Womack, "Sea Ray Cites Slow Market for Boats, Lays off 10 Percent of Workers at ET Plants," *The Journal*, 7 July 1990.
21. National Marine Manufacturers Association (NMMA), Market Statistics Division, January 1999.
22. Roger Giles, e-mail correspondence with Jeffrey L. Rodengen, 11 May 2007.
23. Sea Ray Products and Programs manuals: 1991, 1992, 1993.
24. Womack, "Sea Ray Cites Slow Market."
25. "Significant Accomplishments of PACE," 1994 Sea Ray Products & Programs manual, 2 July 1993.
26. Ibid.
27. Wylie Gerdes, "Pulling Up Anchor," *Detroit Free Press*, 19 December 1990.
28. Annette Kingsbury, "Slow Sales Spelled Doom for

Sea Ray," *The Oxford Leader.*

29. Daniel Grantham, "Drydock Approaches for Sea Ray," *The Oakland Press*, 13 January 1991.

30. Michalak, interview.

31. "World-Class Boats from an Industry Leader," *Trailer Boats*, July 1996.

32. 1991 Sea Ray Products & Programs manual.

33. "World-Class Boats."

34. Barrington, interview.

35. International Standards Organization, http://www.iso.org/.

36. Barrington, interview.

37. Stone, interview.

38. Patrick Short, "Luxury by Design," *Sea Magazine*, April 1993.

39. 1992 Sea Ray Products & Programs manual.

40. "Sea Ray, Disney Join Marketing Force," *Boating Industry*, December 1991.

41. "Significant Accomplishments of PACE 1992/1993," 1994 Sea Ray Products & Programs manual, 2 July 1993.

42. Facsimile of ISO 9002 certification by Irish Standards Authority.

43. "Significant Accomplishments of PACE 1994/1995," 1995 Sea Ray Products & Programs manual, 11 June 1995.

44. Barrington, interview; Stone, interview.

45. Ibid.

46. Barrington, interview.

47. Stone, interview.

48. Sea Ray Products and Programs manuals: 1991, 1992, 1993.

49. Stone interview.

50. "Notice of Proposed Rulemaking for Federal Requirements for Propeller Avoidance Measures," 66 Federal Regulation 237, National Marine Manufacturers Association and Houseboat Industry Association, 10 December 2001.

51. Jim Steffens, interview by Jeffrey L. Rodengen, digital recording, 10 May 2007, Write Stuff Enterprises, Inc.

52. 1994 Sea Ray Products & Programs manual.

53. Joel Johnson, "The Compact Jet Boat Market is Booming, as the Influx of 1995 Models Shows," http://www.boats.com/.

54. Steffens, interview.

55. "Sea Ray Leads with This Popular 'Dancer,'" *Trailer Boats*, February 1995.

56. 1994 Sport Cruisers & Signature Sport Boats brochure.

57. "Significant Accomplishments of PACE 1993/1994," 1995 Sea Ray Products & Programs manual, 8 June 1994.

**Chapter Seven Sidebar
High-tech Boatbuilding**

1. Mike Hungerford, e-mail correspondence with T. Wayne Waters, 6 September 2007, Write Stuff Enterprises, Inc.

2. 1990 Sea Ray brochures.

**Chapter Eight
Shipshape and Seaworthy**

1. Rob Parmentier, interview by Jeffrey L. Rodengen, digital recording, 10 May 2007, Write Stuff Enterprises, Inc.

2. National Marine Manufacturers Association (NMMA), Market Statistics Division, January 1999.

3. Rick Stone, interview by Jeffrey L. Rodengen, digital recording, 10 May 2007, Write Stuff Enterprises, Inc.

4. Bill Barrington, interview by Jeffrey L. Rodengen, digital recording, 31 August 2007, Write Stuff Enterprises, Inc.

5. Ibid.

6. Ibid.

7. Parmentier, interview.

8. Ibid.

9. "Significant Accomplishments of PACE 1994/1995," 1996 Sea Ray Products & Programs manual, 6 June 1995.

10. Ibid.

11. "Significant Accomplishments of PACE 1995/1996," 1997 Sea Ray Products & Programs manual, 6 June 1996.

12. Barrington, interview.

13. Ibid.

14. Wiley Poole, "Family Outing, Sea Ray 240 Sundeck Motorboat," *Trailer Boats*, March 1996.

15. John Clemens, Show-Stopper, *Motorboating & Sailing*, February 1996.

16. Brunswick Corp. Quarterly Report 10-Q, Securities and Exchange Commission, SEC File 1-01043, Accession Number 14930-95-12, 7 November 1995.

17. Jeff Kurowski, "Brunswick's Sea Ray Eyes

Baja," *Boating Industry*, February 1995.

18. Barrington, interview.

19. Brunswick Corp. Annual Report 10-K, Securities and Exchange Commission, SEC File 1-01043, Accession Number 950131-97-2142, 28 March 1997.

20. David Leonhardt, "Perelman to Buy Boston Whaler for $20M," *The Boston Globe*, 25 June 1993; Barrington, interview.

21. Barrington, interview.

22. Ed Boncek, interview by Jeffrey L. Rodengen, digital recording, 3 December 2007, Write Stuff Enterprises, Inc.

23. Barrington, interview.

24. Boncek, interview.

25. "Sea Ray Introduces 'Legacy,' the Marine Industry's First Certified Pre-owned Boat Program," Sea Ray news release, 22 July 1996.

26. "Sea Ray Dealers Go Online with New RayNet System for Improved Customer Service," Sea Ray news release, 22 July 1996.

27. 1997 Sea Ray Marketing & Media Planner, 22 July 1996.

28. "Boat of the Year," *Boating Magazine*, December 1996.

29. John Clemans, "No Compromise," *Motor Boating & Sailing*, July 1997.

30. Sales InfoGram, 1997 Sea Ray Products & Programs manual, 7 October 1996.

31. Ibid.

32. Jim Barron, "Overnight Sensation," *Trailer Boats*, January 1997.

33. Marketing InfoGram, 1997 Sea Ray Products & Programs manual, 7 October 1996.

34. Marketing InfoGram, 1997 Sea Ray Products & Programs manual, 8 May 1997.

35. Chris Caswell, "The Secret of Sea Ray," *Robb Report*, July 1997.

36. The Robb Report Collection, http://www.robbreportcollection.com/.

37. 1998 Retail Price List, 1998 Sea Ray Products & Programs manual, 25 July 1997.

38. Roger Giles, interview by Jeffrey L. Rodengen, digital recording, 10 May 2007, Write Stuff Enterprises, Inc.

39. Roy Attaway, "Special Delivery," *Motor Boating & Sailing*, March 1999.

40. Capt. Chris Kelly, "Three Dancers," *Power & Motoryacht*, February 1999.

41. "Sea Ray Names Global Sales Chief," *Knoxville News-Sentinel*, 16 October 1998.

42. Barrington, interview.

43. Giles, interview.

44. Darlene Brady, "Sea Ray to Represent Italy's Azimut: Sea Ray President Says Alliance Gives Dealers More Flexibility," *Boating Industry*, January 1999.

45. "Sea Ray's Dave Marlow is Chairman of the Board for ABYC," Sea Ray news release, 19 March 1999.

46. "Sea Ray's Dave Marlow Appointed to National Boating Safety Advisory Council," Sea Ray news release, 11 March 1999.

47. "Sea Ray Boats is First Company to Receive Horizon Award," Sea Ray news release, 6 April 1999.

48. Ibid.

49. "Significant Accomplishments of PACE 1999/2000," 2000 Sea Ray Products & Programs manual, 19 June 1999.

50. Roger Giles, e-mail correspondence with T. Wayne Waters, 11 May 2007.

51. "Significant Accomplishments of PACE 1999/2000," 2000 Sea Ray Products & Programs manual, 19 June 1999.

52. Ken Harrell, interview by Jeffrey L. Rodengen, digital recording, 10 May 2007, Write Stuff Enterprises, Inc.

53. Ibid.

54. Ibid.

55. Ibid.

56. Sean Hao, "3 Area Companies Seek County Tax Breaks, Sea Ray May Add 400 Jobs at New Plant," *Florida Today*, 31 July 1999.

57. Kevin Falvey, "Art Exhibit," *Boating Magazine*, October 1999.

58. Kevin Falvey, "Blue Chip," *Boating Magazine*, September 1999.

59. Joe Skorupa, "Rising Sun," *Boating World*, November 1999.

**Chapter Eight Sidebar**
**Sea Ray Owners Club**

1. Sea Ray Owners Club, http://owners.searay.com/sea_ray_owners_club.asp/.

2. Ibid.
3. Ibid.
4. Ibid.
5. Ibid.

**Chapter Eight Sidebar**
**Evolution of the Sundancer**

1. Peter Bohr, "The DA was a Sundancer," *Sea Magazine*, April 1995.
2. Capt. Chris Kelly, "The Sundancer Also Rises," *Power & Motoryacht*, February 1999.

**Chapter Eight Sidebar**
**Evolution of the Master Dealer**

1. Ed Boncek, interview by Jeffrey L. Rodengen, digital recording, 3 December 2007, Write Stuff Enterprises, Inc.
2. Rick Stone, interview by Jeffrey L. Rodengen, digital recording, 10 May 2007, Write Stuff Enterprises, Inc.; 1994 Sea Ray Products & Programs manual, 7 July 1993.
3. Mike Burke, interview by Jeffrey L. Rodengen, digital recording, 10 May 2007, Write Stuff Enterprises, Inc.
4. Ibid.
5. Nancy Luster, interview by Jeffrey L. Rodengen, digital recording, 19 November 2007, Write Stuff Enterprises, Inc.
6. Ibid.
7. Liz Walz, "Back to the Future," *Boating Industry*, June 2007.
8. Boncek, interview
9. Ibid.
10. Luster, interview.

**Chapter Nine**
**Changing Course**

1. Jim Steffens, interview by Jeffrey L. Rodengen, digital recording, 10 May 2007, Write Stuff Enterprises, Inc.
2. 2001 Sea Ray Products & Programs manual, 15 July 2000.
3. Ibid.
4. Ibid.
5. "Introducing Sea Ray's Proprietary Multiple Insert Technology," Sea Ray internal documentation, July 2001.
6. Walter Perlmutter, "A Visit with a Giant of the Boat Industry," *Sarasota Herald-Tribune*, 28 October 2000.
7. Bruce Thompson, interview with Mike Hungerford, Summer 2001.
8. "Brunswick to Form Boat Group; McCoy Named Group President," PR Newswire, 31 October 2000.
9. Rick Stone, interview by Jeffrey L. Rodengen, digital recording, 10 May 2007, Write Stuff Enterprises, Inc.
10. 2002 Sea Ray Products & Programs manual, 28 June 2001.
11. Bill Barrington, interview by Jeffrey L. Rodengen, digital recording, 31 August 2007, Write Stuff Enterprises, Inc.
12. 2002 U.S. Recreational Boat Registration Statistics, National Marine Manufacturers Association, http://www.nmma.org/.
13. Annual Retail Unit Sales Estimates 1980–2000, National Marine Manufacturers Association, http://www.nmma.org/.
14. Barrington, interview; Sea Ray Boats Annual Sales, internal documentation.
15. Rebecca Ferrar, "President of Sea Ray has Auto-Industry Background," *Knoxville News-Sentinel*, 27 December 2002.
16. "Sales Slump Prompts Boat Maker to Cut More Jobs," *Knoxville News-Sentinel*, 25 April 2001.
17. Ibid.
18. "Introducing Sea Ray's Proprietary Multiple Insert Technology."
19. Ibid.
20. Ibid.
21. Ibid.
22. Ibid.
23. "300 Sundancer," Sea Ray news release, 12 July 2001.
24. Stan DeLozier, "Sea Ray Cuts 74 ET Jobs," *Knoxville News-Sentinel*, 10 August 2001.
25. "Sea Ray Reports Record Sales at Ft. Lauderdale Boat Show," PR Newswire, 5 November 2001.
26. "Brunswick to Buy Hatteras for $80 Million in Cash," *The New York Times*, 25 October 2001.
27. 2002 Annual Retail Unit Sales Estimates, National Marine Manufacturers Association, http://www.nmma.org/.
28. Morgan Stinemetz, "Navigator Well Worth the Wait," *Sarasota Herald-Tribune*, 9 March 2002.
29. Sea Ray Boats Annual Sales, internal documentation.

30. Rebecca Ferrar, "Sea Change," *Knoxville News-Sentinel*, 10 October 2004.
31. "Brunswick to Invest $22 Million in Region," Knoxville Chamber of Commerce news release, 12 October 2004.
32. Rebecca Ferrar, "President of Sea Ray has Auto-industry background."
33. Jim Hendricks, "Pony Express," *Trailer Boats*, 1 July 2003.
34. Ibid.
35. Rebecca Ferrar, "Sea Change," *Knoxville News-Sentinel*, 10 October 2004.
36. Ibid.
37. Ibid.
38. "Sea Ray's RIMFIRE Selected for Innovation in Manufacturing Process Award for the 2003 Excellence & Innovation Awards," *Advanced Materials & Composites News*, 19 January 2004.
39. "Brunswick Completes Purchase of Warranty Firm," *The Business Journal of Milwaukee*, 7 April 2004.
40. "Sea Ray Boats to Feature Delphi Switch Technology on Industry-First Application of Auxiliary Controls," *Financial News*, 27 September 2004.
41. 2005 Sea Ray Products & Programs manual, July 2004.
42. Rebecca Ferrar, "Incentives Anchor Boat Jobs for ET; $22 Million Project at Brunswick's Sea Ray Plants in Knoxville, Monroe to Add 200 Jobs," *Knoxville News-Sentinel*, 14 September 2004.

43. Ibid.
44. Rebecca Ferrar, "Sea Change."
45. Ibid.
46. Richard Thiel, "Boat Test: 2005 Sea Ray 48 Sundancer," *Power & Motoryacht*, April 2005.
47. Pete McDonald, "Winning Smile," *Boating*, August 2005.
48. "Sea Changes; Nothing is the Same Here, Sport," *Gold Coast Bulletin* (Australia), 30 December 2005.
49. "Sea Ray Express Cruisers Awarded Prestigious J. D. Power and Associates Award for Third Time," Sea Ray news release, 24 February 2005.
50. Sea Ray Boats Annual Sales, internal documentation.
51. Rob Parmentier, interview by Jeffrey L. Rodengen, digital recording, 10 May 2007, Write Stuff Enterprises, Inc.
52. Stone, interview.

**Chapter Nine Sidebar
Sea Ray International**

1. Rae Line, http://www.raeline.com /.
2. Jozef Wiszniewski, interview by Jeffrey L. Rodengen, digital recording, 4 October 2007, Write Stuff Enterprises, Inc.
3. Ibid.
4. Robert VanNorman, interview by Jeffrey L. Rodengen, digital recording, 28 August 2007, Write Stuff Enterprises, Inc.

5. Ibid.
6. Ibid.
7. Shane Stanfill, interview by T. Wayne Waters, 26 November 2007, Write Stuff Enterprises, Inc.
8. 2007 Sea Ray Products & Programs manual, 24 August 2006.
9. Ibid.
10. Ibid.

**Chapter Nine Sidebar
MarineMax: Sea Ray's No. 1
Dealer Network**

1. Michael Sasso, "Billion-Dollar Babies," *The Tampa Tribune*, 24 December 2006.
2. Hoover's (MarineMax, Inc.), http://www.hoovers.com/.
3. Michael Farrell, "Consolidators at the Gate," *Boating Industry*, July 1998.
4. Bill McGill, interview by Jeffrey L. Rodengen, digital recording, 31 August 2007, Write Stuff Enterprises, Inc.
5. Richard Bassett, interview by Jeffrey L. Rodengen, digital recording, 13 February 2008, Write Stuff Enterprises, Inc.
6. Ibid.
7. McGill, interview.

**Chapter Ten
A Half Century of Building Boats**

1. Rick Stone, interview by Jeffrey L. Rodengen, digital recording, 10 May 2007, Write Stuff Enterprises, Inc.
2. 2008 Sea Ray Yacht brochure.

3. Jay Coyle, "Swingin' Sixty," *Yachting*, April 2006.

4. Jeffrey Moser, "BOAT TEST: 2006 Sea Ray 60 Sundancer," *Power & Motoryacht*, June 2006.

5. "Peter B. Hamilton Named President–Brunswick Boat Group; John E. Stransky Named President–Life Fitness Division; Warren N. Hardie Named President–Brunswick Bowling & Billiards," Brunswick Corporation news release, 27 February 2006.

6. David Keim, "Executive Chain Reaction," *Knoxville News-Sentinel*, 28 February 2006.

7. Dustan McCoy, interview by Jeffrey L. Rodengen, digital recording, 19 December 2007, Write Stuff Enterprises, Inc.

8. "Terry McNew Returns to Lead Sea Ray Product Development, Engineering; Zimmer to Head Quality and Manufacturing Technology," Sea Ray news release, 20 April 2006.

9. McCoy, interview.

10. Ian Williamson, e-mail interview with T. Wayne Waters, 30 April 2008, Write Stuff Enterprises, Inc.

11. Stone, interview.

12. "Sea Ray Launches Completely Redesigned Web Site," Sea Ray news release, 24 April 2006.

13. "310 Sundancer," Sea Ray news release, 22 August 2006.

14. J. D. Power and Associates, http://www.jdpower.com/.

15. "2007 55 Sundancer," Sea Ray news release, 23 January 2007.

16. 1998 Sea Ray Products & Programs manual, 15 July 1997.

17. "Sales Department Organizational Changes," Sea Ray Sales InfoGram, 6 February 1997.

18. 2000 Sea Ray Products & Programs manual, 9 July 1999.

19. "Sea Ray Living Earns Gold in the Mercury Excellence Awards Competition," Sea Ray news release, 24 February 2006; "Sea Ray Living Earns Three 2006 Gold Millennium Awards," Sea Ray news release, 12 May 2006.

20. "Sea Ray AquaPalooza Set to Make On-Water History," Sea Ray news release, 16 June 2006.

21. "Sea Ray AquaPalooza Set to Make On-Water History … AGAIN!" Sea Ray news release, 21 June 2007.

22. "AquaPalooza Set to be Larger and Louder in 2008," Sea Ray news release, 19 May 2008.

23. Rodney Bensz, interview by Jeffrey L. Rodengen, digital recording, 12 September 2007, Write Stuff Enterprises, Inc.

24. Rod Malone, interview by Jeffrey L. Rodengen, digital recording, 13 September 2007, Write Stuff Enterprises, Inc.

25. Michael Silence, "Sea Changes at Brunswick," *Knoxville News-Sentinel*, 20 January 2007.

26. Robert VanNorman, interview by Jeffrey L. Rodengen, digital recording, 28 August 2007, Write Stuff Enterprises, Inc.

27. Ken Harrell, interview by Jeffrey L. Rodengen, digital recording, 10 May 2007, Write Stuff Enterprises, Inc.

28. "Terry McNew Returns to Lead Sea Ray Product Development, Engineering; Zimmer to Head Quality and Manufacturing Technology," Sea Ray news release, 20 April 2006.

29. VanNorman, interview.

30. Dwight Cobble, interview by Jeffrey L. Rodengen, digital recording, 10 May 2007, Write Stuff Enterprises, Inc.

31. Forrest Weyant, interview by Jeffrey L. Rodengen, digital recording, 10 May 2007, Write Stuff Enterprises, Inc.

32. Bob Scott, interview by Jeffrey L. Rodengen, digital recording, 10 May 2007, Write Stuff Enterprises, Inc.

33. Gary Montavon, e-mail interview with T. Wayne Waters, 30 April 2008, Write Stuff Enterprises, Inc.

34. Ibid.

35. 2008 Sea Ray Products & Programs manual, July 2007.

36. "The Sea Ray 330 Sundancer—Beyond the Horizon," Sea Ray news release, 9 August 2007.

37. Kevin Falvey, "American Way: Winning is a Habit," *Boating*, September 2007.

38. "The Sea Ray 47 Sedan Bridge—On Top of the World," Sea Ray news release, 9 August 2007.
39. "The Sea Ray 290 Amberjack—Ultimate Crossover Athlete," Sea Ray news release, 9 August 2007.
40. "The Sea Ray 290 Sundeck—Extended Family Welcome," Sea Ray news release, 14 August 2007.
41. "The Sea Ray 205 Sport—Back and Better than Ever," Sea Ray news release, 14 August 2007.
42. "The Sea Ray 175 Sport—Innovative New Styling for 2008," Sea Ray news release, 14 August 2007.
43. "The Sea Ray 210 Select Fission and 230 Select Fission–Air Apparents," Sea Ray news release, 14 August 2007.
44. "Zeus Technology and New Sea Ray Models Receive Rave Reviews at Sea Ray Dealer Meeting," Sea Ray news release, 6 August 2007.
45. "CMD Announces Zeus Propulsion System Has Shipped to Launch Partners," Cummins-MerCruiser Diesel press release, 2007.
46. Mercury Marine, "Want Nothing but the Best? Start at the Core," http://www.mercurymarine.com/.
47. "Mercury Axius Claims IBEX Innovation Award," Mercury Marine news release, 12 October 2007.
48. McCoy, interview.
49. Stone, interview.
50. VanNorman, interview.
51. Stone, interview.

52. Ibid.
53. Nancy Luster, interview by Jeffrey L. Rodengen, digital recording, 19 November 2007, Write Stuff Enterprises, Inc.; Mike Burke, interview by Jeffrey L. Rodengen, digital recording, 10 May 2007, Write Stuff Enterprises, Inc.
54. Burke, interview.
55. Ibid.
56. Ibid.
57. Ibid.
58. Ibid.
59. Correspondence with T. Wayne Waters, 2008.
60. Burke, interview.
61. Liz Walz, "Back to the Future," Boating Industry, June 2007.
62. Stone, interview.
63. VanNorman, interview.
64. Sea Ray Boats Annual Sales, internal documentation.
65. "The New Sea Ray 300 Select EX—Super Action Hero," Sea Ray news release, 12 January 2008.
66. "The New Sea Ray 210 Sundeck Offers Everything and More," Sea Ray news release, 11 January 2008.
67. "The New Sea Ray 350 Sundancer Comes with Hidden Benefits," Sea Ray news release, 13 February 2008.
68. Cobble, interview.
69. Liz Walz, "Back to the Future."
70. Stone, interview.
71. Ibid.
72. Walz, "Back to the Future"; E-mail correspondence with Mike Hungerford.
73. Burke, interview.

74. McCoy, interview.

**Chapter Ten Sidebar**
**Sea Ray Mission Statement**

1. Sea Ray, http://www.searay.com/.
2. Ibid.

**Chapter Ten Sidebar**
**Sea Ray Superlatives**

1. Sea Ray marketing materials.

**Chapter Ten Sidebar**
**Dealer Feedback**

1. Pete Beauregard, Sr., interview by Jeffrey L. Rodengen, digital recording, 23 August 2007, Write Stuff Enterprises, Inc.
2. Ibid.
3. Pete Beauregard, Jr., interview by Jeffrey L. Rodengen, digital recording, 23 August 2007, Write Stuff Enterprises, Inc.
4. Ibid.
5. Wakeen's Family Boating Center, http://www.wakeens.com/.
6. Joe Wakeen, interview by Jeffrey L. Rodengen, digital recording, 22 October 2007, Write Stuff Enterprises, Inc.
7. Ibid.
8. Barry Bensz, interview by Jeffrey L. Rodengen, digital recording, 12 September 2007, Write Stuff Enterprises, Inc.
9. Rodney Bensz, interview by Jeffrey L. Rodengen, digital recording, 12 September 2007, Write Stuff Enterprises, Inc.
10. Ibid.

11. B&E Marine, http://
www.bemarine.com/.
12. Rod Malone, interview
by Jeffrey L. Rodengen,
digital recording,
13 September 2007,
Write Stuff Enterprises, Inc.
13. Ibid.
14. Ibid.
15. Sail & Ski Center,
http://www.sailandski.com/.
16. Malone, interview.

# INDEX

Page numbers in italics indicate photographs.